CLASSICAL EDINBURGH

CLASSICAL EDINBURGH

A City Divided

Alan Balfour

FHB | FIRST HILL BOOKS

FIRST HILL BOOKS
An imprint of Wimbledon Publishing Company
www.anthempress.com

This edition first published in UK and USA 2023
by FIRST HILL BOOKS
75–76 Blackfriars Road, London SE1 8HA, UK
or PO Box 9779, London SW19 7ZG, UK
and
244 Madison Ave #116, New York, NY 10016, USA

British Library Cataloguing-in-Publication Data
A catalogue record for this book is available from the British Library.

Library of Congress Control Number: 2022921006
A catalog record for this book has been requested.

ISBN-13: 978-1-83998-789-2 (Hbk)
ISBN-10: 1-83998-789-8 (Hbk)

Cover Credit: Regent Bridge from Calton Road image (1895),
photographer unknown. With permission from CANMORE, National
Record of Historic Environment, HES Collection.

This title is also available as an e-book.

Thus, the broad and comely approach to Prince's Street from the east, lined with hotels and public offices, makes a leap over the gorge of the Low Calton; if you cast a glance over the parapet, you look direct into that sunless and disreputable confluent of Leith Street; and the same tall houses open upon both thoroughfares. This is only the New Town passing overhead above its own cellars; walking, so to speak, over its own children, as is the way of cities and the human race.

Robert Louis. Stevenson, Edinburgh: Picturesque Notes

[1] Overleaf and cover. Looking up at Regent Bridge from the Low Calton.

To my mother and father whose lives were shaped in large measure by all that follows.

Contents

Prologue

As I looked through my sister's papers after her funeral in 2013, my ignorance of the family's history became startlingly clear. There on a death certificate I saw for the first time my paternal grandfather's name and learned that he had married twice and that my father had one half-brother and three half-sisters of whom I knew nothing. I then realized I could not name either of my grandmothers. It was at that moment that I decided to write this history of our two families, the Finlays and Balfours.

The only grandparent who had any presence in my childhood was my mother's father James Finlay. He was killed in action in Flanders in 1918. I have no memory of my mother ever mentioning her mother. Inexplicably, neither my father nor his sister ever mentioned or discussed their parents. So, with scant evidence to go and with the help of the extraordinary Scottish government website *Scotlands People*, and one formative memory from childhood, I devoted myself to the task, and one fact quickly became increasingly clear, the histories of my two families could not be more different, one, my mother's sometimes affluent, the other, my father's always in poverty.

This work is both a family history and a social history of Scotland with a particular focus on Edinburgh. The families are mine, traced from their roots in seventeenth century into the twentieth. However, all their wandering and failures, and births and marriages, are in themselves of no importance; they are merely the actions of helpless actors (one not so helpless) caught in the midst of changing worlds and realities. I have embedded their lives into the larger forces in a changing Scottish culture, climaxing in the creation of the New Town of Edinburgh, one of the eighteenth and nineteenth century's most extravagant romantic fantasies. It was a reality shaped by the leaders of the Scottish Enlightenment to give identity to a capital of a nation in name only, after the closing of the Scottish parliament with the Union of the Crowns in 1707.

This New Town became a vast idealized reality, which could only have been achieved in a Scotland that was and remains essentially feudal. All the lands surrounding the walls of the old city were the inherited properties of a few aristocratic families who were able, free of constraint, to sustain a succession of developments for over eighty years creating a continual stream of wealth for the landowners and their successors, and in the process producing extreme poverty for those left behind.

By the mid-nineteenth century, a very different reality emerged out of the need to accommodate the poor and the rising workforce in the city's new industries. This resulted in street after street of monotonous, identical tenements, a joyless demeaning world in stark contrast to the lively grandeur of the housing in the new town. The medieval tenements of city's old High Street were once called 'slums built to last a thousand years', and in many ways the extensive tenements of the industrial city from the nineteenth and twentieth century can equally be said to represent the prospect of people divided for a thousand years. It will be argued that such divisions are unavoidable and can be found in many cities, but it is the extent and the willfulness of the planning that make the Edinburgh example so potent.

I

Poverty, Filth and Bondage

'How long can it be suffered', wrote John Wesley in his Journal in 1770: 'that all manner of filth should be flung into the streets? How long shall the capital city of Scotland and the chief street of it stink worse than a common sewer'?[1]

From the Journal of John Wesley

Paul Sandby, In the Grassmarket 1758: Drag Cart and Horse

---

1. Wesley, John, *The Journal of John Wesley* 1703–1791; Parker, Percy Livingstone, 1867–1925, editor, Chicago: Moody Press.

Edinburgh is fortunate to have a series of drawings of the people on the streets of the city by Paul Sandby. They were made in the 1750s. Sandby had come to Scotland in 1747 to join his brother in Edinburgh as a military cartographer. The drawings were done for his own pleasure, recording moments that he found of interest as he strolled the streets of the city – a drag cart and horse in the Grassmarket, the crowd at an execution, a horse fair on Bruntsfield Links and what appears to be several men relieving themselves against a wall while their lady companions stand by. It is believed that he learnt printmaking in the city and was sufficiently respected to be employed to teach drawing to the architect Robert Adam before he set out on a grand tour of Europe.[2] The

Paul Sandby: 'Drawn at the Execution of John Young in the Grassmarket, Edinburgh' 1751.

2. https://www.scotsman.com/art-review-paul-sandby-1-769301

drawings show lively animated groups in colourful and elaborate dress – many plaid shawls round the shoulders. These were the people who every day lived with and tolerated the muck in the city. (The drawings were published as part of larger collection in 1765, and in 1768 he became one of the founding members of the Royal Academy.)

Filth: In an extensive correspondence *Letters from Edinburgh in 1774*[3] (published in 1776) the young English journalist Edward Topham wrote:

> This town has long been reproached with many uncleanly customs. A gentleman, who lately published his travels through Spain, says that Madrid, some years ago, might 'have vied with Edinburgh in filthiness'. But if a stranger may be allowed to complain, it would be, that in these wynds, which are very numerous, the dirt is sometimes suffered to remain two or three days without removal and becomes offensive to more senses than one. The magistrates, by imposing fines and other punishments, have long put a stop to the throwing anything from the windows into the open street: but as these allies are un- lighted, narrow, and removed from public view, they still continue these practices with impunity. Many an elegant suit of clothes has been spoiled; many a powdered, well-dressed

---

3. Edward Topham, *Letters from Edinburgh, Written in the Years 1774 and 1775: Containing Some Observations on the Diversions, Customs, Manners, and Laws, of the Scotch Nation, during a Six Months Residence in Edinburgh: In Two Volumes, Volume 1* Watson 1780.

Paul Sandby: Horse Fair on Bruntsfield Links, 1750.

Paul Sandby: Finding Relief 1750.

maccaroni[4] sent home for the evening: and to conclude this period in Dr. Johnson's own simple words, 'Many a full-flowing periwig moistened into flaccidity'.

This is the world of my father's family, the Jamiesons; it could be him standing next to Sandby's horse and cart. My father was given two surnames, Jamieson and Balfour, and the Jamieson[5] are the first in my family to be recorded in Edinburgh, living for almost a century in the filthiest parts of the city. The earliest confirmable record is the

---

4. 'Macaroni' in mid-eighteenth-century England was a fashionable fellow who dressed and even spoke in an outlandishly affected and epicene manner. The term pejoratively referred to a man who 'exceeded the ordinary bounds of fashion' in terms of clothes, fastidious eating and gambling. He mixed Continental affectations with his English nature, like a practitioner of macaronic verse (which mixed English and Latin to comic effect), laying himself open to satire.

5. Jamieson comes from the ancient Dalriadan clans of Scotland's west coast and Hebrides islands. The name comes from 'son of James'. Earliest use is recorded on the Isle of Bute.

birth certificate of one Alex. Jamieson born in Edinburgh on 25 July 1739:[6]

> *The Alexander Jamieson Indweller & Elspeth Dawson his spouses, a son Alexander W[it.]. James Jamieson, Baxter [Baker?] & Richard Johnstone, Soldier in the Castle born Inst. (25 July 1739).*[7]

There is no address and no occupation given, 'Indweller' simply means someone from the city. The first substantial family document is the birth record of his son, a third Alexander Jamieson, in March 1767:

> *Alex. Jamieson, Carter at Wyndmylne & sp. Janet Thornton a son Alex. born 26th last. Witt. Andr. Henderson, Wright, Adam Hall Carter*

The birth took place in Edinburgh, and he was baptized within St Cuthbert's Parish, presumably in the recently built Chapel of Ease which had opened in 1754 to serve the poor on the South side of the city. St. Cuthbert's is the oldest religious foundation in the city, dating from the eighth century. This short entry in the church records is surprisingly informative on the senior

---

6. There are earlier records going back with less certainty to Alexander's father, born on 29 February 1716. The church document gives his parents as William Jamieson and Margaret McAllay living in the village of Gargunnock near Stirling. And perhaps before that to the birth of his father William to Alexr. Jamieson and Helen Thomson, in the village of Tulliallan, east of Stirling on 14 June 1691. These are the earliest I have found.
7. All the italicized records of births, deaths and marriages have been transcribed from the actual church and public documents available in the Scottish Government website *Scotland's People*.

Alexander Jamieson. He was a carter of goods, either with a barrow or with a horse and cart, a lowly but necessary occupation, living and plying his trade on Wynd Mylne, a street referred to in a seventeenth-century *Derivation of Edinburgh Street Names*[8] as the *calsav leid and fra the Societie port to the Wynd mylne,* which translates as: 'the causeway led to and from the Society Port to Mylne's Wynd'.[9] The Society Port was the old Bristow gate into the city from the south, leading on to Candlemaker Row and Cowgate. Mylne's Wynd or Mill Wynd was a passage from the Cowgate to the High Street – a few openings down from St Giles. It was deep into the filthiest part of the old city.

The younger Alex next appears in the 1785 record announcing the birth of his son, George Jamieson, from Old Parish Registers dated 16 February 1785:

> *Alex. Jamieson, Shoemaker and Helen Brown his spouse, High Kirk parish a son Born 16 February last, named George – Bapt. in Church*

High Kirk of Edinburgh, also misleadingly called St Giles Cathedral, is the principal place of worship of the Church of Scotland in Edinburgh. In the eighteenth century, as elsewhere in Edinburgh, there would have been a chapel for the poor nearby. Mention of the High Kirk parish is evidence that the family was still living in the streets around the old High Street, the poorest part of the medieval city, which became ever poorer as the New Town evolved.

---

8. *History and Derivation of Edinburgh Street Names.* Charles B. Boog Watson, Edinburgh (Scotland).
9. Ian Forde www.fons-scotiae.com/home.html

A view of the High Street in the 1870s showing the Cannongate home of the last leader of the Catholic Church in Scotland Cardinal Beaton, now demolished, in the sixteenth century briefly housed the High School.

Henry Graham's *The Social Life of Scotland in the Eighteenth Century*[10] is a brilliant evocation of life in Edinburgh or *Auld Reekie*,[11] in all its distinct qualities:

> The height of Edinburgh's glory was before the Union of 1707, in the days when meetings of the Scots Parliament drew to the capital nobles and persons of quality from every county, when

---

10. Henry Grey Graham, *The Social Life of Scotland in the Eighteenth Century*. London: Adam and Charles Black, 1901
11. *Auld Reekie* 'old smoky' in Scots, a once popular name for Edinburgh.

periodically the city was full of the richest, most notable, and best-bred people in the land, and the dingy High Street and Canongate were brightened by gentlemen in their brave attire, by ladies rustling in their hoops, brocade dresses, and brilliant coloured plaids, by big coaches gorgeous in their gilding, and lackeys splendid in their livery.

For the capital of a miserably poor country, Edinburgh Had...

Edinburgh had then a wonderful display of wealth and fashion. After 1707 all this was sadly changed. 'There is the end of an auld sang', said Lord Chancellor Seafield in jest, whether light or bitter, when the Treaty of Union was concluded; but it was a 'song' that lingered long in many regretful memories behind it. No more was the full concourse of men and ladies of high degree to make society brilliant with the chatter of right honourable voices, the glint of bright eyes from behind the masks, the jostling of innumerable sedan-chairs in the busy thoroughfare, where nobles and caddies, judges and beggars, forced their way with equal persistency. Instead of the throng of 145 nobles and 160 commoners, who often with their families and attendants filled the town with life and business, [the town was empty] they went to Westminster.

No wonder the Union was especially unpopular in Edinburgh, for it deprived the city of national dignity carried from citizens their

fashions and spoiled their trade. A gloom fell
over the Scots capital: society was dull, business was duller still, the lodgings once filled
with persons of quality were left empty – many
decayed for want of tenants, some fell almost
into ruin. For many a year there was little social
life, scanty intellectual culture, and few traces
of business enterprise. Gaiety and amusement
were indulged in only under the censure of the
Church and the depressing air of that gloomy
piety which held undisputed and fuller sway
when the influence of rank and fashion no
longer existed to counteract it.

But the few visitors from England were
impressed far more by its dirt and dinginess
than by its quaint beauty, by the streets which
were filthy, the causeways rugged and broken,
the big gurgling gutters in which ran the refuse
of a crowded population, and among which
the pigs poked their snouts in grunting satisfaction for garbage. By ten o'clock each night the
filth collected in each household was poured
from the high windows, and fell in malodor-
ous plash upon the pavement, and not seldom
on unwary passers-by. At the warning call of
'gardyloo' [*Gardez l'eau*] from servants preparing
to outpour the contents of stoups, pots, and cans,
the passengers beneath would agonisingly cry
out 'Hud yer hand' but too often the shout was
unheard or too late, and a drenched periwig and
besmirched three-cornered hat were borne drip-
ping and ill-scented home. At the dreaded hour

when the domestic abominations were flung out, when the smells (known as the 'flowers of Edinburgh') filled the air, the citizens burnt their sheets of brown paper-to neutralise the odours of the outside, which penetrated their rooms within. On the ground all night the dirt and ordure lay awaiting the few and leisurely scavengers, who came nominally at seven o'clock next morning with wheel-barrows to remove it.

In the flats of the lofty houses in wynds or facing the High Street the populace dwelt, who reached their various lodgings by the steep and narrow 'scale' staircases, which were upright streets. On the same building lived families of all grades and classes, each in its flat in the same stair – the sweep and caddie in the cellars, poor mechanics in the garrets, while in the intermediate stories might live a noble, a lord of session, a doctor, or city minister, a dowager countess, or writer; higher up, over their heads, lived shopkeepers, dancing masters, or clerks [...]

The long precipitous stairs were crowded all day long with men, women, and children belonging to the various flats passing up and down – masons, judges, dancing masters, countesses, barbers, and advocates, all encountered each other in the narrow passage. Besides the residents there was the stream of porters carrying coals, the Musselburgh fishwives with their creels, the sweeps, the men and women conveying the daily supply of water for each flat, barbers' boys with re-trimmed wigs, the various people bent on business or on pleasure, on errands and visits for the several landings, all jostling unceremoniously as they squeezed past one another. It was no easy task for brilliantly dressed ladies to crush their hoops, four or five yards in circumference, up the scale-stairs, or to keep them uncontaminated by the dirt abounding on the steps. So confined were some of the stairs that it was sometimes impossible, when death came, to get the coffin down; and when a passage was too narrow for the tenant of a house so situated to get entry through the adjacent house and bring the coffin down its more commodious stair. Nor was the cleanliness of those un- salubrious abodes above suspicion, and it was not uncommon for lodgings to be advertised as possessing the special virtue of being 'free from bugs'.

Eight o'clock was the breakfast hour, with its substantial meal of mutton, collops, and fowl, with libations of ale, and sometimes sack, claret, or brandy – tea not being used at that meal till about 1730. The citizen shut his shop, or left his wife to tend it, when the St. Giles' bells rang at half-past eleven – a well-known sound which was known as the 'gill-bells', because each went to his favourite tavern to take his 'meridian', consisting of a gill of brandy, or a tin of ale. Little

did these citizens heeded the music-bells, which
meanwhile overhead were playing the bright
charming tunes lo which wiser folk were all
listening. The dinner hour was at one o'clock till
1745, when it was being changed to two, though
the humbler shopkeepers dined at twelve. The
wonted fare in winter was broth, salt beef, boiled
fowls; for only the wealthy could afford to get
fresh beef at high prices until the summer, when
the arrival of any supply of beef for sale was
announced in the streets by the bellman.

By two o'clock all citizens wended their way
down their respective stairs to their places of
business, reopened the doors, and hung up the
key on a nail on the lintel – a practice which
afforded the notorious burglar. Deacon Brodie,
in 1780, opportunities of taking impressions of
the keys on putty. By the early afternoon the
streets were crowded, for into the main thoroughfare the inhabitants of the city poured.
Later in the century an Englishman describes
the scene: 'So great a crowd of people are
nowhere else confined in so small a space,
which makes their streets as much crowded
every day as others are at a fair'. There were
few coaches, fortunately, in the narrow steep
streets; but there were sedan-chairs swaying
in all directions, borne by Highland porters,
spluttering Gaelic execrations on those who

impeded their progress. There were ladies in
gigantic hoops sweeping the sides of the causeway, their head and shoulders covered with
their gay silken plaids, scarlet and green, their
faces with complexions heightened by patches,
and concealed by black velvet masks which
were held close by a string, whose buttoned
end was held by the teeth. In their hands they
bore huge green paper fans to ward off the sun;
by their side hung the little bags which held
the snuff they freely used their feet shod in red
shoes, with heels three inches high, with which
they tripped nimbly on the steep decline and
over filthy places. There were stately old ladies,
with their pattens on feet and canes in hand,
walking with precision and dignity; judges with
their wigs on head and hats under their arm;
advocates in their gowns on way to the courts
in Parliament House; ministers in their blue
or gray coats, bands, wigs, and three-cornered
hats. At the Cross (near St. Giles') the merchants assembled to transact business, and to
exchange news and snuff-boxes; while physicians, lawyers, and men about town met them
as at an open-air club and joined citizens in the
gossip of the city.

*Edinburgh, Procession up the
High Street 1793, David Allen
(National Gallery of Scotland).*

In the town there was a fine camaraderie – the friendliness and familiarity of a place where everyone knew everybody. There existed a special neighbourliness among them all. In the several 'landings', descending in dignity as they ascended in height, dwelt on the same stair peers, lords of session, clergy, doctors, shopkeepers, dancing-masters, artisans, while in the cellar lodged the water-caddy, the sweep, and the chairman. The distress of the poor neighbour on the stair became the concern of all, and poverty in the 'close' was relieved in common friendliness. The very beggars were old friends and exchanged jokes with his lordship going to the Parliament House.

> From early morning, when they awoke on the doorsteps on which they had slept, till night, when they lighted the way in the dark streets with paper lanterns, the caddies were to be seen – impudent, ragged, alert, and swift – carrying messages and parcels to any part of the town for a penny – very poor, but marvellously honest, for whatever was stolen or lost when in custody of these caddies was refunded by their society. They knew every place and; they could toll who had arrived lust in town, where they lodged, and how long they were to stay, they were invaluable as detectives, for the haunts of the lowest and the doings of the thieves were as familiar to them as the names of the guests at the Lord President's supper party the previous night, and the condition of insobriety of each gentleman when he stumbled home in the morning.

> [...] There was also the assembly in the West Bow, in a flat facing the grim and haunted

lodging of the wizard Major Weir and in the
narrow lane, from four o'clock, there was a
crowd of sedan-chairs with their gaily attired
occupants, the noisy mob pressing to witness
the fine sight, the objurgations [harsh repri-
mand] in safe Gaelic of competing chairmen,
the clanking of the swords of gentlemen in
bright silken coats. Up the winding turnpike
stair to a flat, ladies ascended, holding up
their hoops to gain difficult entrance by the
narrow passage. For these articles of rai-
ment were enormous and capacious, as young
Robert Strange the Jacobite engraver found,
when beneath the hoop of his betrothed, the
vigorous-minded Isabella Lumsden, he sought
concealment from his pursuers, while she sat
quietly spinning in seeming innocence before
the baffled searchers.

[...] Into the middle of the 18th century families
of all ranks – from the highest to the lowest –
continued to lived close to one another, in the
High Street and Canongate and in all the lanes
in between – in the same tenement or 'land' of
nine or ten flats, as they had for centuries. But
about 1775 the fashionable and wealthy began
to migrate to the suburbs and stately houses in
the New Town; they withdrew from the filth of
the old town – Auld Reekie and the ill-flavoured
wynds in the High Street, where high and low
had for ages dwelt companionably together.
The poor remained behind in the old quarters,
and the rich when they left did not retain their
homely interest in them. Now, therefore, when
poverty came, public assessments were made to

relieve it; when beggars increased the law was enforced to suppress them.

It seems most likely that decay and disease in the old city caused George Jamieson to leave in 1813 for Peebles and marry:

> *Compeared [Scots law: to appear in court personally]*
> *George Jamieson Labourer, and Margaret Murray,*
> *daughter of Archibald Murray, who produce Marriage*
> *Lines dated Lauder 9th July 1813. They were rebuked*
> *for irregularity and absolved and their marriage ordered*
> *to recorded.*

An irregular marriage, they had been living in sin before the wedding. George, at the age of 29, was a labourer. Margaret was seven years younger than George, her birth recorded in 1792 in Peebles.

> *Peebles 29 July 1792 Margaret Murray, daughter to*
> *Archb'd Murray Indweller in Peebles and Joan Kidd his*
> *spouse was baptized by the Rev. Dr. Will'm Dalgliesh*
> *Min. of the Gospel at Peebles witnesses John Scott and*
> *Thomas Bog both weavers in Peebles the child born 13th*
> *July 1792*

In the year of Margaret's birth, 1792, 'Wild ideas about liberty and equality, projected by the French Revolution, having reached Peebles, and affected some young men, and the council take the subject into consideration, and declare their horror of 'the seditious writings and open efforts of the turbulent designing for the subversion of our present, and in favour of republican government'. There is no indication of the father's trade, and again 'indweller' simply meant a person of the parish, not a stranger. However, the witnesses were both weavers, an increasingly important industry in Peebles, an indication of where George would find employment.

Peebles and the Tweed, from Neidpath Castle Engraving by William Miller after P Paton.[12]

Peebles:[13] William Chambers, in *A History of Peeblesshire*[14] published in 1843, gives intimate detail of life in the town at the time of the marriage. He begins by being surprised that the Old Town contains no *bastel-houses*, farmhouses fortified to defend against border raids, adding 'a circumstance indicative of its general desertion previous to the

---

12. Published in Sir Wallter Scott, *Waverley Novels* vol. viii (Abbotsford Edition).
13. There is a belief that that area was settled in British, or, at latest, in Romanized British times but nothing survives. The village, a favourite of Scottish king, Over the years it has divided its loyalties between England and Scotland.
14. *A History of Peeblesshire* by William Chambers of Glenormiston. Edinburgh and London: Willaim and Robert Chambers Publishers, 1843.

wars which ensued on the death of Alexander III'. These were the border wars that began in the early fourteenth century and did not effectively end until the Union of the Crowns in 1707. He continues:

> [...] nor does it possess any ancient remains, excepting the ruins of the two old ecclesiastical structures. It consists chiefly of a humble class of dwellings, some of them thatched, as is still common with suburbs in several Scottish towns. Ascending from the lower to the higher part, we find the ancient spacious market-place, circumscribed only by the encroachment of some modern buildings on its southern side. This open space was in the centre of Peebles before it attained to the character of a royal burgh, or suffered from the devastating border wars [...]

> At this and a later time, the parochial succour to the poor was on that niggardly footing which at length provoked the establishment of the new poor-law system. Besides the native poverty, too modest to make itself known, mendicancy of every kind was still common – aggravated, indeed by the mishaps of the war. Old soldiers with wooden legs, and blinded of an eye from the campaign in Egypt; sailors with one arm, and long queues hanging down their backs, who were always singing ballads about Lord Nelson and his marvellous battles; houseless nondescripts carrying wallets for an 'awmous' [Scottish for alms] of meal; blue-gowns, who presented themselves with professional confidence; and real or affectedly lame aged women, who were carried about on hand-barrows from

door to door, were all a pest to the community, and continued their perambulations in defiance of a functionary, designated the 'beggar-catcher,' who was specially appointed for their suppression.

Besides these mendicants and peripatetic minstrels, natural idiots, or 'daft folk' as they were called, haunted the town and county, some harmless and amusing, and others vicious and troublesome. Among the amusing class, none was more welcome as a temporary visitor than 'Daft Jock Grey', a native of Selkirkshire, which, as well as the adjoining counties, he wandered over during the first twenty years of the present century, and who is generally considered to have been the original of Scott's 'Davie Gellately'. There was at least some resemblance between the real and imaginary character. Jock was a kind of genius, had a great command of songs, and wholly or partly composed a ballad, which, commencing with an allusion to his own infirmity, recited in jingling rhymes the names and qualities of a number of those whose houses he frequented in his migrations between Hawick and Peebles. He was also a mimic, and as such gave acceptable imitations of the style of preaching of all the ministers in his rounds. The great novelist could not fail to know and be amused with Jock and his harmless drolleries.

Shortly after the recommencement of the war, in 1803, Peebles became a depot for prisoners of war on parole; not more, however, than twenty or thirty of these exiles arrived at this early period. They were mostly Dutch and

Walloons, with afterwards a few Danes – unfortunate mariners seized on the coast of the Netherlands, and sent to spend their lives in an inland Scottish town. These men did not repine. They nearly all betook themselves to learn the art of hand-loom weaving, at that time a flourishing craft in Peebles. At leisure hours, they might be seen fishing in long leather boots, as if glad to procure a few trouts and eels, and, at the same time, satisfy the desire to dabble in the water. In 1810, a large accession was made to this body of prisoners of war, by the arrival of upwards of a hundred officers of an entirely different quality – French, Poles, and Italians, in a variety of strange and tarnished uniforms, fresh from the seat of war. Gentlemanly in manners, they made for themselves friends in the town and neighbourhood; those among them who were surgeons occasionally assisting at medical consultations. It added somewhat to their comfort that the occupant of the Tontine Hotel, Mr Lenoir, was a French-Belgian. During their stay, they set up a private theatre in an upper apartment of the building now used as a Corn Exchange, in which they enlivened the town by performing gratuitously some of the plays of Corneille and Moliere.

And in the years after the Jamieson marriage, Chambers wrote that

domestic accommodation was still on a very imperfect scale. The apartments were small and few in number; many houses even of a good kind, consisting only of a kitchen, parlour, and bed-closet. In perhaps not more than two dozen dwellings were there any carpets; horn spoons were giving way to pewter; and silver forks were of course unheard of. There was no reading-room, and the two or three newspapers which arrived daily or semi-weekly [from Edinburgh], were handed about in clubs. The transit of goods from Edinburgh was conducted by a few carriers' carts, which were sometimes obstructed for days by heavy snow-storms in winter. On one occasion of this kind, there was a dearth of salt in the town for a fort night.

He describes the improving means of getting from Peebles to Edinburgh – of great importance to Jamieson:

The species of stage-carriage employed on the road between Peebles and Edinburgh, at the beginning of the 19th century, was a plain wooden vehicle placed on two wheels, and was without springs. William Wilson's Caravan, as this primitive species of carriage was called, was drawn by a single horse, which walked the distance, 22 miles, stoppages included, in the space of ten hours. It left Peebles at eight o'clock in the morning, and arrived at the Grassmarket, Edinburgh, at six o'clock in the evening. The fare charged for each passenger was 2s. 6d. The Caravan, which was in operation as late as about 1806, was superseded by the Fly, which resembled an old-fashioned post-chaise. It accommodated three insides, and one outside on an uneasy swinging seat, along with the driver – fare, inside, 1s. 6d. The Fly was drawn by two horses, and, including a stoppage of an hour at Howgate, they made out the journey in five hours. As this machine went only one day, and returned.[15]

'How long can it be suffered', wrote John Wesley in his Journal in 1770: 'that all manner of filth should be flung into the streets? How long shall the capital city of Scotland and the chief street of it stink worse than a common sewer'? the next, it accommodated no more than twelve passengers in the week. and, at particular times, to secure a seat, passengers required to be booked a week in advance. Yet, as only the more affluent classes could afford to take places in the Fly, many persons adopted a less legitimate course. Walking a short way out on the public road, they tried the chance of getting a ride by bribing the driver with a shilling; and by a hangy [from hanging on]) of this kind.[16]

George and Margaret Jamieson[17] reappear several years later in Dalkeith with the record of the birth of a daughter:

1832 Elizabeth Jamieson: George Jamieson, Merchant, and Margaret Murray, his spouse, had a daughter born on the 5th March, and baptized on the 18th of the same month, by the name of Elizabeth, in the presence on the congregation

---

15. And this surprising detail: 'Shortly before the period here referred to, there was a tax on clocks and watches, and from the returns of the surveyor, the following facts are learned concerning the number of these articles in Peeblesshire in 1797. In the town of Peebles, 15 clocks, 19 silver, and 2 gold watches; in the country part of the parish, 4 clocks, 5 silver, and no gold watches. In the whole county, town and parish of Peebles included, 106 clocks, 112 silver, and 35 gold watches'.
16. Ibid., William Chambers.
17. 3rd great-grandparents.

Peebles High Street, 1900.

Dalkeith was close enough to Edinburgh, and this fitted him to explore the possibility of returning and finding work in the city. It does show that George is successful enough to call himself, merchant. Given his family connection, it would seem most likely that he was a 'webster', selling woollens made in Peebles.[18] 'The webster called at houses of gentry, farms, and peasants, to buy their yarn,

---

18. On his second daughter's death certificate in 1905, her father's occupation is given as 'traveling packman', a very different occupation than cloth merchant. In the last years of nineteenth century horse transport was expensive and most rural roads were unmade, so the packman carried his goods on his back in packs that could weigh as much as a hundredweight. As well as fabric the packs contained 'a treasure trove of bits and pieces, everything from household goods to horsehair wigs, all neatly arranged in drawers. Since the customers were practically all female, the best-sellers were almost always beauty products'. It was hard life and this suggests he died in poverty.

which he and his men wove into checks or sheeting. The Webster bartered his stuff, when bleached and finished, at the doors of his customers for more home-made yarn, carrying on his own or his pony's back loads of tempting webs to exchange by stiff bargains, or with pawky cajolery, for the thread'.[19]

Subsequent records show that George and Margaret had a second daughter Isabella, born in 1838. Isabella became my great-grandmother when she married Willian Balfour in 1866.

Balfours in Fife: The Balfours have had a long and distinguished history in Fife; the name is believed to be derived from the lands of Balfour, in the parish of Markinch, formerly belonging to a family which were long heritable sheriffs of Fife. Balfour Castle was built upon their ancient possessions, in the vale or strath of the Orr, a tributary of the Leven, near their confluence. *Bal-orr* is the original name, and is used more often by the older manuscript writers, and is variously stated to be from the Gaelic *Bal foidh* or, the town at the foot of the Orr (the *dh* in *foidh* is silent) or *Baile Fuar*, the cold place/town, (which could refer to any number of places in Fife). Many forms of the name are found in medieval manuscripts in Scotland, and examples of such are Balfure/Balfor/Balfour.[20]

At the beginning of the eighteenth century, there were a greater number of heritors in Fife named Balfour than of any other surname.[21] A heritor was a privileged

---

19. Ibid., *The Social Life of Scotland in the Eighteenth Century.*
20. In his *Memoria Balfouriana*, Sibbald, the Royal geographer (who wrote the texts for Slezers Theatrum Scotiae), states the family of Balfour is divided into several branches, of which those of Balgarvie, Mountwhanney, Denmylne, Ballovy, Carriston and Kirkton are the principal.
21. Five contained no less than 13 landed Balfour properties in, viz., the Balfours of Burleigh, of Fernie, of Dunbog, of Denmylne, of

person in a parish in Scots law. In its original meaning, it signified 'the proprietor of an heritable subject'.[22]
In Scotland, until the early twentieth century, the term
'heritor' was used to denote the feudal landholders of a
parish. Historically landholding in Scotland was feudal
in nature, meaning that all land is technically 'owned'
by the Crown, which, centuries ago, gave it out – feued
it – to various tenants-in-chief in return for specified
services or obligations. Similarly, these tenants-in-chief
gave parcels of land out to lesser 'owners', and the resulting reciprocal obligations too became financial – feudal
dues – or notional. In effect, they were the gentry of the
Scots countryside, with legal privileges and obligations,
and like the gentry in other countries, the heritors ruled
the countryside.[23] There were a few Balfour gentry or
landed proprietors, but many Balfour peasants took the
name from the owners of the land. And since the earliest
recorded history, they would have been subjects of the
feudal elite.

The Scottish Government's website *Scotland's
People* allowed me to trace my Balfour family to the village of Torryburn in the eighteenth century. There were

---

Grange, of Forret, of Randerston, of Radernie, of Northhank, of
Balbirnie, of Halbeath, of Lawlethan, and of Banktown, Torry
and Boghall, Kinloch are also landed properties of the Balfours.
Most were almost contiguous properties stretching from central
Fife to the Firth of Tay.

22. The occasional female landholder so liable was known as an
heririx.
23. They were responsible for justice, law and order in their district
and for keeping the roads in good repair. They were responsible
for appointing and paying – the minister and the schoolmaster,
and for maintaining the church, manse and schoolhouse. They
also had to provide for the poor of their parish. For all this they
levied a rate on all the heritors in the parish – and often included
non-heritor tenant farmers in the rate.

no records of the name Balfour in births, marriages or deaths in Torryburn before 1737. (In searching for where the Balfours were living in the seventeenth century, no clear pattern emerges. I presumed there would be many Balfours in Dunfermline, the closest major town to Torryburn, but the only frequency of Balfours is in east central Fife in such towns as Kettle and Ceres, much closer to the ancient Balfour estates than Torryburn.)

Torryburn

My part of the Balfour clan then emerges in central Fife in the early eighteenth century and can be presumed to have been in servitude to the feudal estates for centuries before that, but it is in Torryburn that they enter the historical record, and it is Torryburn that shapes their lives and character for well over one hundred years. It lies on the north bank of the Firth of Forth. The area's significance in history begins just a few miles west of Torryburn in the town of Colours.

> It is known that Agricola crossed the Forth and marched his troops to the Tay [in 140 CE]. Mr David Beveridge,[24] the historian of Culross, thinks it possible that the Roman general, on his way to the Tay, embarked his troops in galleys at Borrowstounness, and, landing them at Culross, proceeded onwards to Perth via Saline, Cleish, and Kinross. It was in the year [424 a.d] that Pope Celestine sent St Palladius on a mission of conversion to the Scots. Palladius made

---

24. Culross and Tulliallan Volume 1, by David Beveridge, is a replication of a work published before 1885, Books on Demand.

a missionary tour through Scotland, and on reaching Culross he is said to have discovered St Serf or Servanus, who had founded a religious establishment there. Palladius consecrated and ordained St Serf a bishop. And by ancient tradition around this time, mid 6th century, it was the birthplace of the Scottish Apostle St Mungo.

In 1217 Malcolm, the seventh Earl of Fife, founded the monastery, the ruins of which are still extant. The monastery was dedicated to the Virgin Mary and St Serf, and the monks belonged to the Cistercian order founded by St Benedict of Clairvaux. [...] Earl Malcolm, in 1229, long before the building was completed, gave a grant of the lands of Crombie, in the parish of Torryburn, to the Abbey; and lands in many parts of Scotland were subsequently seized, on very flimsy pretexts, to maintain the Abbey of Culross in all the splendour and glory common to the monasteries of the time.[25]

An indication of the town's significance comes from Slezer in *Theatrum Scotiae*,[26] who produced three elaborate drawings of it. In this view from out on the water of the Firth of Forth, the village is depicted very much as it remains to this day. It shows a grand house in the centre of the village, and on the hill above the ruins of the Abbey and the Abbey House. Sibbal's attached this commentary:

---

25. Andrew Cunningham *Romantic Culross, Torryburn, Carnock* [...] 1902.
26. *THEATRUM SCOTIA: Containing the PROSPECTS* [...] by John Slezer, Captain of the Artillery Company [...] London: Published by John Leake. MDCXCIII.

Hath its Name from Cul, which signifies a
Bank or Border, and Rosse, which was the
ancient Name of Fife because it lies in the
Western Corner of that Shire. It is situated on
a Descent at the side of the River of Forth, its
Chief Commodities being Salt and Coals. That
which chiefly adorns it, is the stately Buildings
of the Earl of Kincardine; with the Gardens
and Terrace Walks about it. having a pleasant
Prospect to the very Mouth of the River Forth.
Near unto these Buildings are to be seen the
Ruins of an Ancient Monastery.

The abbey was reduced to ruins during the
reformation

John Slezer's drawing and Sibbald's text are dedicated to Right Honourable Alexander Earl of Kincardin,
Lord Bruce, a descendant of King Robert the Bruce, the
most powerful family in the area. After the Reformation
of 1560, the lands and properties of Culross Abbey passed
to the Colville family. George Bruce's cousin, Alexander
Colville, was appointed as Commendator of the Abbey.
In 1575, he granted the 25-year-old George Bruce a lease
to restore and operate the colliery at Culross, which by
this time had fallen into disuse. Bruce was chosen 'for his
great knowledge and skill in machinery such like as no
other man has in these days; and for his being the likeliest
person to re-establish again the Colliery of Culross'.

The existing Castlehill Shaft stood on the coast
a short distance to the west of Culross. The problem was
that the coal seam it was exploiting led out under the River
Forth. Bruce's solution was revolutionary. He constructed
an artificial island in the River Forth to a height of well
above the high-water mark, and on it sank a shaft to a

depth of 40 feet […] He drained the mine by the Egyptian wheel system. The wheel was driven by three horses and consisted of an endless chain of 36 buckets. The experiment was a success. The pit's location in the river meant that ships could tie up alongside and be loaded with coal direct from the mouth of the shaft.[27]

George Bruce built the grand house shown in the Slezer drawing, strongly Dutch in character, begun in 1593 during the reign of the first Queen Elizabeth, not completed until 1611 when the throne had passed to the Scottish James VI and 1st of England. It had and still has painted ceilings and ornament. In 1608, his kinsman Edward Bruce built an elegant Renaissance palace. (Bruce had played a formative role in bringing the Scottish King to the throne of England.) The complex of buildings, called Abbey House, was to form a quadrangular with square angle pavilions on the corners. Construction was begun in 1608, but only two sides were completed. It is also the subject of the Slezer engraving, and a much-reduced fragment remains. This is one of the earliest Renaissance buildings in either Scotland or England and a grand demonstration of the worldliness and romantic ambition of the Scottish aristocracy. Inigo Jones, England's formative classicist, produced his first designs for buildings in the same year. The architect is unknown. However, it is a premonition of the idealizing imagination of the Scottish enlightenment that would give flower in the Edinburgh New Town.

The Bruces were among the most powerful of the Scottish feudal lord, the grandeur in which they lived was in absolute contrast to the lives of many they exploited, none more so than the large workforce labouring in their mines.

---

27. http://www.scottishmining.co.uk/497.html

Slezer, Theatrum Scotiae:
View of Culross from the
Forth, 1693.

In 1606, in the period of the mines' greatest productivity, Edward Bruce pressed the Scottish king, James VI, to issue the *Anent* (Scotti: concerning) *Salters and Coalyers Law* that condemned all those families working in the salt and coal mines to being enslaved by the owners, in perpetual bondage. A law that remained in effect for almost 200 years.

Salters and Coalyers Law: The actual words of the King are not in dialect, but in the written language of the Scots' educated elite and was presumably what James VI sounded like when he arrived in St James Palace.[28] The law as laid down in the words of the king:[29]

---

28. Consider that this was composed in 1606, the year Shakespeare wrote his Scottish play Macbeth to gain favour with the new King. Nowhere in that text does he attempt to emulate the Scottish language.
29. https://en.wikipedia.org/wiki/Colliers_and_Salters_ (Scotland)_ Act_1606

1606 King James the Sext.

Anent Salters and Coalyers

OUR SOVERAIGNE LORD, and Estates of this present Parliament, statutes and ordeins, that na person within this realme hereafter shall hyre or conduce any Salters, Coalyears or a coal-bearers, without a

George Bruce's Culross Palace

35

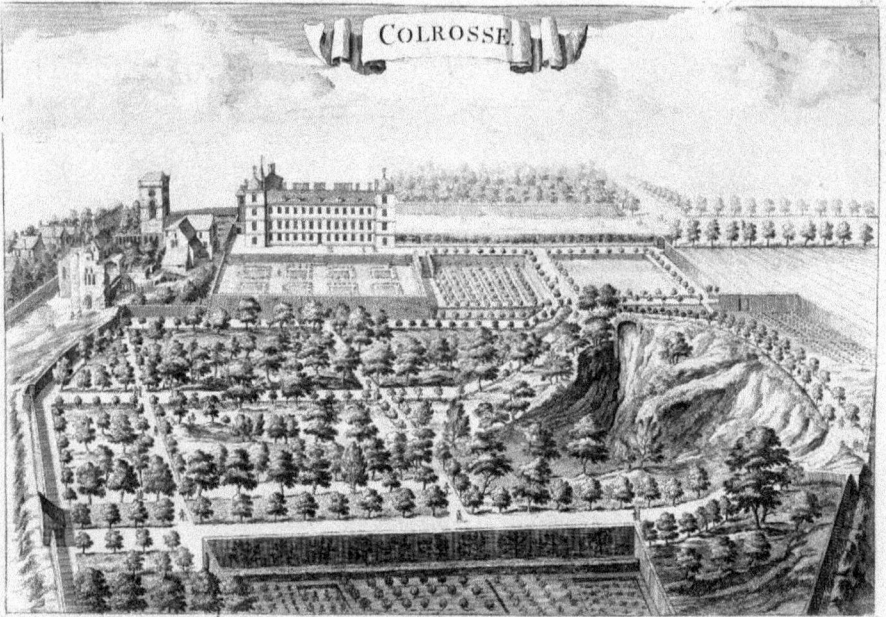

COLROSSE

Slezer, Theatrum Scotiae:
'Colross' Abbey House, 1993.

sufficient testimoniall of their Maister whom they last served, subscryved with his hand, or at least sufficient attestation of ane reasonable cause of their removing, made in presence of ane Baillie, of ane Magistrat of the part where they came fra. And in case any recesue, fee, hyre, supplie or intertaine any of the saids Coalyears, Salter or a Coal-bearers, without ane sufficient testimonie, as said is. The maisters whom fra they came, challenging their servants within yeare and day, that the partie from fra they are challenged, shall delyver them back againe within twentie foure houres, under the paine of ane hundreth pounds, to be payed to that persons whom fra they passed, and that for ilk person; and ilk tyme that they or any of them shall happen to be challenged, and not delyvered, and said is. And

Abbey House in the 1960s before restoration.

the said Coalyears, Coal-bearers and Salters to be esteemed, reput and halded as theives, and punished in their bodies, Viz. Sa many of them as shall receaue forewages and fees. And the saids Estates of this present Parliament, giues power and commission to all maisters and awners of Coal-heughs and pannes, to apprehend all vagabounds and sturdie beggers to be put to

London could barely understand him when he arrived at the Court of Westminster, but the illiterate mining and salter communities across central and eastern Scotland would understand when this was read to them, and it would have been read and repeated until everyone knew that they were being condemned to a form of slavery.[30]

---

30. The slave trade with the British American colonies also began in the early decades of the seventeenth century (with strong Scottish involvement) made slaves the human property of the owners to be bought and sold as needed, which was essentially the situation in Scotland, except they were not traded, but in all other respects their lives were controlled by the owners.

In his *Social Life of Scotland in the Eighteenth Century*,[31] Grey writes:

> Hateful as coal labour everywhere was in those days, specially hateful was life to all engaged in Scotch coal-pits – colliers, coal hewers, and bearers. They lived in serfdom, compelled by law to labour their whole life without hope of freedom. This was the condition also of all who worked in salt pans and of many in mines. If the land was sold they passed with the pit to the purchaser as part of his property. If the son or daughter of a collier or coal hewer once went to work he or she was 'thirled' to it for life. If a workman ran away or gave his services to another coalmaster, he was accounted by an ingenious twist of the law a thief, and punished for having stolen himself, who was his master's property. With such a miserable prospect before them, it seems marvellous that any Salter or coal hewer should ever have permitted his children to enter such a service and endure such a thraldom. But servitude made them an hereditary caste aloof from society.
>
> There existed the strange practice of binding their infants over to the master at the time of baptism, in presence of the minister and neighbours as witnesses; a when a thriftless collier was in sore need of money to defray christening festivities, he often sold the freedom of his son to the employer, who gave arles or earnest money

---

31. Ibid.

to the father, promising to provide his baby serf
thereafter with a garden and house, and protec-
tion in sickness and age. From that hour the
'arled' child was recognised as bound for life
to the pit. This extraordinary state of bondage, sanctioned by Scots law since 1606, there
was no attempt to abolish till 1775, when an
Act was passed to emancipate all who after that
date 'shall begin to work as colliers and salters';
and all those already working who were under
twenty-one years of age were to be set free in
seven years, and those between twenty-one and
thirty were to be liberated in ten years.

An act of 1775 Act noted that the Scottish coal and
salt workers existed in 'a state of slavery or bondage'
and sought to address this. Although the Act noted 'the
reproach of allowing such a State of Servitude to exist in
a Free Country', it sought not to do 'any injury to the present Master' and the Act changed little. It took a further
Act, the Colliers (Scotland) Act 1799 (c.56), to liberate the
remaining mine workers from the conditions created by
the law of 1606. And the mining industry collapsed in
the first decades of the nineteenth century. This appeared
to have been the direct result of the loss of cheap bonded
labour, than with the seams of coal running out. (Though
more than 200 years have passed, I believe the legacy of
these laws is still present in the deep social divisions that
mark Edinburgh and central Scotland into the present.)[32]

---

32. There are parallels between the *Anent Salter and Coalyers and Salters
Laws* and the rise of the slave trade. The Scots in the early seventeenth century began to import tobacco from Virginia, an industry dependent on slavery. And by the end of the century, Scottish
landowners shipped their unwanted clansmen to the new world.

The first record of the Balfours in Torryburn is from 9 July 1737. James Balfour and Margaret Bawd were married when the *Anent Salter and Coalyers and Salters Laws* were very much in effect,

> *James Balfour & Margaret Bawd both from this parish, give up their names to be proclaimed*

Margaret's surname Bawd, even in broad Scots, would have meant a brothel keeper; this must have been either a deliberate or unfortunate mistake by the beadle. One Margaret Bald, of the right age, was born in Dunfermline in 1720,[33] and in 1738 the first Balfour child was born in Torryburn.

> *Aug 5th James Balfour & Margaret Bald had a son named Robert*

Robert subsequently married Helen Nicol in 1762 and had a son also named Robert in 1770.[34] And this third Robert married Mary Erskine in 1787[35] and had a

---

33. 30/11/1720 Dunfermline
    Robert Bald had a woman child born to him of his wife Christian Harrower upon the nineteenth day & baptized on the thirteenth day called Margaret. Witnesses John Anderson & David Bald.
34. 31/07/1762 Torryburn
    July 31st Robert Balfour and Helen Nicol both in this parish gave up their names to be proclaimed in order to marriage
35. 30/09/1770 Torryburn
    Sept. 23rd Robert Balfour and Helen Nicol had a son born Baptized 30th named Robert

son named Thomas in 1791,[36] and a second son, my fifth grandfather named Andrew in 1795:

> *Torryburn June 1795*[37] *Robert Balfour and Mary Erskine had a son Born Bapt. Named Andrew*[38]

Thus, a succession of Balfour families throughout the eighteenth century and into the nineteenth would have inevitably been tied and laboured either in salt panning and coal mining and later weaving; there was nothing else. And Graham's *Social Life in Scotland in the 18th Century* gives a bleak description of life in such small towns as Torryburn:[39]

> The houses inside and outside were filthy,
> though the dirt of their homes, of their food, and
> of their persons did not distress them, except in
> the familiar disease which too often came over
> their bodies. They loved this state; it kept them
> warm; it saved them trouble; and they enshrined
> their tastes in their sayings – 'The mair dirt the
> less hurt', 'The clartier the cosier'. The exposure
> to all weathers outside and to peat reek within,
> which filled the room with smoke and feathered
> the rafters with soot, made their skin hard,
> brown, and withered, and old-looking before
> their time. The dress of the people was of the

36. 17/07/1791 Torryburn
    Baptism Anno 1791 July 6 Robt. Balfour & Mary Erskine had a son born, bapt. 17th named Thomas
37. Marriages Anno 1787
    Nov 2 Robt. Balfour & Mary Erskine both in the parish
38. In 1799, a daughter Margaret was born.
39. Ibid.

rudest and roughest – the women having coarse
home-made drugget, a matted mixture of wool,
spun as it came in natural state from the sheep's
back – usually no gown, but a short woollen
petticoat down to the knees, and their feet were
destitute of shoes or stockings. the farmers' wives
and daughters with 'toys' or head-covering of
coarse linen, and a tartan or red plaid covering
head and shoulders. On Sundays only women
wore their shoes; and so unaccustomed were
they to the use of them, they seemed to hobble
as they walked; so they usually carried-them
in their hands till they came within sight of the
church, when they put them painfully on.

The Scottish Census taken in 1841 reports on my family
living on the High Street in Torryburn Fife: head of the
family Andrew Balfour, brother of Thomas, aged 45, a
sawyer and his wife Jane Williamson and their children:
son Andrew, aged 20, a damask weaver, son Robert and
William (my great step-grandfather) was then aged nine.
And in 1841, the Poor Law Commission held a 'Poor Law
Inquiry'[40] into living conditions in Torryburn
The report concluded:

The population of Torryburn now consists
principally of hand-loom weavers; formerly they
had extensive salt pans, and coal works. They
have still the dregs of that population amongst
them. These, and the low rate of wages paid
to the weavers, have sunk the condition of the

---

40. 1843, Poor Law Commission Extracts from *Poor Law inquiry*
  (*Scotland.*) Appendix, part III.

population very much stationary. The appearance of the houses of the paupers, in point of comfort, is very little inferior to that of the houses of the lowest class of independent labourers. Besides the allowances from the parish funds, which the witness thinks inadequate, a good deal is done for the poor by private charity and contributions are made for them also in coals, so that their condition, on the whole, is perhaps as favourable as in any other part of Scotland; but not equal to what the wants of the poor require.

The witness does not think that there is an adequate provision made for the education of poor children. He is not aware, however, that many are suffered to grow up altogether destitute of education; but he believes that a considerable number must be educated only imperfectly. The feeling of independence, or self-respect, among the lower classes in the parish, is not very strong. They are quite willing to receive parochial relief when they can obtain it; but he knows some cases where the parties must be very ill provided for, and where they struggle, nevertheless, to support themselves independently of parochial aid. Such parties are, he thinks, generally speaking, much above mediocrity in moral worth, and appear to be more under the influence of religious principle.

(On a visit to Torryburn in 2017, it was hard to have any sense of what life would have been like in the past. The concern above was survival in the daily drudgery in the harbour, the mines and the salt pans. I looked in vain for

The graveyard Torryburn Church, 2017 the tombs of the Balfours in the graveyard, for their bodies since 1730 must be lying in rest here. The church was abandoned, and the land was up for sale.[41])

These are the earliest records for both sides of my father's family, the Jamiesons, and the Balfours. The Jamiesons had worked for decades to make a life in the squalor of the old town, being forced to leave because of

---

41. *The New Statistical Account of Scotland for Fife*, FHL book 941 B4sa, 2nd series, vol. 9. 1843, notes that: 'The parish church was rebuilt in 1800 and is located at the east end of the village of Torryburn. It is too small for the population. There are no Seceding or Dissenting places of worship in the parish and the majority of the people profess to adhere to the Established Church. In 1836, the number professing to belong to other denominations was 160 of which 126 were United Secession, 17 Relief Church, 10 Original Burghers, 3 Reformed Presbyterians, and 2 Episcopalians. They likely attend services in Dunfermline'.

the conditions, and returning when the opportunities of the New Town beckoned. These generations of Jamiesons were poor but energetic enough to keep moving to find employment and support families. There is no evidence that the Balfours were ever condemned to the bondage of the *Salter and Coalyers Laws*, as many in Torrymburn would have been, though they would have been subject to an abusive culture that the law created. Because of the poverty and an existence devoid of opportunities, the Balfours, with the rest of Torryburn, as Poor Law Inquiry put it: 'have sunk the condition of the population very much stationary'. And this his was so until my paternal grandfather, William Balfour, left Torryburn for Edinburgh in the 1860s.

The history of my mother's family could not have been more different […]

II

Ambition

As I have admitted when I began this search, I knew nothing about either my mother or my father's family and could name only one of my grandparents – my mother's father James Finlay. It was his grandfather, also named James Finlay, whose marriage announcement from 1829

> *James Finlay, writer,[1] Hanover Street, St Andrews*
> *Parish & Elspit Wallace Same place of Parish, Procla.*
> *no objections.*

raised a most intriguing question: How had he managed at the time of his marriage to become a law clerk and live on Hanover Street, the most prestigious part of the Edinburgh New Town? There was not any evidence of previous wealth or status. What was the source of his good fortune?

Two memories, both are fragments from conversations with my great aunt Susie Finlay Bell. She is the only person I can remember speaking to me about family history when she looked after me when my mother was ill. I now think that these were conversations she wished

---

1. 'Writer' in this context is an old word for lawyer or attorney in Scotland and solicitors in Scotland would have been known as 'writers'.

me to keep to myself. They have come back to me often, why I wonder should these few fragments of conversation have seemed significant enough to remain embedded in my mind for more than 70 years? They have been held in my memory as vignettes, recreations of moments in time, blurred scenes in which I'm a passive witness. In the first, I am there with my great aunt in her bedroom – I must have been eight or nine. She was opening a little jewel box and taking out a faded piece of parchment. I thought it was a letter – unfolding it, I saw it was a family tree, obviously old, written in sepia ink with the heavy marks of a quill pen. And there, near the top of the page, there was a name framed in a box, and below a sentence, 'physician went to the West Indies [...] of whom nothing more has been heard'. I see it clearly to this day.

The second is a memory of a promise, just words and an image of an old lady in a black dress leaning forward, and she may have told me several times, 'when you are old enough', she said, 'you will be eligible for a scholarship to Dr. Bell's Madras school'. She had married in 1911, a railway clerk named James Bell, and I assumed that Dr Bell had some connection to her husband's family. Driven by the notion, hope even that there could be a connection to such as Alexander Graham Bell, I tracked down Bell's ancestors as far as the documents would allow and got nowhere – no famous ancestor. I then typed in Dr Bell's Madras School. And Wikipedia immediately gave me the website of 'Dr Andrew Bell (educationalist)' and led me to a marble monument in Westminster Abbey with the inscription:

> Sacred to the memory of Andrew Bell D.D.
> L.L.D. Prebendary of this Collegiate Church: the
> eminent founder of the Madras System of educa-
> tion, who discovered and reduced to successful
> practice the plan of mutual instruction; founded

upon the multiplication of power, and the division of labour, in the moral and intellectual world, which has been adopted within the British Empire as the national system of education of the children of the poor. In the principles of the Established Church Dr. Bell was born in the city of St Andrew's N.B.27th of March 1753. Appointed minister of St Mary's church Madras 1789, Master of Sherburn Hospital 1809, Prebendary of Westminster 1810. Died 27th of January 1832.

The Andrew Bell Monument, Westminster Abbey

And quickly thereafter to a biography in three volumes: *THE LIFE of THE REV. ANDREW BEL,*[2] and this massive work – much of it tedious reading – has been the key to unlock the earliest recorded history of my mother's family, providing it with extraordinary detail.

I was still made anxious by the ease with which the Bell biography quickly enabled me to find unmistakable blood ties between the Bell family and my mother, and then was astonished to read, early in the first volume, a sentence that came back to me from my childhood. The sentence:

> [...] Captain Caivillie had one son who went to the East Indies as a physician, and of whom nothing more has been ascertained [...]

My memory was wrong in one significant detail – it was to the Dutch East and not the West Indies into which his son disappeared, not surprising as his father was Dutch. Bell, it appears, threw nothing away, and these three volumes were formed out of a mass of material which took over two years to sift through and somewhere in the midst of it all must have been that same folded piece of paper which was so carefully opened by my great aunt. [3]

---

2. *THE LIFE of THE REV. ANDREW BELL, D. D. L.L.D. F. As. S. F.R.S.E.D. Prebendary of Westminster, and Master Sherburn Hospital Durham. COMPRISING THE HISTORY OF THE RISE AND PROGRESS OF THE SYSTEM OF MUTUAL TUITION.* The First Volume by Robert Southey, Esq., P.L., LL.D. The Two Last By His Son, The Rev. Charles Cuthbert Southey, B.A. Oxford. London: John Murray; Edinburgh: William Blackwood & Sons. M.DCCC.XLIV.

3. In my notes for the book before discovering the Bell biography, I wrote 'It was a hand-written chart a family tree, with several branches ending with my aunt's father in the mid 19th century.

Captain James Caivillie:[4] Thus, it revealed the earliest roots of my mother's family, which goes back to Holland around 1670 with the birth of my 7th grand-father Jacobus (James) Caivillie. He is recorded as having been one of the Horse Grenadier Guards in the army of William III, which invaded England in 1688. Although it was an invasion without much opposition, the Dutchman came prepared for war. He put out to sea with 53 warships carrying 1,700 cannons – a massive amount of firepower – followed by hundreds of transport ships carrying an army of 20,000 men, 7,000 horses with Jacobus Caivillie among them. Ten fire-ships loaded with combustible materials were ready to be set ablaze and steered into the ranks of English ships if there was opposition – there was none. This vast fleet set sail on November 1, out into the North Sea and then westwards into the Channel, its progress marked by threatening salutes of cannon fire. Up on deck, regiments of soldiers stood in full formation, and trumpets and drums played martial music for hours on end – a highly effective display of 'shock and awe'. It took three

---

At the top was an entry enclosed in a box with a name I can't recall, but the words below have stayed in my mind and in my imagination ever since – physician went to the West Indies [...] of whom nothing more has been heard'. This sentence was in my mind several years ago as I walked down Cuba Street in Havana and saw a plaque on a handsome classical building; it read 'Carlos J Finley Savior of the city from the scourge of yellow fever'. Alas, I concluded 'I have since been unable find any connection between the savior of Havana and our family'.

4. I have a suspicion the name Caivillie may have been a nickname; he was indeed a cavalier – significantly Dutch family names were not required until 1811 when Emperor Napoleon annexed the Netherlands. Prior to then, the use of names based on the first names of parents or grandparents was much more common – in that case, his Dutch name could have been Jacobson.

days for the news of the impending invasion to arrive in London, by then the number of ships had been inflated to 700. London was restless and filled with rumour and confusion as to why the English Navy was making no attempt to engage the Dutch fleet.

The last half of the seventeenth century was a continuous series of disasters in England, beginning with the execution of Charles I in 1649, for many an act against God. This was followed by the harsh and dictatorial republic under Cromwell until the English monarchy was restored in 1661 by the crowning of Charles II (he had been crowned King of Scotland in 1651). Then plague ravaged the land between 1665 and 1666, leaving over 100,000 dead, but sparing Scotland. And the final tragedy, the Great Fire of 1666, destroyed much of medieval London.

In the 1670s, France and England were allied against Holland, and Charles signed a treaty with French King Louis XIV in which he agreed to convert to Catholicism and support France's war against the Dutch in return for subsidies. The secret clauses stated that Charles would convert to Catholicism 'as soon as the welfare of his realm will permit', which he did on his deathbed. He died in 1685 childless and was succeeded by his brother, who became James II of England and Ireland and James VII of Scotland. He was an active Catholic who alienated the Anglican bishops in England and advocated toleration for Catholics but not for rebellious Presbyterian Covenanters in Scotland. With the Dutch forces on English soil James, despite being offered French support and his army's numerical superiority, declined to attack and gave in. He was captured by the Dutch and allowed to travel to France into the shelter of the French king.

In Scotland, the invader king was titled Willian
II, but was widely referred to as King Billy, and he had
to quickly organize a response to the deposed James trying to regain the Scottish throne: this had the support
of Catholic-leaning clan chiefs. An Oath of Allegiance
to William was demanded of the chiefs, and a Royal
Proclamation offered a pardon to anyone taking the Oath
with severe reprisals for those who did not. Most did, but
failure to sign in time was a pretext for William's troops
to attack the MacDonald's of Glencoe. Many were killed
in the attack, and 40 women and children died later of
exposure after their homes were destroyed. This would
forever cloud the Scottish reign of King Billy.

By 1688, the King had withdrawn most of his
troops in Scotland to join the combined forces of Europe
in the Nine Years' War against France.[5] Which leads to
the question assuming he was part of the Scottish cam-
paign, why did James Caivillie, return to Scotland after
1697, and according to the Bell biography became a wine
importer? Returning not just to Scotland but to the small
university town of St. Andrews? *The Ordnance Gazetteer of*

---

5. Often called the War of the Grand Alliance, a conflict between
   Louis XIV of France and a European coalition of Austria, the
   Holy Roman Empire, the Dutch Republic, Spain, England and
   Savoy. It was fought in Europe and the surrounding seas, Ireland,
   North America and in India, which ended in the treaty signed in
   William's Dutch Place Ryswick, in 1697, after which his armies
   were disbanded. The treaty not only gave victory to the Dutch
   but helped William consolidate power in Scotland. Note, he is
   Lieutenant Caivillie not Captain, and I learn that lieutenant is
   the equivalent of a captain in the land services. The marriage
   announcement for Caivillie's daughter Bettie to James Robertson
   (my 5th great grandparents) begins with a reprimand. Though
   the document says April, the parish records give the date as 24
   August 1721.

Scotland: A Survey of Scottish Topography, Statistical, Biographical and Historical published between 1882 and 1885 records that the town was so impoverished in 1697 that a proposal was made to remove its university to Perth. Among the reasons given:

> [...] there was not a foot of side pavement in any of the streets; filth and squalor abounded unchecked; cows and pigs grazed in front of the colleges; the venerable ruins were fast going, by neglect, to decay, and were littered with rubbish; the lines of the public streets were continually broken by awkward abutments of ungainly houses; there were few visitors of any distinction, even to the splendid links, which lay with all its vast capabilities almost untrodden; and, generally, St Andrews, considering the prestige of its antiquity as an ecclesiastical capital, and its rank as a seat of learning, was at the lowest pitch of miserable neglect and decay.[6]

It could not have been the attraction of such a place but a combination of love and opportunity that brought the captain to the town. There had been trade between the coastal towns of Fife and Holland for centuries, but to establish a business importing wine to an impoverished town may be an invention of subsequent generations. However, it is of interest that he chose to import wine rather than Dutch gin then flooding England, displacing

---

6. A historical perspective, drawn from the *Ordnance Gazetteer of Scotland: A Survey of Scottish Topography, Statistical, Biographical and Historical*, edited by Francis H. Groome and originally published in parts by Thomas C. Jack. Edinburgh: Grange Publishing Works, between 1882 and 1885.

beer as the drink of the masses and causing great harm to that nation's health. The Scots didn't need gin, they had whisky and claret was a favourite drink of the wealthy and the noble.

In 1699 Captain Caivillie married Isobel Greig. They subsequently had three children, one son Anthony and two daughters, Bettie and Margaret, which gives me the name of he who went to the Dutch East Indies and vanished, it was Anthony, born in 1705.

> *1705 Caivillie January 15 Lieutenant James Caivillie[7] and Isobel Greig have a son baptized called Anthony, Witnesses James Rymer and Baillie Morris.*

Daughter Bettie Caivillie married James Robertson in 1721. (It was one of the many so-called irregular marriages in the family for which they were fined.)

> *Jm. Robertson & to be cited The session being informed that Jm. Robertson and Bettie Caivillie[8] are Cohabiting together they appoint them to be cited the next session day. The meeting lead with prayer All St Andrews April fifth ten and twenty-two after prayer*

The Robertsons had had three daughters, Margaret, Agnes and Euphemia. Agnes married Robert Birrell, a shipmaster, Margaret became the wife of Bailie (Alexander) Bell (the biography notes that her friends disapproved) and Euphemia – my 5th Great Grandmother – married

---

7. Named Lieutenant James Caivillie, not captain. Captain would have implied he had a ship.
8. There are several spellings of Caivillie, but I have used the *s* form from this document.

Laurence Norie, a merchant. All were living in St Andrews.

Alex Bell and Margaret Robertson marry after cohabiting in 1747:

> *This Day the Committee appointed to meet at Alex Bell's*
> *house gave in their report the tenor which follows viz. At*
> *Alec Bell's house in St. Andrews October 22, 1747 hora*
> *tertia post meridien, after prayer led by John McCormick*
> *mod. the committee appointed by the session in the*
> *forenoon met according to appointment, the said Alex*
> *Bell and Margaret Robertson being present, the modera-*
> *tor enquired of them upon what grounds they did cohabit*
> *together as if they were man and wife with any proclama-*
> *tion of Banns. Upon which they produced a paper signed*
> *at Edinburgh October 12, 1747 subscribed by one who*
> *calls himself William Jamison, minister Certifying that*
> *Alex Bell and Margaret Robinson foresaid were married*
> *by him,[9] witnesses signing the said paper were Roger*
> *Gibson and Margaret Ferrier. After which the mod.*
> *having rebuked them for their irregularity took them both*
> *engaged to adhere to one another as man and wife and the*
> *said Alex Bell laid down three Shilling's Sterling as the*
> *Clark and the Beadle dues fine*

And 14 years later, in 1761, Margaret's sister Euphemia Robertson married Laurence Norie, again after cohabiting:

> *Laur. Norie paid L6.6..This day Laurence Norie and*
> *Euphemia Robertson summoned compared [?]and*

---

9. There is the implication that many so-called ministers willing for a fee, to offer instant marriage certificates.

*produced marriage lines dated Edin. 11ᵗʰ Curr. and sub-
scribed by one Dannett who stiles himself as a Minister.
They were rebuked for their Irregularity and taken bound
to adhere to one another and behave Dutifully as husband
and wife all the days of their lives. The said Laurence
Norie has put down his fine of half guinea, which was
put into the hands of John Morris purser and of which
he is ordered to pay the Clerk and Beadles One pound five
shilling Scot, as their due.*

In the laws of the Scottish kirk, both the Bell and Norie
marriages were also irregular – they had lived in sin.
Scotland was famous for its distinctive marriage arrangements, which owed much to pre-Reformation canon law,
and were based on principles of mutual consent rather
than religious ceremony, there was tolerance of both 'regular' and 'irregular' marriages, though the church could
impose a fine, which they did in both cases:

> [...] fines imposed on members of the congre-
> gation for any fault or misdemeanour – above
> all for immorality – greatly supplemented the
> parochial funds. These penalties varied accord-
> ing to the frequency or the heinousness of the
> sin, and also according to the social standing of
> the offenders, whose scandal should be further
> expiated by appearing on the stool of repentance
> and being rebuked from the pulpit. To escape
> this latter shame and ordeal, the higher classes
> commuted their penance into a sum of money
> to the Session, and the laird was often absolved
> in private while the servant was condemned in
> public. As the century advanced, and decency
> and common sense opposed the open form of

penance, the practice of exacting money fines
became more usual, and the funds of parishes
were so much enlarged that a third or a half
of its supplies was derived from punishment of
transgressors of morality. [10]

Thus, my mother's family was formed out of unions
between the Robertsons and the Nories,[11] and shaped by
the impoverished but ambitious culture of St Andrews.
(Captain Caivillie's other daughter Margaret married
into a military family, the Mercers.[12] Though her family
moved away, Margaret Caivillie died in St Andrews in
1777 and would have remained close to her sister Bettie.)

St Andrews: A vivid description of St Andrews
in the years Captain Caivillie arrived in the town is in the
Theatrum Scotiae,[13] the work of the aforementioned John
Slezer and Robert Sibbald. Slezer was named by Charles
II, as 'Surveyor of his Majesties Stores and Magazines',
which involved compiling detailed surveys of the country's fortifications. This led to the production of a series

---

10. Ibid, *Social Life of Scotland in the Eighteeneth Century.*
11. The name Norrie (or Norie, or Norry, or Nory, or Norre, or Nore)
    originated in Orkney, and means 'a Northerner' or, more spe-
    cifically, 'someone from Norway', indicating that it referred to
    someone who settled in Orkney from that country. References to
    the name go as far back as Thomas Nory who held the land of
    Corchrony.
12. Whose grandson Alexander Caivillié Mercer was a British artil-
    lery officer famous for his command of G Troop Royal Horse
    Artillery in the thick of the fighting at the Battle of Waterloo,
    and most significantly as the author of *Journal of the Waterloo
    Campaign*; the vivid record of the fighting (still in print). Mercer
    painted many delicate and charming watercolours while serving
    in Canada; they are now in the National gallery of Canada.
13. Ibid., *THEATRUM SCOTIA.*

of engravings of views of castles, abbeys, towns and seats of the nobility. (He could well have met fellow Dutchman Caivillie.) The written descriptions are by Sibbald, Geographer Royal for Scotland, another appointment by Charles II; both were planned as parts of what was to be an *Atlas of Scotland*.

The first volume was produced in 1693. Sibbald's text:

> Saint Andrews, in Latin, Andreanopolis, or Fanum Sancti Andreae, has its Name from St. Andrew, whose Bones are said to be brought hither from Patras, a Town in Peloponnesus, by Regulus a Grecian Monk, Anno 368 a Man in that Age much esteem'd for Piety, as appears by the Church dedicated to him, and called after his Name. From him also (as ancient Writers report) this Town was at first called Regimund, that is, Mons sancti Reguli; for we read that Oengus, or Ungus, King of the Picts, did grant to God and Saint Andrew, That he should be Head of all Churches within the Jurissdiction of the Picts. Likewise, it is manifest from Old Manuscripts, that this was the principal See of the Culdai, who had the care and management of Holy Things from the first reception of Christianity in those Parts.

> Alexander the I King of Scotland, founded a Priory here for the Monks of the Order of St. Augustine, the Government of the Picts being abolished in Britain; and Kenneth III transferred the Episcopal See from Abernethie to St. Andrews, about the Year 850.

Slezer's, View of St Andrews
1693

Faeics Guitatis Sancti ANDREÆ

ect of The Town of St ANDREWS.

This City is the Metropolis of the whole
Kingdom, and the See of an Archbishop, who is
Primate of all Scotland. It lies towards the East
with a pleasant Prospect to the Ocean, having
a Harbour for Ships, the Sea near it plentiful in
Fishes, and Fields wholesome and spacious.

There yet remain the Marks of Venerable
Antiquity, the Ruines of the Cathedral Church
and Monastery, which do abundantly testifie
their Ancient Glory and Magnificence. The
Town itself is situate in a Plain, from East to
West, with a most pleasant Prospect to the
German Ocean. It had a very strong Castle of
Old, whose Rubbish and Ruines are yet to be
seen upon the Rocks on the Sea-side towards
the North. It has Streets straight and broad,
stretching East and West, whereof two lead to
that once famous Abbey of Canons Regular of
the Order of St. Augustine, situate toward the
East and South-East, the Wall surrounding this
Abbey being yet intire, and of hewen Stone,
with many Towers and Turrets which give it the
Resemblance of a King's Palace.

The remains of Saint Andrew (in Christian tradition,
brother of the Apostle Peter, born in Galilee in BCE) that
were alledgedly brought to the town are recorded as having
included an arm, kneecap, three fingers and a tooth. And
it was this assortment of bones that led to the construction
of a massive cathedral in 1160, shaped by French vision
and craftsmen. It became the largest place of pilgrimage in
medieval Scotland, attracting pilgrims, trade and wealth
from across Europe. St Andrews was, up until the late
medieval period, the ecclesiastical capital of Scotland.

The cathedral was destroyed in 1559 by what the
Scottish Gazetteer calls a rascal multitude' of Reformers:

> [...] who had been urged on to their work of
> destruction by four successive days of the fiery
> eloquence of John Knox in those famous ser-
> mons against idolatry, wherein he: `did intreet
> [treat of] the ejectioune of the buyers and the
> sellers furthe of the temple of Jerusalem, as it is
> written in the evangelists Matthew and John;
> and so applied the corruptioune that was then
> to the corruptioune in the papistrie; and Christ's
> fact to the devote [duty] of thois to whome God
> giveth the power and zeill thereto, that as weill
> the magistrates, the proveist and baillies, as the
> commonalty, did agree to remove all monuments
> of idolatrie, whilk also they did with expeditioun.

It concludes that 'in a single day the magnificent building
which had cost so many years of labour and so much toil
and thought was utterly ruined'.

The university was created in 1410 as a part of
the cathedral when a group of Augustinian clergy, driven
from the University of Paris by the Avignon Schism and
from the Universities of Oxford and Cambridge by the
Anglo-Scottish Wars, formed a society of higher learning in St Andrews and the continual presence of the university sustained the status of the town no matter how
impoverished.

Bell's father Alexander was a barber and wigmaker, from the Bell biography:

> [...] the house in which he lived, and which
> was his own, stood in South Street, on the east

side of the town or parish church, and adjoining it. It consisted of two stories, with an outer staircase supported by wooden pillars, and a wooden projection into the street. This served for his shop, and there he enjoyed his afternoon lounge

A photograph from 1845 shows a house as described, a hundred years after Alex. Bell bustled around the town, by then taken over by the poor of St Andrews – fisherwomen, the poorest of the poor. (This was taken by the pioneering early photographers David Octavius Hill and Robert Adamson.[14] Adamson was born in St Andrews.)

Hill & Adamson: North Street
St Andrews 1845

14. Robert Adamson was a polymath whose knowledge of chemistry advanced early photography in partnership with the artist David Octavius Hill. They produced some 2,500 calotypes between 1843 until Adamson's untimely death in 1848.

The most compelling descriptions of life in a Scottish town at the time of the marriages is given in *The Social Life of Scotland in the Eighteenth Century*. It was written by Graham Henry Grey in the last decades of the nineteenth century and published in 1901:

> No carpets covered these floors, and, indeed, even after the middle of the century many houses of pretension remained without them, except in the public rooms. The bedrooms rarely had grates, the fuel of turf or peat being kindled on the wide-open hearth; and only some of the chambers were what were called 'fire-rooms', for many were destitute of fireplaces. The beds were closed like a box in the wall, or in recesses with sliding doors, which imprisoned and stifled the sleeper; others stood out in the room with curtains of plaiding which the household had spun, as protection from the cold and draughts which came from ill-jointed windows and doors with ill-fitting 'snecks'.

> As houses were incommodious and hospitality wass exuberant, it was usual for two gentlemen or two ladies, however unknown to each other they might be, to sleep together, lying overwhelmed with the burden of from six to ten pair of Scots blankets. Even in the drawing-room it was usual to have a closed bed, which was used by the guests.

> It was in the bedroom the family lived chiefly. There they took their meals, there they saw their friends, there at night the family gathered round the hearth, with its high-polished brass

South Street St Andrews, with St Rules Tower in the Distance, Hill and Adamson 1845.

grate, which stood detached from the back and sides of the fireplace ornamented with tiles. There the girls spun, and lads learned the rules of Despauter's Latin Grammar; and only after 'family exercises' did the household disperse, and the heads of the family were left to rest and to sleep in the exhausted air.

The food consisted incessantly of broth, or kail, of beef or mutton, the broth being made of 'groats', which were oats stripped of their husks at the mill, or of bear or barley which had been beaten at the-knocking-stone in the morning, and hence known as 'knockit bear', for as yet barley mills were not introduced into Scotland. Only in summer or autumn could fresh meat be had; for, as all the cattle were kept under cover during winter and spring, and fed on straw or mashed whins, the flesh of the half-starve emaciated brutes was utterly worthless as food. To obtain a supply for store at Martinmas,

therefore, the 'mart' was killed; each household
had cows and sheep slaughtered and salted sufficient to last till next May; and on this salted
Turnips – neeps as they were always called –
were only in a few gardens; onions were in none,
being all imported from Holland or Flanders;
and only at the residences of a few rich and
enterprising gentlemen were potatoes grown.

When breakfast was served, at eight o'clock, he
was ready for the substantial fare of 'skink' or
water gruel, supplemented by collops or mutton,
aided with ale. The bread consisted of oatmeal
cakes or barley bannocks: wheaten bread was
scarce, and rarely used except as a dainty. To
accompany this simple but not attractive repast,
there was strong ale in ample supply, and sometimes sack or claret, which was good and cheap
at a shilling the chopin when it came duty-free
from France. To serve for the family, there was
in many a household only one glass or tankard,
which was handed on to the next person in succession as each finished his draught.

At seven or eight o'clock came supper – a substantial meal of the dinner type, with ale and
claret. But before that repast was the essential
'four hours', the name being derived from the
time of refreshment in every house from the
highest to the lowest. Ladies took their ale and
wine; and if there were guests, as a delicacy a
few slices of wheaten bread were cut and handed
with cake to the company. Tea rare. The guests
were apt to convey their food to their mouths at
the end of their knives

Even in houses of high position the women servants went without shoes or stockings, clad in short worsted petticoats or dresses of coarse plaiding. Their wages were about 15s. to 20s. a year, supplemented by a gown or a pair of shoes, which were chiefly worn on Sunday at kirk. At home, or even to kirk and market, a gentleman went about in homespun clothing and home-made woollen shirt,which had been spun by his wife, family and servants, and woven by the village 'wabster'. While the plain-living and quiet-fashioned were content to go to kirk in the black kelt coat of their ladies' making, others, though they went about in the morning in greasy nightcaps, coats out at elbows, and dirty night or dressing-gowns, in public appeared in their coat and waistcoat trimmed with silver or gold, their silk stockings and jack-boots, with peri-wig or Families wig, surmounted by the laced three-cornered hat [...] But however desirous to be in fashion, every Scots lady had that essential part of national costume, the plaid, wrapped loosely about the head and body, made either of silk or of wool with a silken lining of bright green or scarlet, while the common people wore their gaudy-coloured plaids of coarse worsted.

There was little coin in circulation in the coun-try [...] not sufficient for the currency needs of the country; gold was never seen; silver was exceedingly scarce, especially after all the Scots coinage had been called in subsequent to the Union. The default of Scots or English money, foreign coins were in ready use, and money which came from Holland, Spain, and France was welcome, though it was far from plentiful, because the imports much exceeded the exports. Leg-dollars, rix-dollars, guilders and ducatoons were of service as home currency; but these became still scarcer, owing to their being drawn to England for the wars [...] The blacksmith, and the joiner were allowed as part wages so many firlots of oats or of barley; and sometimes the pay of mechanics about the house was reckoned in so much grain a year and in the scarcity bonds and bills were negotiable as substitutes. Accordingly, in the parish poor-box, during the course of a year, met a strange fraternity of coins of all ages, peoples, and tongues – most of them shapeless, illegible, diminutive – from doits to turners, from placks to bawbees, from 'Irish harps' to 'English clipped money'; while lying among their poor neighbours might be found a Spanish rix dollar, or Flemish guilder. Kirk-Session records of these days teem with bitter lamentations over the poverty-stricken sin.[15]

Andrew Bell, born 1753:

*Bell Andrew to Alexander Bell periwig maker&
Margaret Robertson[16] his spouse, born on the 27th March
1753 and baptized on the 1st of April thereafter by
Mr. John Mair. Witnesses William Lonsdale & John
Wallace*

---

15. Ibid., *The Social Life of Scotland in the Eighteenth.*
16. The biography makes but one further comment on Bell's mother Margaret: 'She was of an eccentric disposition; a little of this tendency appeared in some of her children; it assumed the character of decided insanity as she advanced in years, and conclusive proof of this appeared by her putting an end to her own life'.

South Street St Andrews from St Rules Tower, Hill and Adamson 1845

St Andrews may have been impoverished, but there must have been enough wealth to support Bell's wigmaker father and a shipwright by the name of Finlay (my mother's maiden name). It would have been the shipping trade with Europe and to a lesser degree the university that created whatever affluence there was, successors of James Caivillie's wine imports and the like. Surprisingly there is no evidence of the town being shaped or enhanced by the presence of major feudal estates so dominant elsewhere in Scotland.

The university could not have been expected to support wigmakers and shipwrights, it had but a handful

of professors and its buildings were crumbling and was
often beset by civil and religious disturbances. In a particularly acute depression in 1747, severe financial problems triggered the dissolution of one of its colleges.[17]
Throughout this period, student numbers were low; when
Samuel Johnson visited in 1773, there were fewer than
100 pupils. This was the year Alex. Bell's son Andrew
aged 20 graduated and considered his future in a town
devoid of opportunity.

    The Bell biography is quite exact: 'In his own
country, narrow circumstances were likely to render his
advancement difficult and slow; he looked to the colonies,
therefore, as a more promising spot, and having received
some offers from Virginia which it was thought advisable to accept, embarked for America in the twenty-first
year of his age'. It is notable that the modest society of St.
Andrews, some might call it rural, was able to inspire the
ambitions of a young man to consider travelling across
the world and reinventing himself. [...] he sailed from
Glasgow, early in the year 1774. There is no part of his
life [...] which so little is known, as the first five years of
his residence in America. It appears that he was engaged
in tuition for the most, if not the whole of that time, and
that he went out with some definite engagement of this
kind; but what that engagement was, or even where, there
are now no means of ascertaining.[18]

---

17. St Leonard's, whose properties and staff were merged into St
Salvator's College to form the United College of St Salvator
and St Leonard. (It was to St Salvator's College that that my
seventeenth-century relation Walter Glendie, endowed a bursary in 1690.)
18. Ibid., Bell biography.

It seems not to have been difficult for a well-educated, ambitious young Scotsman to find sponsorship to the English colonies in the early 1770s, even at the start of the Revolutionary War. These were years when 'Glasgow's Tobacco Lords', as these merchants were called, were handling more than half the tobacco being imported into Britain. So important was tobacco to Glasgow that the city's merchants showed their support for the American cause in successfully pressuring the burgh corporation not to submit a loyal address to the King after the first battles in the American War of Independence. Well into the war years, there were continual sailings from Glasgow to Baltimore, the port for the great tobacco-growing areas in Virginia.

The details of his life in Virginia become clearer from the year 1779, when he engaged as private tutor, at a salary of £200 a year [a significant sum] in the family of Mr Carter Braxton, who was then a wealthy merchant of West Point, Virginia.[19]

Bell, it can be assumed, lived and carried out his duties on the Braxton estate, Chericoke in King William County, Virginia. Braxton, an aristocratic Virginia planter, had through inheritance and marriage acquired large amounts of land and numbers of slaves. He both cultivated and traded tobacco, and his family had traded slaves with the West Indies.[20] Along with Thomas Jefferson, he was part of the Virginia delegation to the Continental Congress and served from February until August 1776. In that capacity, he signed the Declaration of Independence. Although Braxton supported independence, he published

---

19. Ibid., Bell biography.
20. Persons with the name Carter Braxton since the end of the Civil War have been, and are, African American, presumably descendants of slaves on Braxton's plantation(s).

a pamphlet that challenged the democratic ideas of John Adams and, as a result, was sent home from the Congress. Several aspects of Bell's employment seem significant. First, Bell was hired in 1779, four years after the first military engagements in the American Revolutionary War – the battles of Concord and Lexington, and three years after the Continental Congress, the governing body of the United States during the Revolution, in which Braxton served. Second, Jefferson would have been a visitor to the estate, and Bell would surely have been witness to some of the formative debates in the shaping of the new nation. Third, even before he returned to England, Braxton was loaning money to the Revolution and funding shipping and ordering his vessels to engage in privateering attacks against the British. Soon after Bell left Virginia, the British retaliated, destroying many of Braxton's ships and ravaging his plantations.

Carter Braxton[21]

---

21. Ole Erekson, Engraver, c1876, (Library of Congress).

Consider that Bell was housed in Chericoke, a vast planter's mansion, furnished in the most exquisite Georgian taste, living with a family of Virginia aristocrats in one of the largest plantations in the Colony with hundreds of slaves. And, further that his employer Braxton, was an acquaintance of Thomas Jefferson and he likely met other leaders in the Revolutionary War; his journals make no mention of any of this, no acknowledgement that he was witness to the most significant revolution in modern history. In his journals, he sums up his American experience with a detailed list of all the money he was owed. (His concern with money is a persistent issue throughout the biography, and for my family, this is of more than passing interest because in the end we were modest beneficiaries of his acquisitiveness.)

The biography notes that his employment with 'Braxton continued about two years, and then, in consequence of the political state of the province, he thought proper to return to his own country for a while'. He sailed back to Britain in spring of 1781 after agreeing to continue tutoring Braxton's sons in Europe, from the biography:

> His connexion with Mr. Braxton was not broken by this removal, that gentleman being (in his own words) induced by the high sense he entertained, after two years' experience, of Mr. Bell's morality and great abilities as a tutor, to send his two younger sons, Corbin and Carter, under his care to Europe.[22]

There is a remarkable coda to his colonial adventure; on his return journey to England, he was shipwrecked on the

---

22. Ibid.. Bell bio.

coast near Halifax, Nova Scotia, and fearing death, wrote
a will in his pocketbook; which in part stated:

> 27th, [March 1771.] Revised this book, and, set-
> tling all my accounts, I owe nothing to any man
> in America ; and declare, on the word of a man
> who expects death, that Mr. Braxton owes me
> by bond 25,634 lbs. of tobacco, and upwards of
> £10 sterling; praying them to forward my bills of
> exchange in their hands to my father, Bailie A.
> Bell, of St Andrews, North Britain, as I hereby
> give them power ; as also that they will remem-
> ber that he and his heirs are my proper heirs.
> (Signed) 'Andrew Bell'.[23]

Despite falling into bankruptcy in part because of attacks
on his assets by the British forces, Braxton continued to
pay Bell modestly for supervising his son's studies at the
University of St Andrews; however, he reports regretfully
that Braxton never repays the major debt owing. Whether
Bell was aware that this was because of Braxton's ruin is
not recorded. Again, it is surprising that Braxton's sons
travelled to Scotland at the height of the Revolutionary
War with the American coast blockaded by the British
Navy.

    Bell's restless career was a continual search for
wealth and influence. A mere five years after returning to
Britain, an acquaintance of his father:

> [...] proposed to him that, instead of content-
> ing himself with a scanty subsistence at Leith
> and looking forward to indefinite hopes of

---

23. Ibid., Bell bio.

> preferment in England, he should go to India,
> where there was every probability that he might
> turn his talents and acquirements to good
> account as a philosophical lecturer, and in the
> way of tuition […] and promised him introduc-
> tion to the persons in authority there.

He sailed for India in 1787 and returned to Britain in 1796. Before leaving, he was told that his success would be greatly enhanced by having a doctoral degree, so he asked the University of St. Andrews to confer such a degree and was disappointed when they willingly named him Doctor of Medicine, a field in which he had absolutely no knowl-edge. And after nine years in India, he returned to England as a celebrity, having created 'a process of teaching school age children, rich and poor, in which pupils wherever pos-sible become the teacher' – the Madras System. And as was his way he returned with a small fortune.

Bell's concern with money and influence appears to have been the driving force in his life, certainly as strong as his faith. His life in the years that follow has little connection to the family history, as he hunts the nation for well-paid religious positions, and puts great energy into promoting his teaching system. His preaching and writ-ings on education made him a favourite of the aristoc-racy, becoming sufficiently celebrated for Queen Victoria to invite him to tea. He became wealthy and in his later years bequeathed a small part of that wealth to save my family from destitution.

The Finlays and the Bells: While he was wan-dering the world, my mother's family the Finlays,[24] thrived

---

24. Finlay is an Old Scottish name, from the Gaelic personal name Fionnlagh, which is composed of the elements fionn, meaning 'white, fair', with laoch, warrior or hero. The name was early

in eighteenth-century St Andrews. They were recorded in Parish records well back in the seventeenth century. The eighteenth-century records for my family begin with birth of Thomas Finlay in 1726 to Alex Finlay and Agnes Barchlet in Leuchars, a town within a morning's walk to St Andrews. This same Thomas Finlay had a son with Margaret Mackie named James Finlay in St Andrews around 1750. And James married Elizabeth Wood[25] in the Parish of St Andrews and St Leonards in 1768. The record shows that they also had been living irregularly:

> *The superiors being informed the James Finlay and*
> *Eliz. Wood have been irregularly married. They appoint*
> *the following [Church] committee to inquire into the mat-*
> *ter and in case[?]that they found it so.*

The connection between the Bells and the Finlays is further revealed in a document from the charters and miscellaneous writs in the records of the Burgh of St Andrews. Translated from Latin, it records a meeting on

---

reinforced by the Old Norse personal name Finnleikr, composed of the elements Finn, and leikr, meaning 'play, sport'. As a personal name, 'Finlay' is first recorded in circa 1070 as Fionnlaoich, and in the *Book of Leinster*, the name of MacBeth's father is spelled Findlech (1070); Fynlai was provost of Stirling in 1327. In the Western Isle of Lewis, the fairies are called in Gaelic Muinntir Fhionlaidh. The first recorded spelling of the family name is shown to be that of Andrew Fyndelai, Chaplain of Brechin, which was dated 1526, Register of the Church of Brechin, during the reign of King James V of Scotland, 1513–1542. Scotland is a small world, and Andrew Fyndelai might link to other family threads in Brechin.

25. 1747 Birth of Elizabeth Wood Tuliallan – some distance from St Andrews?? Her mother was a Mercer – possibly a connection the English Mercers.

2 July 1782, 'called by the provost the city to choose men who would act as 'curators during the minority of Andrew Finlay (Findlay), minor lawful son of the deceased William Finlay (Findlay), shipmaster in St Andrews. His death is not mentioned in the parish records, presumably because he was lost at sea and the body was not recovered. Andrew, the male twin whose birth is recorded above, would have been fourteen years old when the document was drawn up.

A *curator ad litem* is a legal representative in Scots law appointed by a court to represent, during legal proceedings, the best interests for a child or for a person who is mentally or physically incapacitated. In the eighteenth century, such individuals need have no legal training. The names proposed: 'nearest of kin on the father's side; Mr. Andrew Bell M.A. and Laurence Norrie (Norie), merchant in St Andrews, nearest of kin on the mother's side'.[26] Here we see all parts of my eighteenth-century family in St Andrews gathered together, including the soon-to-be the illustrious future Reverend Bell, who just returned from Virginia. It shows Andrew Bells' closeness at that time to his family.

> Andrew Finlay names and chooses the following men to act as curators during his minority, any two whereof constituting a quorum – James Finlay, wright, Alexander Bell, wigmaker and former bailie, and the Rev. Mr. George Hill'. Note that Andrew Bell is missing, he would have already planned to leave the city and his father was a willing substitute. The agreement is also a document of the surprisingly extensive holdings

---

26. Charters and miscellaneous writs in the records of the Burgh of St Andrews.

of the deceased mariner Willian Finlay; 'over
12 acres of arable land in small plots all around
the town, as we'll as property on the southern
main street of the town'.[27]

---

27. The estates comprise the following: The fourth part of 1 acre 3
roods of land lying among the priory acres in the territory called
Wester Rufflets bounded between the common way leading to
Cupar to the north, and the common way leading to Kirkaldy
to the south;

2 acres of arable land lying in the said priory of St Andrews
in the territory called New Grange, formerly belonging to
John Carstairs elder, bounded by the acres sometime of
Margaret Fairfull to the north, the acres sometime of William
Corstorphine (Carstorphin) to the east, the common way lead-
ing to Pittenweem to the west and the acres sometime of James
Oliphant to the south;

2½ acres among the acres of the said priory in the territory
called Broomfaulds, having Pitmilly (Pitmily) Meadow to the
north, and the lands of Cairnsbank (Cairns) to the south;

1 acre of land with pertinents lying among the priory acres in
the territory called the Canongate;

3½ acres of arable land with pertinents lying among the lands
of Easter and Wester Granges;

2 roods of arable land with pertinents lying among the priory
acres in the territory called Hallow Hill bounded by the acres
sometime of Thomas Carstairs to the east, Dickson's Den and
the Cannongate to the south, the commonalty of Balone (Ballon)
and Kiness Burn to the west and north, all which lands lie within
the parish and regality of St Andrews, sheriffdom of Fife

1 acre in Wester Sandyhill between the acres of the deceased
[blank] Reid and now [blank] to the west, the to the south, the acres
of William Kidd to the north and the common way to the east;

A fourth part of the tenement under and above, back and fore
with the yard crofts and pertinents on the south side of South
Street, St Andrews, bounded by the tenement belonging to the
deceased John Wilson, then to the heirs of William Duncan and
now to [blank] to the east, [blank] to the south, the tenement
sometime of Robert Jack now of John Wemyss to the west, and
the tenement lately sold to the said John Wemyss to the north.

These are described in the text with such care that they can be plotted on maps to this day. In conclusion, it states that the Bell and Norie families share the revenue from the properties.

The document is also valuable in giving their occupations: William Finlay, mariner; James Finlay (5th grandfather) wright, and William Gourlay, weaver; Mr Andrew Bell M.A., scholar (proudly adding the Master of Arts to his name), his father Alexander Bell, wigmaker and Laurence Norie, merchant. These were not peasants; they were not farmers or fisherfolk; they were all involved in respected and relatively remunerative occupations. The senior Bell would earn his keep tending to the stylish wigs of the small but affluent community of the church and the university. Given the size of the town, he may have been the only one. The scholarly Andrew Bell's education would make his fortune, while the others were in various ways involved with the trade, the ships and shipbuilding around the port.

This is another photograph of St Andrews by David Octavius Hill and Robert Adamson, taken in the fall of 1845. It is a view of the harbour, a scene that had changed little since the 1770s when the men of both families gathered to look after the interests of the minor Finlay. This port was the main stage of the family's business activities throughout the eighteenth century. The photograph is an artful composition: two small brigs in the foreground frame the views of the tower of St Rule, immensely tall for the eleventh century, built to guide pilgrims arriving by sea to visit the relics of Saint Andrew[28] and in the centre the ruined East facade of the cathedral. It is low tide and

---

28. St Rule is believed to have carried the relics of St Andrew from the Greek island of Patras to this remote coast of Fife.

the ship keels are sitting in the mud. A solitary figure on a broken wall is staring at the sea. The ships are of similar size, but are different; the one on the left is single-masted. A coastal smack was possibly operating on regular runs to Edinburgh. On the right, a square-rigged Brigantine was designed to carry all manner of cargo in the tramp trade without a fixed schedule or published ports of call. The masts and elaborate rigging on the boat on the right are the centuries-old technology of sailing, still in use decades after the introduction of steam power. Though indistinct, there appear to be men working on both ships and on the quay carts and horses waiting to receive the cargo; one is just visible behind the gaff-rigging on the right. The buildings appear ancient; on the left, a warehouse with more trundle carts outside. The two-storey terraces could be homes with workshops on the ground floor.

It may be that this group of families were among the most actively involved in the business of the port; they were traders, merchants, sailors and shipwrights, all successful within the limited opportunities of St Andrews. It was here that James Caivillie established a trading business with Europe around 1700. He was called a wine importer, which would suggest trading with France, yet the traditional exchange for small harbours around the coast of Fife was Holland, which would have been the obvious choice for a Dutchman like Caivillie. It was here that the merchant Laurence Norie did business exporting wool, animal skins, salted fish, sheep, horses, and even oxen, and on return, possibly importing a wide variety of goods. From Germany and from the Netherlands would come Jenever (gin), vinegar, linseed, clover seed, madder, smalts and small manufactured items such as stone bottles, pencils, paper, mirrors, spectacles, weapons and cutlery. There would have been small quantities of luxury goods such as linens and silk, carpets and tapestries and there would have been an occasional ship arriving from much further south carrying port wine, oranges, lemons, figs and nuts, onions, cork. Norrie may have exported the product of his kin, the weaver William Gourlay; there is no indication of what he wove, but at the time, Fife was producing high-quality damask for export in these years.

James Finlay is described as a 'wright', which in the eighteenth-century Scottish English means 'skilled woodworker'. Who would have employed a skilled woodworker in St Andrews, accepting that the University had no money? The answer, James Finlay was a ship carpenter or shipwright – choosing timbers, laying the keel and building and repairing the boats that were essential to both trade and to the fishing fleet. And this shipwright would have occasionally gone to sea with his brother, and it was from this harbour that shipmaster William Finlay sailed, presumably to his death, leaving the young Andrew fatherless.

In 1777, a very young Andrew Finlay was a witness to the birth of a second James Finlay.

James son to James Finlay, Wright in this city (St ANDREWS) and Elizabeth Wood, his spouse was born on the 1ˢᵗ of April 1777 and baptized on the 6ᵗʰ by Doctor Gillespie before these witnesses, Conveener Finlay and Andrew Finlay Jnr.

And this second James Finlay was apprenticed as a shipwright to his father and, around 1803, married May, the daughter of Laurence and Euphemia Norie. In 1805, a third James Finlay (Great, Great Maternal Grandfather) was born in Yarmouth, Norfolk, while he was serving in the Fife Militia.

*Finlay in 1805} James son James Finlay Lieutenant
in Fife Militia and May Finlay his wife was born at
Yarmouth Norfolk, 15th baptized, 22nd Aril 1805, BY
Mr. Crichton Minister of Forces* [29]

James Finlay's birth was registered twice. Though born
in 1805, he was given a Scottish baptism in 1811, with
a brother named Andrew Bell Finlay, perhaps showing
the eagerness with which the Finlays wished to please the
illustrious Dr Andrew Bell. (Andrew Bell Finlay's death
was recorded in St Andrews on 22 December 1814.) Recall
Euphemia Robertson Norie was Andrew Bell's aunt, his
mother's sister. And May Norie Finlay, his second cousin.
Such an intertwined family. My mother's name was May
Finlay.

     With Napoleon's Army massing on the French
coast just across the English Channel, the British had
to mobilize. Thousands of troops were sent to positions
around the south-east of England, ready to counterattack.
The Fife Militia was just one of the scores of such regiments marching to and fro over the countryside. (They
didn't see battle, but were used with much complaint, as
prison guards.) Finlay's Fife Militia arrived in Yarmouth
in November 1804, and the third James was born the following April. Lieutenant Finlay had enlisted in 1803 and
resigned in 1808, returning to St Andrews and to penury.
This is stated in the biography without explanation, but

---

29. There was a second entry, a second child born in 1809, Charles,
who must have died in infancy *Finlay in 1809} Charles son of James
Finlay, adjutant to the 2nd Reg. of the Fife Local. Rev Dr. Hill Militia and
May Finlay his wife was born at St Andrews on the 15th baptized 21st ditto
1809 October. Witnesses Laurie Norie & Mrs. Norie?*

his inability to find work could have been the direct result of the war blocking trade with the continent and the mariners and the ship-owners, along with the shipwrights became destitute. At which point, Andrew Bell, now Dr Bell again re-enters the picture.

The Rev, Andrew Bell, Master of Sherburn Hospital Originator of the Madras System. After William Owen. (National Galleries of Scotland)

The Bequest: In Chapter 40 of the third volume of Bell's biography is a topic titled 'His allowance to his relations'. It admits:

We have hitherto heard little or nothing concerning Dr. Bell's relatives in Scotland. He had, indeed, been a wanderer during so large a part of his early life, that the ties which bound him to his native country were naturally somewhat weakened, and, it must also be remembered, that the sphere in which he now moved was considerably above that in which he had been born ; moreover, with the exception of Miss Bell, (the 'gentle Jessy' of his early letters,) [his sister] he had no other very near connexion living. He was not, however, unmindful either of her or of his other relations; and I shall take this occasion of his present visit to St Andrews, to recount, briefly, his proceedings with respect to them, for some years past.

[...] In January 1812, [Bell] received a letter informing him that Mrs. Finlay [my fourth great grandmother)] and her family were left almost destitute by the death of her husband, (who had at one time been adjutant in the coast militia, and had subsequently taken up the trade of carpenter, to which he had been brought up,) and that a subscription was about to be made for them.

James Finlay Cabinet Maker has died on the 8th of January 1812

In consequence of this, he wrote to Mrs. Cook, making enquiries as to what arrangements were likely to be made: to which she replied, that the widow was going to live with her father and

mother; and added, that the subscription had
fallen far short of what had been looked for. Dr.
Bell's answer is very characteristic of his cautious mode of proceeding. 'At present', he writes,
'I can commit myself or even my name in no
shape to poor Mrs. Finlay; but I beg that you
will appropriate my last remittance (till I supply its place) of £10 to her, in such weekly or
monthly sums as you see fit. But I must particularly request, that you will state that you act, in
what you give, by no specific instructions from
me, and that this sum comes, as it really does,
from another quarter'.

Mrs Cook, in her next letter, tells him it was impossible
to conceal the source of this supply from Mrs Finlay, who
expressed great gratitude for it. It continues:

[...] Soon after this, the College bursary, of
which Dr. Bell was patron, (which was worth
about £12 a-year,) was given for the use of Mrs.
Finlay's son, James. As, however, he was only six
years old, there was some difficulty in managing
this, so as not to infringe upon the regulations of
the founder's will. 'I need not assure you', writes
Professor Hill to Dr. Bell, 'that, from motives of
benevolence, joined to our esteem and regard for
you, my colleagues and I were most desirous of
serving your relation, young Finlay. Our difficulty was this: – From one passage in the deed of
mortification, Miss Bell was of opinion, that the
Glendee bursary might be enjoyed by a boy at
school. But after a careful perusal of the whole, we
were satisfied that the founder meant to require
the bursar to be at college, though he wished him

to continue at the humanity class till he should be
qualified to begin the study of Greek and philosophy. To allow a boy of six years old, however, to
enter the humanity class, would have been a gross
abuse, and therefore we determined to propose
to you, as patron, to leave the bursary vacant till
Finlay shall be capable of becoming a student,
we, in the meantime, paying the amount of the
bursary to Mrs. Finlay, for the behoof of her son'.

In the following September, Mrs Cook wrote Bell,
informing him of the death of Mrs Finlay, my third great
grandmother and mother of the third James Finlay, then
aged 8, after a lingering illness and of the almost complete destitution in which her children were left. In his
reply, he said he was unable to decide what he could do
for the family at present and requested some further information as to what arrangements were likely to be made.
Accordingly, Mrs. Cook suggested that, if an annuity
of from £20 to £30 per annum could be, in any way,
secured to them, this, with what their other friends could
contribute, would provide for them until they were able to
support themselves.

*May Norie widow of Mr. James Finlay Cabinet maker,
has died 18th Sept 1814:*

The letter continued:

Dr. Bell, however, still said he was unable to
make any specific pledge on this point, having
'great duties to perform, and heavy obligations
to discharge'; and, not wishing to take on himself any new burdens that might prove incompat-
ible with these, he stated at the same time, that

in case the lawsuit in which he was then involved should come to an end, he might be able to leave £15 per annum at her disposal for the elder [James] Finlay [...]

About the end of 1815, or early in 1816, it was arranged that a fixed sum of money should be remitted to his almoner quarterly, through the British Linen Company's Bank, in order to obviate the occasional misunderstanding of his intentions in these matters [...]

Professor Hill appears to have been very generous to one particular member of the Finlay family. It was Hill who had advised Bell to leave the bursary in place till the young James Finlay would be of age to take advantage of it. And so from 1812 until he came of age in 1824, at age 18, money had been banked annually for his future education.

After May Norie Finlay died, the remaining Finlay children were left in the care of their maternal grandfather Lawrence Norie. He died in 1817.[30] From that time until his marriage was announced in Edinburgh 12 years later in 1829 – the record on James is silent.

James Finlay, writer, Hanover Street, St Andrews Parish & Elspit Wallace Same place of Parish,3 Procla. no objections.

I had read this wedding announcement before discovering the Bell biography and was puzzled. How was it possible that in the 15 years since his mother died, James Finlay

---

30. The children have been taken in by one of the relations, presumably the Nories.

(grandfather of my great aunt Suzy Bell, who raised me as a child) had risen out of poverty and into the ranks of the middle class in Edinburgh? He had studied law, and proved capable enough to call himself 'Writer', an old word for lawyer or attorney in Scotland and found prestigious employment in the public records office of Scotland, Register House. And he was able to bring his new wife to a home in the most fashionable and expensive street in Edinburgh's new town,[31] all by the age of 24. The Bell biography provided the answer – it was all made possible by the beneficence of his great uncle Andrew Bell.

Bell would have known of the wedding and been pleased to see his generosity producing such positive results. And there is evidence that their home on Hanover Street was also owned by Bell. The Finlays left Hanover Street just after Bell's death in 1832, when his estate sold off all his assets to finance the building of Madras College[32] in St Andrews. A building that he believed would ensure that his system of teaching be preserved for the future.

---

31. A letter to Bell when he was considering returning to Scotland two decades before, gives an indication of the money needed to live well in Edinburgh.

    You may purchase an excellent house in the New Town for £800; so that if, beside the funds which supply your income, you had a couple of thousands to purchase and furnish your house, there can be no doubt but that you would have fortune enough to live creditably and provide genteelly for a family.

32. This may have been built on land that was referred to in the document dealing with the dispersal of the properties of William Finlay 'A fourth part of the tenement under and above, back and fore with the yard crofts and pertinents on the south side of South Street, St Andrews'. It was in construction the year Bell died and remains to the present in the heart of the town, but has recently been sold to St Andrew's University. The Madras System has long since disappeared from the curriculum.

(One of the earliest students of the newly founded college was Robert Adamson, the partner in photography of David Octavius Hill.)

Madras College from the inner quadrangle, 1843, (National Galleries of Scotland)

From the early eighteenth century, my two families, the Balfours and the Finlays, were living in the County of Fife. My father's in Torryburn, for centuries, shaped and demeaned by the state of bondage on many of its people. A small, impoverished community deliberately ill-educated and poorly paid with no escape from limited opportunity and drudgery. Compared to St Andrews, an ancient religious foundation, for centuries, a place of pilgrimage from across Europe, and in the eighteenth century, a worldly place with a small but ambitious educated community around the university and a port prospering on the trade with Europe. Untouched and probably unaware of the damage done by the *Coalyers and Salters Laws* and would not have cared if they knew. A community able not only to inspire but also support the ambition of Andrew Bell to travel to Virginia even as the Revolutionary War was beginning. Two Scottish communities, two profoundly different realities and only fifty miles apart!

Into the nineteenth century, Auld Reekie and its New Town will attract and actively shape the lives of both these families.

III

The New Town of Edinburgh

The New Town: The proposal to create a new town was made in 1752, less that 50 years since the Union of the Crowns in 1707 and the end of a Scottish parliament. Fifty years since the city lost both the wealth of the feudal lords who quickly bought houses in London, and the prestige of being a nation's capital. And only seven years since the Jacobite rising in 1745, when the supporters of Bonnie Prince Charlie took and revelled in the city but failed to capture the castle from Royalist troops. A powerless capital and the embarrassment of the Jacobite occupation would have been strongly in the minds and the imaginations of the city leaders as they formed a new vision for Edinburgh.

The origin of the creation of the New Town of Edinburgh can be dated precisely to a pamphlet published in 1752 entitled, *Proposals for Carrying on Certain Public Works in the City of Edinburgh.*[1] It opens with an advertisement to the reader stating that 'on 8 July 1752 the Convention of Royal Burghs had resolve to build a new Merchants Exchange erecting a building on the ruins on the south side of the Parliament-close containing a Borough-room,

---

1. *Proposals for Carrying on Certain Public Works in the City of Edinburgh.* Edinburgh: Lord Gilbert Elliot Minto, 1752.

providing proper Repositories for the public records of the nation, a place for storing national records' as well as carrying out other improvements in the city. According to the advertisement, the need to act was the result of a deadly accident that had left the core of the old city in ruins:

> The narrow limits of the royalty of Edinburgh, and the want of certain public buildings, and other useful ornamental accommodations in this city, have been long regretted. An opportunity of remedying these inconveniences was often wished for, and Providence has now furnished a very fair one. In September last the sidewall of a building six stories high, in which several reputable families lived, gave way all of a sudden. This melancholy accident occasioned a general survey to be made the condition of the old houses; and such as were insufficient were pulled down; so that several of the principle parts of the town [now] lay in ruins.

The proposal was in the form of a lengthy essay offering a passionate argument drawn from history and commerce on the need to renew the city. Above all, the need to make it more than a capital in name only, perhaps even a modest rival to London:

> AMONG the several causes to which the prosperity of a nation may be ascribed, the situation, conveniency, and beauty of its capital, are surely not the least considerable. A capital where these circumstances happen fortunately to concur, should naturally become the centre of trade and commerce, of learning and the arts, of

politeness, and of refinement of every kind. No sooner will the advantages which these necessarily produce, be felt and experienced in the chief city, than they will diffuse themselves through the nation, and universally promote the same spirit of industry and improvement.

Of this general assertion the city of London affords the most striking example. Upon the most superficial view, we cannot fail to remark its healthful, unconfined situation, upon a large plain, gently shelving towards the Thames; its neighbourhood to that river; its proper distance from the sea; and, by consequence, the great facility with which it is supplied with all the necessaries, and even luxuries of life.

No less obvious are the neatness and accommodation of its private houses; the beauty and conveniency of its numerous streets and open squares, of its buildings and bridges, its large parks, and extensive walks. When to these advantages we add its trade and navigation; the business of the exchange, of the two houses of parliament, and of the courts of justice; the magnificence of the court; the pleasures of the theatre, and other public entertainments: in a word, when we survey this mighty concourse of people, whom business, ambition, curiosity, or the love of pleasure, has assembled within so narrow a compass, we need no longer be astonished at that spirit of industry and improvement, which, taking its rife in the city of London, has at length spread over the greatest part of South Britain, animating every art and profession, and

inspiring the whole people with the greatest and
our and emulation.

To illustrate this further, we need only contrast
the delightful prospect which London affords,
with that of any other city, which is destitute
of all, or even of any considerable number of
these advantages. Sorry we are, that no one
occurs to us more apposite to this purpose, than
Edinburgh, the metropolis of Scotland when
a separate kingdom, and still the chief city of
North Britain. [...] Placed upon the ridge of a
hill, it admits but of one good street, running
from east to west; and even this is tolerably
accessible only from one quarter. The narrow
lanes leading to the north and south, by reason
of their steepness, narrowness, and dirtiness,
can only be considered as so many unavoidable
nuisances. Confined by the small compass of
the walls, and the narrow limits of the royalty,
which scarcely extends beyond the walls, the
houses stand more crowded than in any other
town in Europe and are built to a height that
is almost incredible. Hence necessarily follows
a great want of free air, light, cleanliness, and
every other comfortable accommodation. Hence
also many families, sometimes no less than ten
or a dozen, are obliged to live overhead of each
other in the same building; where, to all the
other inconveniencies, is added that of a common stair, which is no other in effect than an
upright street, constantly dark and dirty. It is
owing to the same narrowness of situation, that
the principal street is incumbered with the herb-
market, the fruit-market, and several others;

that the shambles are placed upon the side of
the North-Loch, rendering what was originally
an ornament to the town, a most insufferable
nuisance.

No less observable is the great deficiency of public
buildings. If the parliament-house, the churches,
and a few hospitals, be excepted, what other
have we to boast of? There is no exchange for
our merchants; no safe repository for our public
and private records; no place of meeting for our
magistrates and town-council; none for the convention of our boroughs, which is entrusted with
the inspection of trade. To these and such other
reasons it must be imputed, that so few people
of rank reside in this city; that it is rarely visited
by strangers; and that so many local prejudices,
and narrow notions, inconsistent with polished
manners and growing wealth, are still so obsti-
nately retained. To such reasons alone it must be
imputed, that Edinburgh, which ought to have set
the first example of industry and improvement, is
the last of our trading cities that has shook off the
unaccountable supineness which has so long and
so fatally depressed the spirit of this nation.

The meanness of Edinburgh has been too
long an obstruction to our improvement, and
a reproach to Scotland. The increase of our
people, the extension of our commerce, and the
honour of the nation, are all concerned in the
success of this project. As we have such powerful
motives prompting us to undertake it; so chance
has furnished us with the fairest opportunity of
carrying it into execution. Several of the principal parts of the town are now lying in ruins.

Many of the old houses are decayed; several have been already pulled down, and probably more will soon be in the same condition. If this opportunity be neglected, all hopes of remedying the inconveniencies of this city are at an end.

The proposals:

1. To build upon the ruins on the north-side of the high street, an exchange, with proper accommodations for our merchants.
2. To erect upon the ruins in the parliament-close, a large building, containing such the courts of justice, the royal boroughs, and town-council, offices for the clerks, proper apartments for the several registers, and for the advocates library.
3. To obtain an act of parliament for extending the royalty; to enlarge and beautify the town, by opening new streets to the north and south, removing the markets and shambles, and turning the North-Loch into a canal, with walks and terraces on each side. And provide proper Repositories for the public records of the nation.

And the city acted: A new Merchants Exchange was built called The Royal Exchange. Construction began in 1753 the year after the proposal, and the building was occupied in 1760. The design is credited Robert Adam's older brother John Adam, but it can be assumed that the brothers worked together. As the first neo classical public building in the city, it has to this day strong presence.[2]

The next major steps were more complicated and intertwined:

- Obtain a royalty (the permission of the king) giving the authority to develop the lands to the north,
- Build a bridge forming a great public passage between the old walled city and the potential new town on the north
- Create through competition, a master plan for the future New Town.
- The initiation of the plan would be marked by the construction of the first major public building in Scotland Register House, containing the 'Repositories for the public records of the nation'. It would sit where the Bridge of Communication would meet the promised new town at its north end.

Building the North Bridge or the Bridge of Communication

The Exchange being finished the next object to which the magistrates of Edinburgh and the trustees appointed by parliament for the improvement of the city, turned their attention, was to build a bridge of communication with the

---

2. I worked in this building in the late 1950s, in the attic which housed the studios of the City Architect. On reflection, it is surprising that there was never any discussion of the significance of this major work of architecture, the first classical construction in advance of the creation of the New Town.

*Paul Sandby, circa 1750:
Edinburgh & the Nor Lock
looking north to land on which the
new town would be built. Register
house would be built just left of
center in the view. Tenements of
the old city on the right*

fields on the north, and to obtain over them an extension of the royalty.

This took much longer than planned, because of the action of the holders of the land to the north. However:

> The magistrates of Edinburgh, defeated in their purpose of obtaining an extension of the royalty, set themselves about building a bridge without it. They chose the architect William Mylne, brother to Robert Mylne who built Blackfriars Bridge in London (still in construction when the Edinburgh structure was commissioned). Accordingly, in A, D. 1763, the North Loch was drained, and the mud removed, in order to the finding a proper foundation. The first stone was laid by George Drummond Esq; Lord Provost of Edinburgh, on the 21st of October 1765; but the contract for building the bridge was not signed till the 21st of August 1765. [...] on the 9th August 1769, the vaults, and side walls on the south end of the bridge, gave way, and five people were buried in the ruins The bridge was relieved and repaired, by pulling down the side walls in some parts, and rebuilding them and, in others, by strengthening them with chain bars; by removing the vast load of earth laid upon the bridge, and supplying its place with hollow arches thrown between the convex sides of the great arches; by raising the walls that went across the bridge to an additional height [...] The bridge being thus fortified, there need be no apprehensions about its security.

The bridge itself was made passable A. D. 1772, but the south-west counterfort is but presently (1778) building.[3]

The need for the New Town:

> And it this third proposal [building the New Town] which is the most ambitious which will above all have the benefit of encouraging principle families of the nation to stay longer in Edinburgh: our people of rank would hardly prefer an obscure life at London, to the splendor and influence with which they might reside at home. It is not choice, but necessity, which obliges them to go so frequently to London.

This gives a sense of the urgency felt in addressing the departure of so many of the most wealthy and prominent citizens to London:

> The extending the royalty, and enlargement of the town, make no doubt the most important article. So necessary and so considerable an improvement of the capital cannot fail to have the greatest influence on the general prosperity of the nation. It is a vulgar mistake, that the greatest part of our principal families choose to reside at London. This indeed is true with regard to a few of our members of parliament, and some particular families who were settled there before the union. The rest go only occasionally; and if

---

3. Hugo Arnot. *The History of Edinburgh, from the Earliest Accounts, to the Year 1780* [...] Printed by Thomas Turnbull.

their stay be long, and their expense by consequence greater than this country can well bear,
it must be entirely imputed to the present form
and situation of Edinburgh. Were these in any
tolerable degree remedied, our people of rank
would hardly prefer an obscure life at London,
to the splendor and influence with which they
might reside at home. It is not choice, but necessity, which obliges them to go so frequently to
London. Let us improve and enlarge this city,
and possibly the superior pleasures of London,
which is at a distance, will be compensated, at
least in some measure, by the moderate pleasures
of Edinburgh, which is at home.[4]

It concludes by proposing an act of parliament to annex
'so much land as shall be thought proper on the north-side
of the North-Loch, (on which streets are to be laid out and
houses to be built), to the royalty of Edinburgh'.

In March 1766, more than ten years after
publishing the Proposals, an advertisement appeared
announcing that the ground to the north of the old city
across the Nor Loch had been surveyed and plans would
be called on which to create a 'New Town'. In April, with
the Bridge of Communication [the North Bridge] nearing
completion, came the following request:

Between the High Street of Edinburgh and the
grounds lying to the north of the city [...] the
Lord Provost, magistrates and counsel are desirous to give all encouragement to such persons
as inclined to build upon the ground belonging

---

4. Ibid., *Proposals for Carrying on Certain Public Works in the City of
Edinburgh.*

to the town, upon the North and propose to feu them with all expedition, according to Street scheme to be hereafter made public for preventing the inconvenience and disadvantages which arise from carrying on buildings, without regard to any order or regularity.

This notice is therefore made inviting architects and others to give in Plans of the New Town marking out streets of a proper breadth, and by-lanes in the best situation for the reservoir and any other public buildings be thought necessary; they will be furnished in the Council Chamber with a survey of the grounds and the heights of risings upon the proper scale.

The person whose plans shall be judged most proper, will receive as an award of merit gold-medal, with the impression of the arms of the city of Edinboro, and the freedom of the city in a silver box.

On 21 May 1766 it was noted in the town Council minutes that six plans a been received, and on the second August plan number four, by Mr. James Craig had been adjudged the best by the Lord Provost and Mr. John Adam. After much discussion and presumably many amendments the final version of Craig plan was accepted in 1767.

The Craig Plan: The title block states:

> *THIS PLAN Was begun and carried into Execution Anno 1767 To His Sacred Majesty GEORGE III. The Munificent Patron of Every POLITE and LIBERAL person*

This PLAN of the New Streets and Squares, intended for his ancient CAPITAL of NORTH BRITAIN: One of the happy Consequences of the peace, Security and Liberty his people enjoy, under his mild, and auspicious Government, IS with the utmost Humility Inscribed by His Majesty's – Most devoted Servant and Subject,

JAMES CRAIG

It is signed: Ja. Craig Arch. invent. et delin. and P. Begbie Sculp. And:

Published by Act of Parliament Jan 1st 1768.

At the head of the engraving, framed in flowers and swags, is a poem:

AUGUST, around, what PUBLIC WORKS I see!
Lo' stately Streets, lo' Squares that Court the breeze,
See! long Canals and deepened Rivers join
Each part with each and with circling Main
The whole enliven'd Isle

This text is from James Thompson's *Liberty Part V*[5]. Thompson, who wrote the words for Rule Britannia, whose meaning is much clearer than this. Flanking the engraving are two cleverly imagined views of the New Town under construction.

In the lower right, there are notes from Craig that give the dimension of all the streets. This brief instruction defines the scale and character of the New Town in every exact detail:

> George Street is 100 feet in Breadth, Viz.
> 80 Feet for
> A Causeway & 10 Feet on each side for
> a Footpath Queen Street, Prince's Street,
> Frederick Street, Hanover Street, and Castle
> Street are 80 Feet in Breadth, Viz. 60
> Feet for a Causeway, and 10 Feet on each
> side for a Footpath – NB The Area between the
> Footpath and Building is 8 Feet

So, from this one simple diagram, a new town was made and here it was just a diagram of a possibility. The canal transformed from the Nor Loch running across the bottom of the plan was never developed; however, the arches of the new Bridge of Communication are carefully dotted, though, as noted earlier, it was still under construction in 1768. The plan is marked by the two churches centrally placed at its extreme east and west ends. The place of the church at the east end is shown in front of

5. James Thomson (1700–1748) Scottish poet and playwright, known for his poems 'The Seasons and The Castle of Indolence', and for the lyrics of 'Rule, Britannia!'. The fifth volume of his epic poem 'Liberty' was published in 1736.

an elaborately landscaped garden, the property of one Laurence Dundas, an immensely wealthy landowner and politician. Dundas had the money and the desire to place himself at the centre of this new world and easily persuaded the city to allow him to replace the church with his own house, a small classical palace designed by the London architect Sir William Chambers. There may be more to this than meets the eye. Chambers was Adams' great rival in London and had just received the commission for what became in effect England's Register House, now Somerset House on the Strand. Perhaps the Dundas' decision to hire Chambers was a deliberate snub to Adam?

From the beginning, this was a plan to please the king of this United Kingdom. In its first iteration, a plan was proposed in the form of the Union Jack. And Craig's dedication of the plan to the crown was underscored by naming the streets for the King and family. James Grant has a delicious note on the Royal contribution. Not surprisingly, the proposal had to be reviewed by King George III, and when he looked closely at the drawing, he saw that the main street had been named after the patron saint of the city, St Giles. The King exclaimed, 'Hey, hey! – what, what! St Giles Street! – never do, never do!' (Shades of *The Madness of George III*, this is his voice). The district of St Giles in central London was one of the worst slums in the city; thus he agreed to the name Princes Street, after the future George IV and the Duke of York'.[6]

Apart from Castle Street, because of its view, all the street names are a tribute to the Hanoverian royal family. George had given his name to what was assumed would be the main street of the New Town. The squares at either end of George Street were at first named for

---

6. Ibid., Grant *Cassells Old and new Edinburgh*.

the patron saints of Scotland and England, St Andrews and St George. However, in 1785, responding to pressure from London over the confusion between St Georges Square and George Square, on the south side of the city, it was renamed Charlotte Square, for Queen Charlotte of Mecklenburg-Strelitz (who was never able to shed her German accent). However, beyond the king, this idealized world was conceived to suit the tastes of the pleasure of the king's patrons, the wealthy feudal lords of Scotland.

In *The Making of Classical Edinburgh*, A. J. Youngson's[7] definitive work on the formation of the New Town, he describes Craig's plan as entirely sensible and almost painfully orthodox. Compared to French examples, it is a poor affair – merely two squares joined by a straight central street flanked by two others. There is nothing new in this simple rectangular, but its strength lies in the excellent use of the site.[8] Edinburgh's decision to create a more orderly new town and escape the limits of its medieval past was a latecomer to eighteenth-century city planning. Around 1730, German King Friedrich I initiated the development of an orderly new suburb just west of the old walled city of Berlin, Sud Friedrichstadt. In these same years, the John Woods, father and son, were adding an entertaining classical fantasy to the spa town of Bath, and in the American Georgia Colony Governor James Oglethorpe, planned and built the new town of Savannah in a form that would not only give order and distinction to the colonial culture but would, he believed, mitigate to some degree the inequities caused by slavery. In 1755 a massive earthquake destroyed the Portuguese

---

7. A. J. Youngston *The Making of Classical Edinburgh, 1750–1840* Edinburgh at the University Press, 1966.
8. Ibid., Youngson.

James Craig's plan for New Streets and Squares, intended for the ancient CAPITAL of NORTH BRITAIN 1768. (Wikimedia Commons)

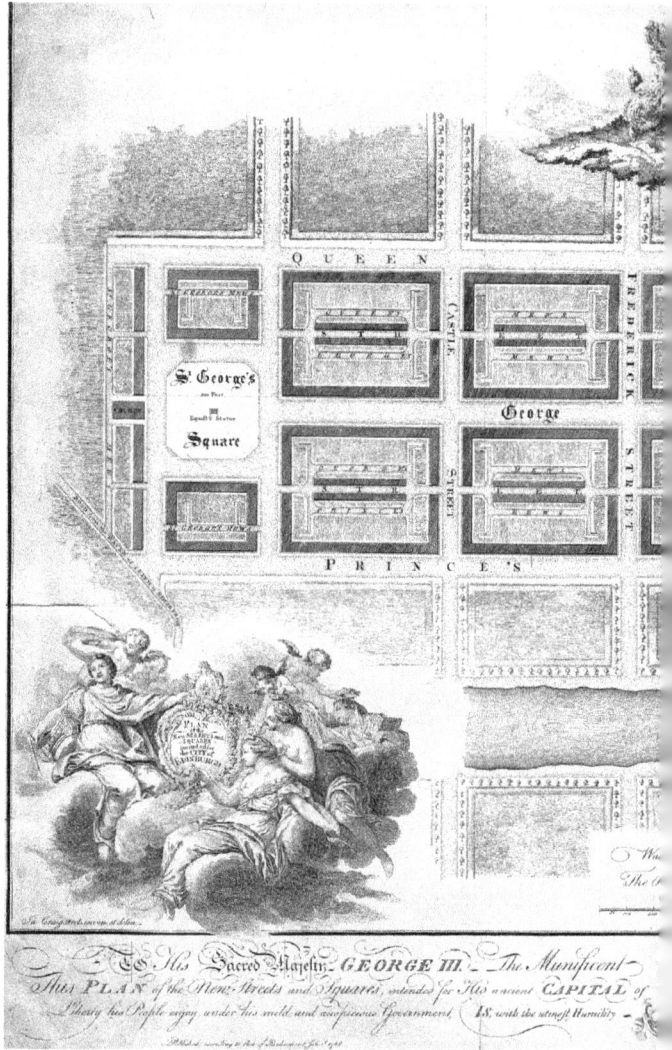

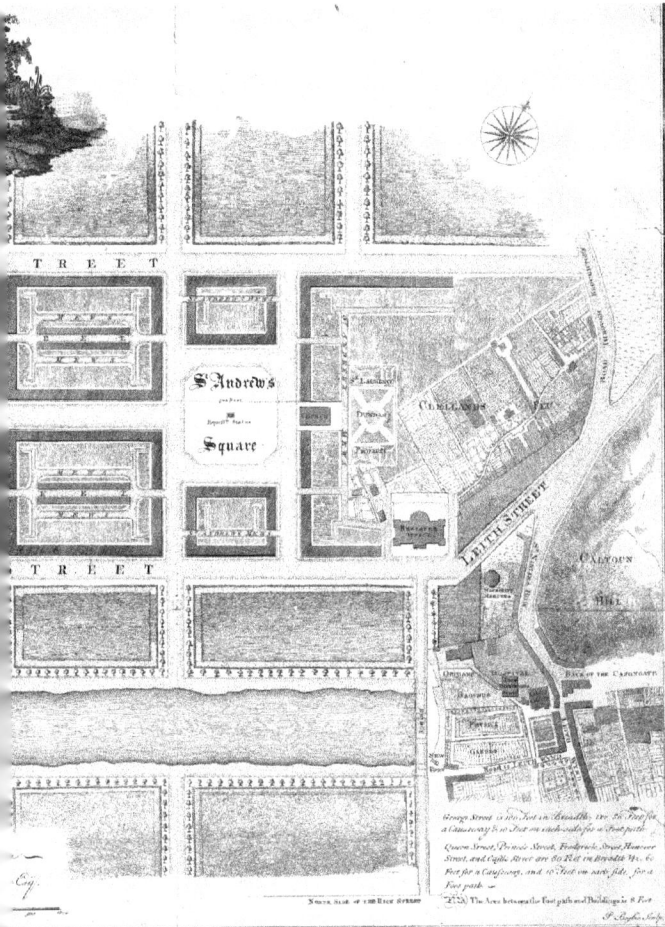

capital, Lisbon, demanding a much more ambitious plan for rebuilding than that envisioned by the cautious city fathers of Scotland's capital. The citizens of Edinburgh were even more cautious than the city fathers:

> So difficult was it to induce people to build in a spot so sequestered and far apart from the mass of the ancient city, that a premium of L20 was publicly offered by the magistrates to him who should raise the first house; but great delays ensued. The magistrates complimented Mr. James Craig on his plan for the New Town, which was elected from several. He received a gold medal and the freedom of the city in a silver box; and by the end of July, 1767, notice was given that 'the plan was to lie open at the Council Chamber for a month from the 3rd of August, for the inspection of such as inclined to become feuars, where also were to be seen the terms on which feus would be granted.

> At last a Mr. John Young took courage, and gained the premium by erecting a mansion in Rose Court, George Street – the first edifice of New Edinburgh; and the foundation of it was laid by James Craig, the architect, in person, on the 26th of October, 1767.[9]

Grant describes the number of ways in which the first owners manipulated the plan to suit their needs:

> Other quaint particulars are remembered, as for instance, Mr. Wight, an eminent lawyer, who

---

9. Ibid., Grant *Cassell's Old and New Edinburgh*.

planted himself in St Andrew Square, finding
that he was in danger of having his view of St
Giles's clock shut up by the advancing line of
Princes Street, built the intervening house himself, that he might have it in his power to keep
the roof low, for the sake of the view in question;
important to him, he said, as enabling him to
regulate his movements in the morning, when it
was necessary that he should be punctual in his
attendance at the Parliament House.[10]

And there on Craig's corrected plan from 1772, at the
north end of the Bridge of Communication, is an outline
of a building with a very distinct form titled 'Register
Office', later known as Register House.

Register House: The need for a building to
store the *'Records of Charters, Records of Parliament, Records
of Privy Seal, Records of Privy Council, &c., and for the more
sure preservation of the ancient charters, Sasins and Records of
Parliament'*, had long been recognized and a report from
1740 describe much of the material to be 'very bad condition, for want of boards to cover them; many of the first
and last leafs of each book being so much obliterat as they
cannot be easily read, and in a little time will be entirely
defaced'.[11]

It continues:

The idea of a New Register House was actively
urged by James Earl of Morton, who died
in 1774, and who was Lord Clerk Register.
Seeing that it was vain to hope for any direct

10. Ibid., Grant *Cassell's Old and New Edinburgh*.
11. Ibid., Grant, *Cassell's Old and New Edinburgh*.

government grant, he obtained L12,000 out of
the money accruing from the forfeited estates
of the Jacobites, and laid it at interest till 1765,
when Robert Adam, architect, and then M.P.
for Kinross, having made a design of the present
building, it was completely approved of, and on
the 27th of June 1774, the foundation stone was
laid, under a royal salute of cannon, by Lord
Frederick Campbell, Lord Register of Scotland.

There is prescience in the actions of the city administration in these years; after considering several sites, they concluded before Craig's plan had been presented that 'the location of such a prestigious public building would turn out to the advantage of the city and will promote fueing[12] out [land offered for development] of the grounds on the north'. Craig would have begun working on his new town plan in 1765 and from the beginning would have known of the project to erect a major public building at the east end of the site. By 1770 he would have received from Adam an outline plan from his first studies for the proposed Register Office.

Two years after Adam produced the final design, his great rival in London, William Chambers, began work on Somerset House. Though much larger in scale than the Register House, both buildings are significant as being the first public buildings in the nation. Public in the sense that they were conceived to serve not the church, not the monarchy neither parliament nor the military,

---

12. *Feu* the most common form of land tenure in Scotland, as conveyancing in Scots law was dominated by feudalism until the Scottish Parliament passed the Abolition of Feudal Tenure etc. (Scotland) Act 2000. In feu holding, there was an annual payment in money in return for the use of the land.

but solely for civic functions. However urgent the need to rehouse the nation's records, completing the building would take decades. Work was suspended at the end of 1778 with the carcass of the building, including the roofs, largely complete, but with significant amounts of work still to be done, when it was observed: '[...] a most magnificent building has been erected for the purpose [of storing records]; but hitherto it has been unfinished, and only occupied by pigeons. Edinburgh may indeed boast of having the most magnificent pigeon-house in Europe'.[13] Alas, the drawing looking north from below the North Bridge [66] does not extend far enough to show the building in

The Register House (Public Records Office) in Edinburgh New Town, Robert and James Adam, 1775.

---

13. Ibid., Hugo Arnot.

The North Bridge and the Register House in 1800 isolation at the edge of an extensive building site out of which the New Town was emerging.

For the next six years, it was a desolate shell of a building, windowless, with the turrets on top of the towers unfinished, and with the dome and the internal vaulting incomplete and empty. Only in 1785, with a further grant from the government, did work start again, and the south wing facing Princes Street was ready for occupation by the end of 1788. Then came the Napoleonic Wars again

halting construction, so it was not until 1822, long after Adam's death, that construction restarted.[14]

In his history of Edinburgh, Arnot gives a precise assessment:

Register House view from the east, unfinished in 1790, (drawing by John Brown from the National Galleries of Scotland, with permission) It is derelict and windowless, weeds growing everywhere, two figures are standing on the rim of the open oculus.

This we consider as by far the most beautiful of Mr Adams's designs. Most of the plans of this eminent architect, either from justice not being done them in the execution, or from the choice of material, of which the fabrics are composed, appear far more beautiful in the drawing, than when realized, but the reverse is the case with the Register Office, which excels the ideas we form of it from the plan. Although the work is not yet completed, in the following description we speak of it as finished. The front of the

14. Ibid., Grant, *Cassell's Old and New Edinburgh* Vol.1.

Robert Adam: Register House, section through the domed hall, around 1770. (Wikimedia Commons)

building, which is forty feet back from the-line
of Prince's Street, and directly facing the bridge,
extends from east to west 200 feet and when the
supplementary part of the plan shall be completed, it will be 200 feet square. In the middle
of the front there is a small projection of three
windows in breadth, where four Corinthian
pilasters support a pediment, in the centre of
which are the arms of Great Britain. At each
end there is a tower projecting a little beyond the
rest of the building, having a Venetian window
in front, and cupola on the top; and the front
is ornamented from end to end, with a beautiful Corinthian entablature. In the centre of the
building is a dome of wooden work, covered
with lead; the inside is disposed into a saloon of
fifty feet diameter, and eighty high, lighted from
the top by a copper window of fifty feet diameter. The roof is divided into compartments,
elegantly ornamented with stucco-work. There
are arches in the wall disposed into presses
for holding of the records; the access to them
is by a gallery, which runs around the whole
apartment.[15]

One element that Arnot does not mention is the strange
statue of George IV watching the proceeding from a side
arch, not merely effeminate, but in its general demeanour
somewhat resembling the Virgin Mary.

---

15. https://blog.nls.uk/robert-adam-rome-and-piranesi/

Robert Adam: Even in his lifetime, Adam was viewed as the most masterly of the neoclassical architects in the eighteenth century. Born in Kirkcaldy into wealth and privilege, he was the son of William Adam, and worked with his father on the design of the first classical building in Edinburgh, the Mercantile Exchange. As he began work on Register House in 1768, he was at the peak of his career defined and shaped by the four years he spent in Europe between 1754 and 1758.

Adam arrived in Florence in 1755, where he was introduced to Charles-Louis Clérisseau, whom Adam paid to accompany him to Rome. He was searching for a project that he could use to establish a reputation in England. Clérisseau proposed documenting the ruins of Diocletian's Palace at Split, easily accessible on the Dalmatian coast. On arriving in Rome later in that year, Adam wrote, 'Rome is the most glorious place in the universal world. A grandeur and tranquility reigns in it, everywhere noble and striking remains of antiquity appear in it'. He stayed till 1757, studying the architecture of the Renaissance city and visiting the excavations of the ruins in the company of both Clérisseau and Giovanni Battista Piranesi, both a decade older than Adam. Adam wrote that Piranesi 'is I think the most extraordinary fellow I ever saw'. And in return, Piranesi told Adam that he had 'more genius for the true noble architecture than any Englishman ever was in Italy'. Calling himself an Englishman was probably quite common in the eighteenth century, where Scotland was often referred to as North Britain. He could not have been better served by his colleagues; they were not only brilliant illustrators, but both inspired in Adam's imagination – in his own words 'the conception of the grand'.

Adam sketched and supervised the documentation of the ruins. He employed two German draftsmen to make measured drawings of the major structures, while Clérisseau produced perspectives. The resulting work *Ruins of the Palace of the Emperor Diocletian at Spoleto* was published in London eight years later in 1764.

From his letters home, it is evident that Adam was not just ambitious but an aggressive social climber quite willing to use his modest wealth to enhance his influence. Adam proposed to Piranesi that he work on an imagined reconstruction of Imperial Rome. Piranesi agreed and would dedicate the work to him if Adam

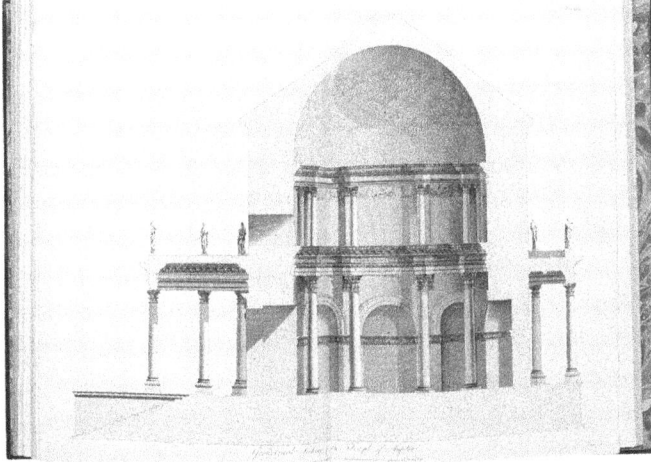

Section through central dome in the Palace of Diocletian from: from Robert Adam and Clerisseau 'Ruins of the Palace of the Emperor Diocletian at Spoleto' published London, 1764.

would purchase a number of copies. This, apparently with Adam's encouragement, led to the creation of the most brilliant fantasy on the power and the multiple realities of the ancient city *Campus Martius Antiquae Urbis*. As promised, Piranesi placed Adam's name prominently in the title block, as well as including a letter of dedication to him in parallel Latin and Italian texts. The work was published with great success across Europe in 1762, and has never ceased to thrill, and it was a combination of Piranesi's dedication and the enthusiastic reception of Adam's work on the Palace of Diocletian, published two years later, that quickly secured his reputation among the aristocracy of England and Scotland.

There is a revealing parallel between Adam paying Piranesi to dedicate the Campo Martius drawings to him, and the occasion several years later in London, when Adam worked on the publication of work on the palace of Diocletian and consciously failed to credit

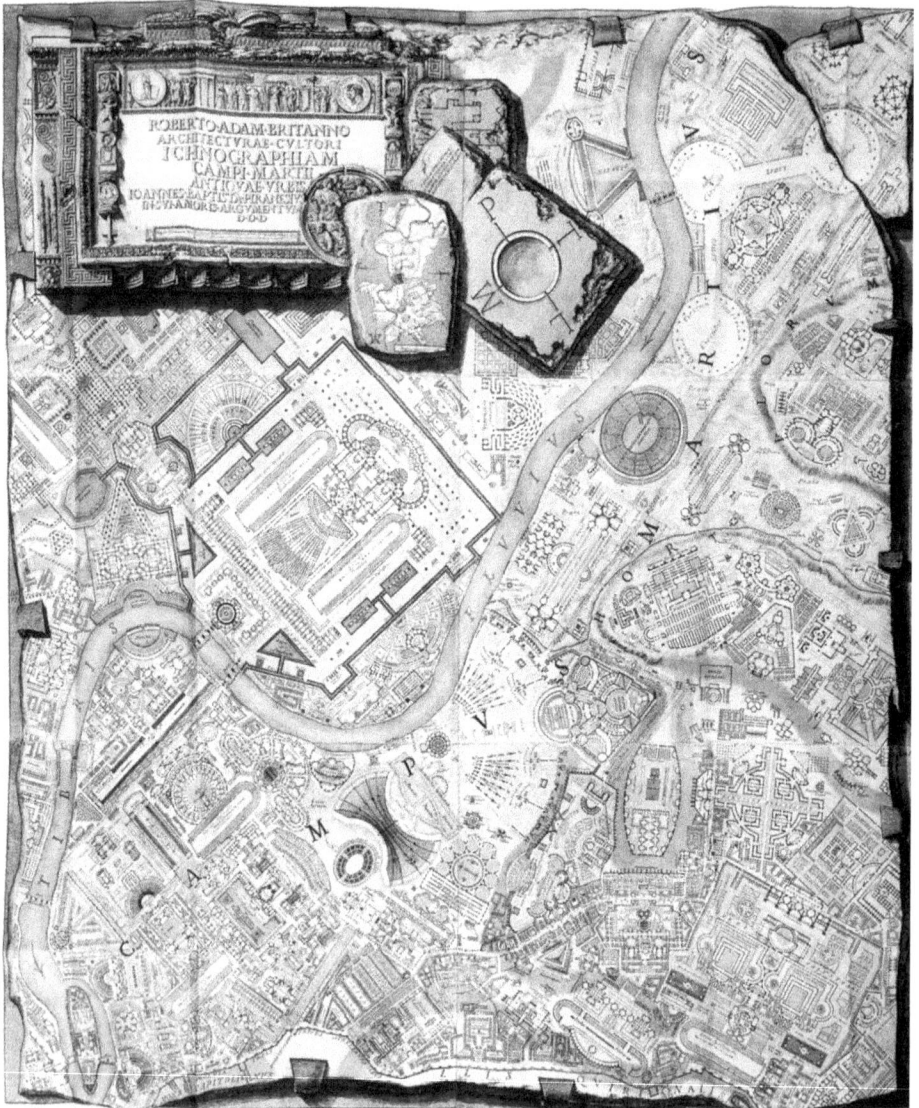

Giovanni Battista Piranesi:
'Campus Martius Antiquae
Urbis'. (Author's copy)

Clerisseau, who had produced most of the drawings from which the engravings were made. By the time of publication, Cerisseau[16] was no longer useful to Adam's ambition, and such an attribution would contradict his claim of sole authorship.

Adam had returned to Britain in 1758 and set up a practice in London with his brother James in 1761, and that same year he was appointed architect of the King's Works (jointly with Sir William Chambers). This seems an extraordinary appointment given that at 33, his only built work had been done with his father.

On the right, Adam and Clerisseau's View of the inside of the [so called] Temple of Jupiter, Plate XXXIII in the Palace of Diocletian[17]

On the left Adam's Dome over the great hall in Register House. (Photo author)

16. Between 1785–1789, Clérisseau assisted Thomas Jefferson in producing designs for the Virginia State Capitol.
    The name Adelphi, chosen to immortalize the Adam 'brotherhood', also became a byword for over-reaching ambition.
17. From *Ruins of the palace of the Emperor Diocletian at Spalatro in Dalmatia*, published London, 1764.

By the time he came to design Register House, he had become enormously successful not only as a consummate designer to the wealthiest, of their houses, their exquisite interiors and luxurious furnishings, but also as a developer and entrepreneur. In the early 1770s, the Adam brothers designed and financed a massive neoclassical terrace of houses on the Thames called the Adelphi. It was inspired by Diocletian Palace and enlarged by the 'concept of the grand'. A grandeur he would attempt to bring later to Scotland's capital. However, the development was a disaster for the Adam family – houses didn't sell, and a Scottish banking crash in 1772 took them to the verge of ruin. Only the sale of their assets saved them from bankruptcy; both the family and Adam's reputation were tarnished.

Given the splendour of his vision for London and his pleasure in the power of Roman-inspired classicism, it is disappointing that his vision for Register House was so modest. There is an echo of Diocletian in the great domed hall at the centre of the complex, but the grand facade announcing the arrival of a new order to all those still held in decrepit walls of old city, it is both sombre and forbidding, more like a prison (which in a sense it was) than a generous stage for a new public order. Perhaps he saw its stern presence as fitting for the Scottish character.

Just a few years after the building was fully opened, probably around 1826, James Finlay entered and would continue working there until his death some 30 years later.

South Bridge:[18] After completing the design for Register House, Adam would occasionally indulge in Piranesian fantasies, small and large, about Edinburgh (though in suitably Scottish strait-laced fashion). The one project which could have given him the opportunity to rival his great terrace in London and produce civic architecture at a scale worthy of the Campo Martius, was his proposal for the extension of the North Bridge.

After the North Bridge opened in 1772, its completion promoted the construction of a further bridge across the ravine of the Cowgate to the south of the ridge on which the Old Town was built. This links the New Town with the growing suburbs to the south. The project was initiated in 1784. The Lord Provost of the city discussed the concept with Adam in London in 1785, following which Adam believed that he was being commissioned to draw up detailed designs for the scheme. He had few commissions in the 1780s due to the failure of the Adelphi, so the development of South Bridge must have seemed an irresistible opportunity, especially since it would terminate in the Register House. The need for the bridge was clear, and from the drawings, Adam saw this as the perfect opportunity to again display 'the concept of the grand'

Early in the summer of 1785, Adam submitted his first design showing long terraces of three-storey buildings, including a colonnaded portico flanking the roadway. Late summer of 1785, he modified the proposal removing the colonnade. The Lord Provost wrote

18. https://sites.scran.ac.uk/ada/documents/southbridge/south
    _bridge.htm

Register House 1845, Hill and Adamson (National Portrait Gallery Print Room).

Robert Adam, South Bridge elevation: first design.

to Adam rejecting his designs. The letter was clear; the trustees were not authorized by the Act of Parliament to agree to designs 'in which the ornamental [*sic*] required to be executed shall in any material degree diminish the value of the ground lots at a public sale'. He asserted that Adam's pleas for a more ornamental design for the arch crossing the Cowgate was a needless extravagance since it would be seen only by carters. [!]

The Adelphi disaster continued to haunt him, and in the view of Lord Provost and his advisors, Adam's proposal was not only unnecessarily grand but also potentially ruinously expensive.[19] Beginning in 1784, South

Adam's vision for the South Bridge drawn in 1786, never to be realized.

19. Money clouded all of Adam's dealing with the city fathers, they objected to his fee being too high and often refused and delayed payment.

Robert Adam, a last fantasy in the manner of Piranesi 1791.

Bridge was built. It was a massive engineering task with 19 stone arches spanning over 1000 feet. Sadly, the mediocre architecture that encloses it to this day completely conceals the drama of the project. This would have been one of the great streets of Europe, but at what cost?

A last fantasy: This drawing dated 1791, the year before his death, is from the collection of the John Soane Museum in London. It is a charming and spectacular vision for a bridge in the form of a Roman viaduct, lined at its upper level with classical buildings. It would have linked Princes Street to Calton Hill and provided a formal entry into the New Town from the South. Below, a massive triumphal arch would have framed the old road from Leith into the walled city. The drawing is strongly reminiscent of a drawing by a young Piranesi from 1750. Not only is this a surprisingly free, late 'visionary' sketch, it also offers details of Adam's heroic vision for the city, with the great pile of his university building in the distance on the right and a series of monuments and public buildings on the left. The vision was not completely lost; it survived in a more modest form in the design of Waterloo Place, and the Roman arch is there in the gracious shape of the Regents Bridge (an early photograph of which forms from the cover of this book),

Clearly inspired by, though not designed by Adam.

Piranesi: An Ancient Port 1749–1750 'Part of a spacious and magnificent Harbor for the use of the ancient Romans opening onto a large market square'.[21]

The Piranesi etching was published as part of a series of architectural and perspective images. In these projects, one sees clearly what inspired Adam's ambition for architecture and the city. However, it is reasonable to accept that the problem was much more with cost than with the architecture; this small nation simply could not in these years have afforded such grandeur. However, in the year before his death, Adam designed the facades for Charlotte Square, at the western terminus of Craig's New Town, and gave the city the most complete and dignified stage for the new citizen.

Adam found little satisfaction with the city's grudging acceptance of his design for Charlotte Square. Construction would not begin until well after his death, and his feelings about Edinburgh and its governance, and Scotland in general, for the that matter, had been

20. From *Opere Varie di Archiettura, prospettive, grotteschi, antichità; inventate, ed incise da Giambattista Piranesi Architetto Veneziano.*

soured by the failure to complete the building of Registrar
House. On his last visit to the city, he would have passed
by it half constructed. He had read the quote and it stung
'Edinburgh may indeed boast of having the most magnificent pigeon-house in Europe'.

Robert Burns in St James Square: This
is a favourite drawing of the old and new city in 1790.
The dome of the Register House is right of centre, and
further right is a wall of tenements. This is the northern part of St James Square, planned by Craig but not
part of the New Town. I walked by Register House every
school day from 1951 to 1956, and I would occasionally
wander into the Square. By then, it seemed a forgotten
place and is now almost all demolished. I was walking
back in time; even now I recall not just the neglect but
the melancholia, the pubs, the tailor shop, the painted
sign for a jeweller over an empty store, the brass plates
remembering abandoned offices unchanged for over a
century.

It was here that the poet Robert Burns lived for a
year in 1788, and it was from here that he would take his
daily walk past the empty Register House, up the North
Bridge to entertain and be entertained in the houses and
taverns on the High Street. He would drink until he could
barely find his way back. There is one surprising tale of
Burns from that year in the *Book of the Old Edinburgh Club*.[21]
It records an event at which Burns was an honoured guest;
the meeting on 31 December 1787, to celebrate the birth
of the Young Pretender, Bonnie Prince Charlie:

21. *The book of the Old Edinburgh Club* (Kindle Locations 2343–2345).
Edinburgh.

Aquatint by John Wells of the central panel from a panorama of Edinburgh produced by Robert Baker in 1792. (Barker invented the word 'panorama' from the Greek pan (all) and horama (view) to describe what he called his comprehensive survey of Edinburgh from the Calton Hill.) The city in the 1790s, the old town is upper left above the North Bridge, the Castle is in the center with the New Town on the right. Register House and its dome is center left. The drawing shows Craig's plan completely built, which is a small fantasy. St James Square to right of the Register House would have been just been built. Look in the distance this was a New Town in the countryside. The single white house below the center, would, a few decades later become the photographic studios of Hill and Adamson.

On this occasion the [...] neighbours were assembled, along with Lawrence Oliphant of Gask, the father of Lady Nairne, and to the supper was bade Robert Burns, then on his second visit to Edinburgh. His acceptance of the invitation, addressed to Mr. Steuart, is dated from his lodgings in St. James's Square, and is in the following terms:

Sir, – Monday next is a day of the year with me hallowed as the ceremonies of Religion, and sacred to the memory of the sufferings of my King and my Forefathers. The honour you do me by your invitation I most cordially and gratefully accept.

He then added a poetic note:

'*Tho'* something like moisture conglobes in my eye, Let no one misdeem me disloyal; A poor friendless Wanderer may well claim a sigh, Still more if that Wanderer were royal.

My fathers that Name have rever'd on a throne, My fathers have died to right it;

Those fathers would spurn their degenerate son, That name should he scorningly slight it.

'I am, sir, your oblidged humble servt., Robt. Burns.

'St. James's Sqr., Weden. even'.

At the meeting, the health of the absent Prince was toasted, carefully omitting the signature and the name of the addressee, doubtless to avoid detection should they have chanced to fall into the wrong hands. I have difficulty reconciling the Burns of 'A Man's a Man for A' That' with the celebration of the birth of the Jacobite

Catholic Charles Edward Stewart. Could Burns have been a Jacobite royalist?

James Finlay: Though the biography is not explicit, it would appear that Bell arranged for an annuity to support the Finlay children, though it does make clear that a bursary was invested in 1812, for the young James till he was of an age to study for a profession. So, from then until he came of age in 1824, money had been banked annually for his future education. Presumably, in that year, he came to Edinburgh, became a law clerk, found accommodation with the help of great uncle Andrew Bell in the smartest street in the New Town and in 1829, he married:

> *James Finlay, writer, Hanover Street, St Andrews Parish & Elspit Wallace Same place of Parish, 3 Procla. no objections.*

It is surprising that the certificate names only the bride and groom – no family present, no witnesses.

For the privileged gentleman, there were several choices for a career. Medicine was very acceptable, but there was no medical school in Edinburgh till the middle of the century. Scots would travel to Leyden or Paris to study. 'The Church' writes a nineteenth-century observer 'was an unattractive career to many a Presbyterian from its austerity and fanaticism'. He continues: 'The law – especially the Bar – was the best profession for a gentleman's son who wished to live by his brains and associate with his equals'.[22] So not only had Finlay risen out of poverty, and entered a profession – he had become a gentleman.

---

22. He adds rather surprisingly 'It was […] in trade that younger sons of good family often sought a livelihood. It was not considered

James' new wife was Elspit Wallace, daughter of Robert Wallace and Elspit Kirk. They married in St Andrews in 1807. She was just 18, which, even for those days, seemed young. The families must have known each other in St Andrews, and Elspit would have been coming of age while James was in Edinburgh. The records give little information on her parents, the Wallaces, but on Elspit's death certificate (named Elspeth on the record), in 1893, her father Robert is described as a veterinary surgeon, an emerging profession in those years. However, from Scotland's first census taken in 1841, Robert and his family, including the two Finlay grandchildren, Elizabeth and James, are living on the north side of Argyle Street, in St Andrews and his occupation is given as 'Blacksmith'.[23] (The ordinance survey map of St Andrews from 1852 does indeed show a smithy on the north side of Argyle Street.)

Hanover Street: News by word of mouth of the wonderous new streets being built in Edinburgh would have excited people in the towns and villages across Scotland, most as decayed and impoverished as the old walled city of the capital. And when James Finlay arrived in the city, he must have felt a sense of awe; it was all so ordered, the vast sandstone terraces of fresh almost white stone, so new, such promise – it was the future. And on to Hanover Street, home for the Finlays would have been

---

below their dignity to become apprentices to shopkeepers, who under the vaguely comprehensive title of 'merchant' might deal in anything from tallow-candles to brocade, from tobacco to Tay pearls. In small low-ceilinged rooms in a second or third fiat in the Edinburgh High Street the best merchants had their shops. Silversmiths, clothiers, woollen drapers, were frequently men of high birth and social position'.

23. I presume the other John was his brother, both 55, twins?

a 'flat' on a common stair.[24] Appropriate for the young Finlays, it was a street of lawyers. The richly detailed book *Old and New Edinburgh*,[25] by James Grant describes the social life in the new streets of the city. On Hanover Street, he tells of the illustrious neighbours surrounding the Finlay in the 1830s:

> [...] in No. 33, now altered and sub-divided, dwelt Lord Meadowbank, prior to 1792, known when at the bar as Allan Maconochie. He left several children, one of whom, Alexander, also won a seat on the bench as Lord Meadowbank, in 1819. No. 39, at the comer of George Street, was the house of Marjoribanks of Marjoribanks and that ilk. No. 54, now a shop, was the residence of Sir John Graham Dalyell when at the bar, to which he was admitted in 1797. He was the second son of Sir Robert Dalyell, Bart, of Binns, in Linlithgow-shire, and in early life distinguished himself by the publication of various works illustrative of the history and poetry of his native country, particularly 'Scottish Poems of the Sixteenth Century, Bannatyne Memorials, Annals of the Religious Houses in Scotland', &c. A few doors farther down the street is now the humble and unpretentious-looking office

---

24. Hanover Street has changed little in these 240 years, and the interior of many of the buildings has remained intact. In preparation for the work, I rented an apartment, or flat as they say in Scotland, just one block west on George Street, and in scale and brightness and elegance it was possible to recover the quality of living in the New Town.
25. Ibid., Grant, Cassell's *Old and New Edinburgh*.

of that most useful institution, the Edinburgh
Association for Improving the Condition of the
Poor, and maintained, like every other charitable
institution in the city, by private contributions.

It certainly was the most useful, but from the evidence, poorly
funded institution. And at No 14 South Hanover Street, was
the City of Glasgow Bank. Grant's depiction of the bank tell-
ing-room, gives a grand sense of the elaborate interiors that
were setting the stage and the plays for this new society – 'in
the style of the Italian Renaissance, lighted by a cupola rising
from eight Corinthian pillars, with corresponding pilasters
abutting from the wall, which is covered by portraits'.

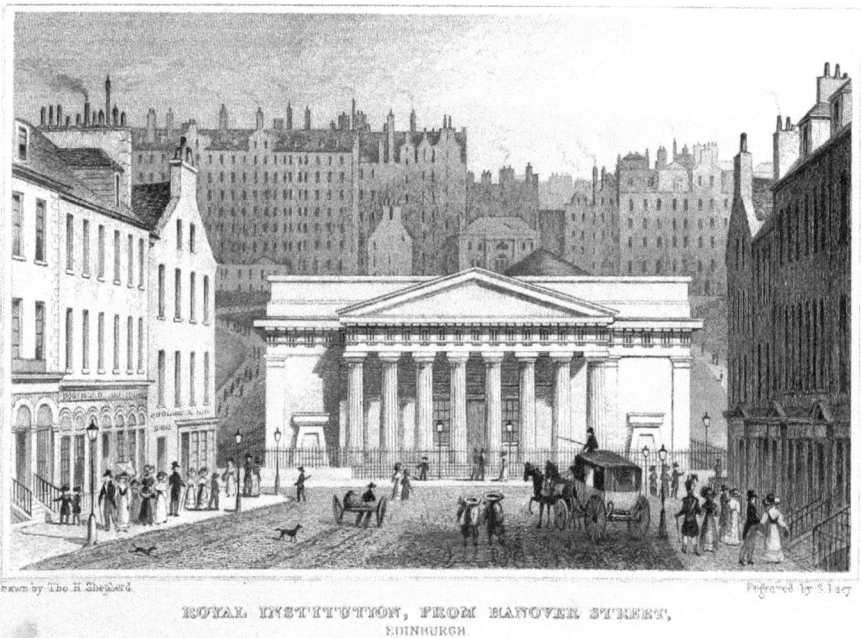

Drawn by Tho.H. Shepherd.   Engraved by S Lacy

ROYAL INSTITUTION, FROM HANOVER STREET,
EDINBURGH.

*'The Royal Intuition from Hanover
Street, Edinburgh' Drawn by
Thos. H Shepherd, 1829*

This view down Hanover Street was published in London on 23 March 1829, the year of the Finlay wedding. Young couples and their children are dressed up and setting out to stroll and shop. The newlyweds could be any of the couples parading on the pavements in grand style. This print was one of the number of popular views of the city, evidence of the national interest of the New Town. The same view appears in a photograph from 25 years later, showing the pediment of the Royal Institution crowned by a colossal statue of Queen Victoria, seated, with crown, sceptre and robes of state, flanked by the eight sphinxes, successfully conceived as the cultural heart of the New Town. The institution was founded in 1819 as the Royal Institution for the Encouragement of the Fine Arts in Scotland and was renamed the Royal Scottish Academy in 1826. It contained several national institutions: The Royal Society, Scotland's national academy of science and letters, the Institution for the Encouragement of the Fine Arts in Scotland, and The Society of Antiquaries of Scotland along with its museum. It also housed the Board of Trustees for Manufactures in Scotland (who owned the building), whose task was the improvement of Scottish manufactured goods, hence the inclusion of a school of design and a gallery of sculpture within its walls. Construction began in 1823 after designs by W. H. Playfair (of whom much more later) and the building opened in 1836.

In 1829 Alexander Bell, in his 82nd year, was at his house in Cheltenham. Though ill much of the time, he remained an active correspondent mainly concerned with preserving his legacy. (Among the many concerns present in his letters was a continuing wish to establish an elementary classical school at Edinburgh.) He spent a great deal of time finalizing his will, including his decision

143

to make: 'over in trust, [...] all other heritable property to which he had a right in Edinburgh, or elsewhere in Scotland', which I assume included the flat on Hanover occupied by the Finlays. The young married couple could not have afforded to live in that part of the city without help. Further evidence of this is that in the year of Bell's death, 1833, they had to move out and find somewhere else to live.

IV

The New Society

Forming the New Society: The Scottish advocate, writer and campaigner Hugo Arnot of Balcormo published his *History of Edinburgh*[1] in 1779. It is the equal of James Grant's commentary on the city, but much pricklier. Arnot had a strong sense of social justice and wrote over many years on tax decisions hitting the poorer part of the population. He is said to have held up for ten years the erection of the city's South Bridge, believing it to be a waste of money. The following extracts from three letters appended to the subsequent editions of the work offer the most telling evidence of the torn social fabric of the city caused by the creation of the New Town. They are signed in the name of the Greek philosopher student of Plato, Theophrastus, and dated 1783 (Arnot died in 1786.)

In introducing the letters, Arnot writes:

> I have often thought that it might not only be
> entertaining but useful, to remark from time
> to time, the vicissitudes of manners in society;
> and, by comparing the present with the past, to
> examine whether, as a people or as individuals
> we were improving or declining. It is frequently

---

1. Hugo Arnot. 1.

'Princes Street with the Commencement of the Building of the Royal Institution in 1825'. The ordered wall of the New Town of the left, the mass of crumbling tenements of the old town on the right: Alexander Nasmyth 1758– 1784. (National Galleries of Scotland)²

2. *Princes Street with the Commencement of the Building of the Royal Institution in 1825.* Alexander Nasmyth 1758–1784 National Galleries of Scotland.

difficult to assign a reason for the material appearance of Edinburgh, the revolutions which take place in the manners of a country, or to trace the causes that have occasioned a change, but in all cases, the first toward investigating the cause, is to state the facts. A plan of this kind frequently repeated, might be of great utility, by leading to cultivation and improvement in somethings, and to correction or prohibition in others, while it would, at the same time, afford a valuable fund of facts for the philosopher, the historian, or the annalist Every person who remembers a few years back, must be sensible of a very striking difference in the material appearance of Edinburgh and also in the mode of mode of living and in the us state a comparison for instance no further back than between probably appear prominent and striking, perceived. So remarkable a change is not perhaps to be equaled in so short a period in any city of Europe, nor in the same city for two centuries, taking all the alterations together.

The dynamic of this change was the mass exodus of the wealthy from the old city to the new, leaving destitution in its wake. The likelihood that this might happen was addressed in the *Proposal*[3] of 1752, but based on the evidence from other cities in Europe, it was thought this would not be a problem for Edinburgh:

---

3. Ibid., *Proposals for Carrying on Certain Public Works in the City of Edinburgh.*

It has been objected, that this project may occasion the centre of the town to be deserted. But of this there can be no hazard. People of fortune, and of a certain rank, will probably choose to build upon the fine fields which lie to the north and south of the town: but men of professions and business of every kind, will still incline to live in the neighbourhood of the exchange, of the courts of justice, and other places of public resort ; and the number of this last class, of men will increase in a much greater proportion, than that of the former. Turin, Berlin, and many other cities, show the truth of this observation. In these cities, what is called the new town, consists of spacious streets and large buildings, which are thinly inhabited, .and that too by strangers chiefly, and persons of considerable rank; while the old town, though not near so commodious, is more crowded than before these late additions were made. The national advantages which a populous, capital must necessarily produce, are obvious.[4]

Arnot then proceeds to offer a series of comparisons, some quite shocking, all testament to a city in the midst of turmoil:

The old rooms received new occupants – pawnbrokers lived where lords of session had dwelt; washerwomen cleaned clothes in chambers where fine ladies had worn them; mechanics, with their squalling brats, occupied apartments

4. Ibid., Hugo Arnot.

whose decorated mantelpieces and painted
ceilings told of departed greatness-rooms where
in bygone days the gayest of the town had met
when they were scenes of all that had been
brightest and merriest of olden life. With the
New Town of Edinburgh began a new social
existence in Scotland.

In 1763 – Edinburgh was almost confined within
the city walls [...] to the south, were fields and
orchards. To the north there was no bridge and
(till of late) the New Town, with all its elegant
and magnificent buildings, squares, rows, courts
&c. did not exist. It may with truth be said, that
there is not now in Europe a more beautiful terrace than Prince's Street nor a grander or more
elegant street than George Street. It is a moderate
calculation to say, that three million Sterling have
been expended on building and public improvements in and about Edinburgh since 1768.

In 1763 – People of quality and fashion lived
in houses which, in 1783, are inhabited by
tradesmen, and people in humble and ordinary
life. The Lord Justice Clerk Tinwald's house
was lately possessed by a French Teacher – Lord
President Craigie's house is at present possessed
bya Rouping wife or Sales-woman of old furniture. Lord Drummore's house was lately left by a
Chairman for want of accommodation.

In 1785 – A bridge to the south, over the
Cowgate Street, was built and the areas for
building shops and houses on the east the
westside of it, sold higher than perhaps was ever
known in the city, even than in Rome, [...]

In 1763 – There were two stage-coaches with three horses a coachman, and postilion, each, which went to Leith every hour from eight in the morning till eight at night and shortened the hour upon the stage: there were no other stage coaches in Scotland, except one, which set out once a month for London, and it was sixteen or eighteen days upon the journey.

In 1785 – There were four or five stage-coaches to Leith every half-hour, which run it in 15 or 20 minutes: [...] to London there are no less than sixty stage-coaches monthly, or fifteen every week and they reach the capital in four days; and, in 1786, two of these stage-coaches reach London in sixty hours, by the same road that required sixteen or eighteen days for the established stage-coach in 1763.

In 1783 – The buildings of the University are in the same ruinous condition that they were in 1763, and the most celebrated University at present in Europe is the worst accommodated. Some of the Professors have even been obliged to have lecturing-rooms without the College for their numerous students

In 1763 – There were about six or seven broth-els or houses of bad fame in Edinburgh, and a very few only of the lowest and most ignorance order of females skulked about at night, A person might have walked from the Castle-hill to the Abbey without being accosted by a single prostitute.

In 1785 – The streets are much more infested with beggars and prostitutes than in any former period of the history of the city, and probably will continue to be so till a Bridewell provided.

In 1785 – The number of brothels and houses of civil accommodation are increased to some hundreds; and the women of the town are more than in an equal proportion. Every quarter of the city and suburbs is infested with multitudes of females, abandoned to vice, and many of them before passion could mislead, or reason teach them right from wrong. Some mothers live by the prostitution of their daughters. Gentlemen, and citizens daughters are upon the town, who, by their dress and bold deportment, in the face of day, seem to tell us that the term Whore ceases to be a reproach.

In 1763 – The Canongate was the foulest quarter of the city, with respect to abandoned women and brothels.

In 1783 – The Canongate, by the vigilance of the magistrates of that district, is the cleanest and most quiet.

Given that he was assessing 20 years of change that long before the full impact from the rise of the new town had been felt, but Arnott is at his most prescient in his view of social progress:

Many of the facts I have now furnished are curious. They point out the gradual progress of commerce and luxury and by what imperceptible degrees society may advance to refinement, nay, even in some points to corruption yet matters of real utility be neglected.[5]

5. Ibid., Hugh Arnot.

In his *Social Life of Scotland in the Eighteenth Century*, Henry
Graham wrote as the houses on Princes Street, George
Street and Queen Street were advancing westward:

> From the old flats descended in gradual exodus
> person of position and quality, who, instead of
> a modest rental of £15 or £20, were able now,
> through advancing wealth and larger incomes,
> to pay £100 for mansions which contrasted
> strangely with the mean and dirty abodes from
> which they emerged. They left those dwell-
> ings where there had been little cleanliness or
> comfort, where fetid air brought sickness and
> death to young lives, where infectious diseases
> passed like wildfire through the inmates of a
> crowded common stair, bringing havoc to many
> a household. Town and town-life underwent a
> revolution, and many a quaintly pleasant and
> picturesque feature of Scottish society soon
> became a mere memory. Fortunately, the old
> taverns lost their 'genteel' company, and gentle-
> men met temperately at home in their spacious
> dining-rooms, instead of in miserable cellars,
> over their mutchkin and glass. The sedan-chairs
> were becoming worn out, like the chairmen
> who had carried in them so many fair occu-
> pants, with towering powdered headdresses,
> to the dance, and for 6d. an hour had shaken
> their burdens over the causeway, and up closes
> where no carriage could enter. These were being
> discarded for hackney coaches that drove swiftly
> along handsome though unfinished streets; but
> for many a year some ladies of the olden type
> still were borne along to their tea-parties in the
> venerable chairs of their grandmothers. By the

close of the century these 'lands', in multitu-
dinous closes were becoming deserted by the
upper classes. Although some clung on tena-
ciously to their patrimonial tenements, the bulk
of quality and fashion had gone to reside on the
other side of the swampy North Loch, quitting
for ever the old haunts where so long a teeming
friendly population of gentle and simple had
dwelt, leaving for ever ancient flats associated
with ages of dirt and dignity, of smells and social
mirth.[6]

This then was the transforming world in which James and
Elspeth Finlay arrived in 1829, a city then more divided
than any could have anticipated or wished. This new
town had sucked all the wealth and creativity out of the
old society leaving behind poverty, disease and decay – in
the midst of which was my father's family. And because
the two parts were so physically separate, the new society including the Finlays, could with ease ignore the suffering, out of sight, out of mind. It had all happened so
quickly.

As he travelled from St Andrews to Edinburgh,
I wonder if James Finlay knew he was entering a dream-
world, a fantasy that would be building around him in his
first decades in the city. The Nelson Monument on Calton
Hill (seen centre, far in the distance) had been completed
just ten years previously. It marked the admiral's victory
at Trafalgar. And close by the construction of the national
monument *A Memorial of the Past and Incentive to the Future*

---

6. Ibid., Graham.

Detail from Nasmyth's Princes Street. A charming view at the east corner of Hanover Street and the relaxed almost casual activity on Princes Street in the years the Finlays arrived. Stagecoaches, carriages and carts ambling along without order save avoiding the pedestrians strolling wherever they wish. The dress of the people and the elaborate store fronts – the equal of London -they thought.

Heroism of the Men of Scotland,[7] had begun in 1826; to the designs of the English architect Charles Cockerell with William Playfair. It was conceived as a full-scale replica of the Parthenon in Athens. James would have seen the work in progress daily from the steps of Register House and witness all coming to a halt in 1829, due to the lack of funds, the project was abandoned. Edinburgh's newspapers described the failure as 'Scotland's Disgrace', 'Edinburgh's Disgrace', 'the Pride and Poverty of

---

7. 'The objective: to adopt the Temple of Minerva or Parthenon of Athens, as the model of the Monument, and to restore to the civilised world that celebrated and justly admired edifice, without any deviation whatever, excepting the adaptation of the sculpture to the events and achievements of the Scottish Heroes, whose prowess and glory it is destined to commemorate and perpetuate, and part of which monument or building must, in terms of the said Act, be appropriated as a church or place of Divine worship, to be maintained in all time coming by the said Association'. From the *Proceedings of the Society of Antiquaries of Scotland. XII. Edinburgh: Neill and Company.*

Scotland' and 'Edinburgh's Folly'. Names which have stuck as have the twelve massive columns when viewed from Princes Street. A massive folly which has a more mysterious and powerful presence than had the monument been completed.

James presumably had been in Edinburgh for several years preparing for the law, whereas Elspeth was new to the city, new in fact to any city and had no friends. The newspapers would have warned her against visiting the old town on the ridge. She was probably unaware of the many prostitutes in the doorways of the Canongate, but may have been tempted by the news of the bathing machines available for hire in the seashore at Portobello. And in this first year, would have been alarmed by her husband's drinking.

These were the years when the New Town was coming fully to life. Writing a century after Arnot, James Grant in *Cassell's Old and New Edinburgh*, wrote nostalgically of what had been:

> Looking at the site of the New Town now,
> it requires an effort to think that there were
> thatched cottages there once, and farms, where
> corn was own and reaped, where pigs grunted
> in styes or roamed in the yard; where fowls laid
> eggs and clucked over them, and ducks drove
> their broods into the North Loch, where the trap
> caught eels and the otter and water-rat lurked
> amid the sedges, and where cattle browsed on
> the upland slopes that were crested by the line
> of the Lang Dykes; and where the gudeman and
> his sons left the plough in the furrow, and betook
> them to steel bonnets and plate sleeves, to jack
> and Scottish spear, when the bale-fire, flam-
> ing out on the Castle towers, announced that

'our ancient enemies of England had crossed the Tweed'. Such, little more than one hundred years ago, was the site of 'the Modem Athens'.

The National Monument, Calton Hill, Edinburgh, the architect William Playfair. Watercolour attributed the architect of the Royal School, Thomas Hamilton circa 1830.[8]

8. I have been unable to discover who owns that marvellous painting or who it is by. I discussed with the headmistress of the New High School, who has a print of the work but knew nothing of its source. The Scottish Gallery offered no help. And I finally met a painting curator at the Scottish National Galleries, who agreed with me mw that it was superb but could not name the artist. It is in my mind too good to be by the architect, Alexander Hamilton, and not quite right for a Turner, though he was painting on the Calton Hill about this time.

Along the line now occupied by Princes Street lay a straight country road, the Lang Dykes – called the Lang Gait in the 'Memorie of the Somervilles', in 1640 – the way by which Claverhouse and his troopers rode westward on that eventful day in 1689, and where in 1763, we read in the Edinburgh Museum for January of two gentlemen on horse-back being stopped by a robber, armed with a pistol, whom they struck down by the butt end of a whip, but failed to secure, 'as they heard some-body whistle several times behind the dykes', and were apprehensive that he might have confederates. The district was intersected by Bearford's Parks on the west, and Wood's Farm on the east, formed the bulk of this portion of the site; St. George's Church is now in the centre of the former, and Wemyss Place of the latter.

[...] The hamlet and manor house of Moultray's Hill are now occupied by the Register House; and where the Royal Bank stands was a cottage called 'Peace and Plenty', from its signboard near Gabriel's Road, 'where ambulative citizens regaled them-selves with curds and cream', and Broughton was deemed so far afield that people went there for the summer months under the belief that they were some distance from town, just as people used to go to Powburn and Tipperlinn fifty years later.

He discussed the new society created by the new town:

By 1790 the New Town had extended west-ward to Castle Street, and by 1800 the

necessity for a second plan farther to the
north was felt, and soon acted upon, and
great changes rapidly came over the customs,
manners, and habits of the people. With the
enlarged mansions of the new city, they were
compelled to live more expensively, and more
for show. A family that had long moved in
genteel or aristocratic society in Blackfriars
Wynd, or Lady Stair's Close, maintaining a
round of quiet tea-drinkings with their neighbours up the adjoining turnpike stair, and
who might converse with lords, ladies, and
landed gentry, by merely opening their respective windows, found all this homely kindness
changed when they emigrated beyond the
North Loch. There heavy dinners took the
place of tea-parties, and routs superseded the
festive suppers of the closes and wynds, and
those who felt themselves great folk when
dwelling therein, appeared small enough in
George Street or Charlotte Square.

The New Town kept pace with the growing prosperity of Scotland, and the Old, if
unchanged in aspect, changed thoroughly as
respects the character of its population. Nobles
and gentlemen, men of nearly all professions,
deserted one by one, and a flood of the lower,
the humbler, and the plebeian classes took their
places in close and wynd; and many a gentleman
in middle life, living then perhaps in Princes
Street, looked back with wonder and amusement
to the squalid common stair in which he and his
forefathers had been born, and where he had
spent the earliest years of his life.

Originally the houses of Craig's new city were all of one plain and intensely monotonous plan and elevation – three storeys in height, with a sunk area in front, enclosed by iron railings, with link extinguishers; and they only differed by the stone being more finely polished, as the streets crept westward. But during a number of years prior to1840, the dull uniformity of the streets over the western half of the town had disappeared. Most of the edifices, all constructed as elegant and commodious dwelling-houses, are now enlarged, re-built, or turned into large hotels, shops, club-houses, insurance-offices, warehouses, and new banks, and scarcely an original house remains unchanged in Princes Street or George Street.

And this brings us now to the Edinburgh of modern intellect, power, and wealth. At no period of her history did Edinburgh better deserve the complimentary title of the modern Athens than the last ten years of the eighteenth and the first ten years of the nineteenth century. She was then, not only nominally, but actually, the capital of Scotland, the city in which was collected all the intellectual life and vigour of the country. London then occupied a position of much less importance in relation to the distant parts of the empire than is now the case. Many causes have contributed to bring about the change, of which the most prominent are the increased facilities for locomotion [...] She was the titular capital of Scotland, and as such, was looked up to with pride and veneration by the nation at large. She was then the residence of

many of the old Scottish nobility, and the exclu-
sion of the British from the Continent, during a
long, protracted war, made her, either for business, society, or education, the favourite resort
of strangers. She was the head-quarters of the
legal profession at a time when both the Scottish
bench and bar were rendered illustrious by a
number of men celebrated for their learning,
eloquence, and wit She was the head-quarters of
the Scottish Church, whose pulpits and General
Assembly were adorned by divines of great eminence and piety. Lastly, she was the chief seat of
scholarship, and the chosen home of literature
and science north of the Tweed', where they
breathed out their tender tale of passion beneath
the fragrant hawthorn'.

Grant illustrates the changes with surprising and delightful details:

The oyster-cellars had become numerous and
were places of fashionable resort. A maid-
servant's wages were about £4 yearly. In 1783 a
number of bathing-machines had been adopted
at Leith. People of the middle class and above it
dined about four o'clock, after which no business was done, and gentlemen were at no pains
to conceal their impatience till the ladies retired.
Attendance at church was much neglected, and
people did not think it 'genteel' to take their
domestics with them'. In 1783 the daughters
even of tradesmen consume the mornings at the
toilet (to which rouge is now an appendage) or
in strolling from the perfumers to the milliner's.

They would blush to be seen at market. The cares of the family devolve upon a housekeeper, and Miss employs those heavy hours when she is disengaged from public or private amusements in improving her mind from the precious stores of a circulating library'.

In that year a regular cock-pit was built for cock-fighting, where all distinctions of rank and character were levelled. The weekly concert of music began at seven o'clock, and mistresses of boarding-schools, &c., would not allow their pupils to go about unattended; whereas, twenty years before 'young ladies might have walked the streets in perfect security at all hours'.

A great number of the servant-maids still continued 'their abhorrence of wearing shoes and stockings in the morning. 'The Register House was un-finished, or occupied by pigeons only', and the Records 'were kept in a dungeon called the Laigh Parliament House'. The High Street alone was protected by the guard.

The New Town to the north, and all the streets and new squares to the south, were totally unwatched; and the soldiers of the guard still pre-served 'the purity of their native Gaelic, so that few of the citizens understand, or are understood by them'; while the king's birthday and the last night of the year were 'devoted to drunkenness, outrage, and riot, instead of loyalty, peace, and harmony', as of old. One of the earliest improvements in the extended royalty was lighting it with oil lamps; but in the Advertiser for 1789 we are told that 'while all strangers admire the beauty and regularity of the New Town, they are surprised at its being so badly lighted and watched at night. The half of the North Bridge next the Old Town, is well lighted, while the half next the New remains in total dark-ness. London and Westminster are lighted all the year through'. Among the improvements in the same year, we read of two hackney-coach stands being introduced by the magistrates-one at St Andrew's Church and another at the Register House; but sedans were then in constant use and did not finally disappear till about 1850.

From another source, Grant records:

[...] By that time the last traces of ancient manners had nearly departed. 'The old claret-drinkers', says a writer in 1824, 'are brought to nothing, and some of them are under the sod. The court dresses, in which the nobility and gentry appeared at the balls and first circles in Edinburgh, together with their dress swords or rapiers, are all [is confusion] for there has been introduced a half-dress – and it is a half-dress: nay, some ladies make theirs less than half; while the swords of the well-dressed men have been dropped for the fist, and the dashing blades of the present day learn to miss, to fib, and to floor, and to give a facer with their mawlies', and other equally gentleman-like accomplishments'. Elsewhere he says 'To prove the more tenacious adhesion of the Scotch to French manners and old fashions, I can assert that for one cocked hat which appeared in the streets of London within

the last forty years, a dozen passed current in
Auld Reekie'.[9]

Then over many pages, Grant offers a detailed street-by-
street description of tenants – shops hotels, clubs and the
people who have moved into this new society. This was
the world of James and Elspeth, where they strolled; these
are the people they passed on the street:

> The houses first numbered in Princes Street
> were in the south portion, which caused the
> legal contention in 1774, and the continuation of
> which was so fortunately arrested by the Court
> of Session, and there the numbers run from
> 1 to 9. No. 2 was occupied in 1784 by
> Robertson, 'a ladies' hairdresser', where, as per
> advertisement Two Irish giants – twin brothers
> – exhibited them-selves to visitors at a shilling
> per head, from four till nine every evening,
> Sundays excepted. [...] In 1811 this house (No.
> 2) and No. 1 were both hotels, the former being
> named 'The Crown', and from them both, the
> 'Royal Eagle' and 'Prince Regent' Glasgow
> stage-coaches started daily at 9 a.m. and 4 p.m.
> 'every lawful day'. Taking the houses of note
> as they occur [...] the first on the north side,
> No. 10 – for some time a famous china empo-
> rium – has had many and various occupants.
> In 1783, and before that period, it was Poole's
> Coffee-house, and till the days of Waterloo was
> long known as a rendezvous for the many mili-
> tary idlers who were then in Edinburgh – the

---

9. Ibid., Grant *Cassell's Old and New Edinburgh*.

veterans of Egypt, Walcheren, the Peninsula, and India – and for the officers of the strong garrison maintained there, till the general peace. In an advertisement, 'Mathew Poole returns his most grateful acknowledgments to the nobility and gentry for their past favours, and begs leave respectfully to inform them that he has taken the whole of the apartments above his coffee-house, which he has fitted up in the neatest and most genteel manner as a hotel The airiness of the situation and the convenience of the lodgings, which are perfectly detached from each other, render it very proper for families, and the advantage of the coffee-house and tavern adjoining must make it both convenient and agreeable for single gentlemen'.

No. 16, farther westward, was [...] occupied as Weir's Museum, [...] One cannot help', says Kincaid, 'admiring the birds from Port Jackson, New South Wales, for the extreme beauty of their plumage; their appearance otherwise exhibits them as not deprived of life'. It is of this collection that Lord Gardenstone wrote, in his Travelling Memoranda 'I cannot omit to observe that in the whole course of my travels I have nowhere seen the preservation of quadrupeds, birds, fishes, and insects executed with such art and taste as by Mr. Alexander Weir of Edinburgh. He is a most ingenious man, and certainly has not hitherto been so much encouraged by the public as his merit deserves'.

The Finlays may have seen an ailing Sir Walter Scott living just one street to the east:

> In 1826 we find Sir Walter Scott, when ruin had come upon him, located in No. 6, Mrs Brown's lodgings, in a third-rate house of St David Street, whither he came after Lady Scott's death at Abbotsford, on the 15th of May in that – to him – most melancholy year of debt and sorrow, and set himself calmly down to the stupendous task of reducing, by his own unaided exertions, the enormous monetary responsibilities he had taken upon himself. Lockhart tells us that a week before Captain Basil Hall's visit at No. 6, Sir Walter had sufficiently mastered himself to resume his literary tasks, and was working with determined resolution at his 'Life of Napoleon', while bestowing an occasional day to the 'Chronicles of the Canongate' whenever he got before the press with his historical MS., or felt the want of the only repose he ever cared for – simply a change of labour.[10]

George Street: While Princes Street was emerging as the destination for shoppers and visitors seeking accommodation, George Street had become, as Craig intended, the most prestigious address in the early years of new Edinburgh. Hanover Street met George Street at its centre, and it would be there that the Finlays would stroll among the wealthiest on Sunday and watch the carriages crowding around Assembly Rooms bringing grandees in all their finery to the ball. This young law clerk must have felt he had sufficient status to feel part of this new society:

10. Ibid., Grant *h*.

ST GEORGE'S CHURCH, FROM GEORGE STREET LOOKING WEST.

[...] Previous to the brilliant streets and squares erected in the northern and western portions of new Edinburgh, George Street was said to have no rival in the world; and even yet, after having undergone many changes, for combined length, space, uniformity, and magnificence of vista, whether viewed from the east or west, it may well be pronounced unparalleled.

In George Street are about thirty different insurance offices, or their branches, all more or less ornate in architecture, and several banks.

St Georges Church from George Street Looking West; drawn by Thos. H Shepherd, 1829.

[...] No. 25 George Street was the residence (from1784 till his death, in 1829), of Mr. James Ferrier, Principal Clerk of Session, [...] he was a keen whist player, and every night of his life had a rubber, which occasionally included old Dr. Hamilton, usually designated 'Cocked Hat' Hamilton, from the fact of his being one of the last in Edinburgh who bore that head-piece. When victorious, he would snap his fingers and caper about the room, to the manifest indignation of Mr. Ferrier, who would express it to his partner in the words, 'Lady Augusta, did you ever see such ridiculous levity in an auld man?'

[...] Robert Bums used also to be a guest at No. 25 and was present on one occasion when some magnificent Gobelins tapestry arrived there for the Duke of Argyll on its way to Inverary Castle. [...] The eldest Miss Ferrier was one of the Edinburgh beauties in her day; and Burns once happening to meet her, while turning the corner of George Street, felt suddenly inspired, and wrote the lines to her enclosed in an elegy on the death of Sir D. H. Blair

[...] No. 45 has long been famous as the establishment of Messrs. Blackwood, the eminent publishers. William Blackwood, the founder of the magazine which stills bears his name, and on the model of which so many high-class periodicals have been started. [...] In October, 1817, he brought out the first number of that celebrated magazine which has enrolled among its contributors the names of Wilson, Scott, Henry

Mackenzie, J. McCrie, Brewster, De Quincey, Hamilton.

[...] No. 49, the house of Wilkie of Foulden, is now a great music saloon; and No. 75, now the County Fire and other public offices, has a peculiar interest, as there lived and died the mother of Sir Walter Scott – Anne Rutherford, [...] a woman who, the biographer of her illustrious son tells us, was possessed of superior natural talents, with a good taste for music and poetry and great conversational powers. In her youth she is said to have been acquainted with Allan Ramsay, Beattie, Blacklock, and many other Scottish men of letters in the last century; and independently of the influence which her own talents and acquirements may have given her in training the opening mind of the future novelist.

[...] In the second storey of No. 108 Sir Walter Scott dwelt in 1797, when actively engaged in his German translations and forming the Edinburgh Volunteer Light Horse, of which he was in that year, to his great gratification, made quartermaster.

[...] The Edinburgh Association of Science and Arts now occupies the former residence of the Butters of Pitlochry, No. 117. It is an institution formed. in 1869, and its title is sufficiently explanatory of its objects.

[...] The Mercantile Bank of India, London, and China occupies No. 128, formerly the mansion of Sir James Hall of Dunglass, Bart.

[...] St Andrew's church stands 200 feet westward of St Andrew's Square; it is a plain building of oval form, with a handsome portico, having four great Corinthian pillars, and built,

says Kincaid, from a design of Major Eraser, of
the Engineers, whose residence was close by. It
was erected in 1785.

[...] Opposite this church there was built the
old Physicians' Hall – the successor of the still
more ancient one near the Cowgate Port. The
members of that college feued from the city a
large area, extending between the south side of
George Street and Rose Street, on which they
erected a very handsome hall, with rooms and
offices, from a design by Mr Craig, the architect
of the new city itself.

[...] 'The New Assembly Rooms, for which
the ground is staked out in the new town', says
the Edinburgh Advertiser for April, 1783, 'will
be among the most elegant of any in Britain'.
In addition to the ballroom, 'there is to be a
tea-room, fifty feet by thirty-six, which will also
serve as a ball-room on ordinary occasions; also
a grand saloon, thirty-eight feet by forty-four
feet, besides other and smaller rooms.

[...] To the assemblies of 1783, the letters of
Theophrastus inform us that gentlemen were in
the habit of reeling 'from the tavern, flustered
with wine, to an assembly of as elegant and
beautiful women as any in Europe'; also that
minuets had gone out of fashion, and country
dances were chiefly in vogue, and that in 1787 a
master of the ceremonies was appointed. The
weekly assemblies here in the Edinburgh season
are now among the most brilliant and best conducted in Europe;

[...] It was in the Assembly Rooms that Sir
Walter Scott, on the 23rd February, 1827, at
the annual dinner of the Edinburgh Theatrical

Fund Association, avowed himself to be 'the Great Unknown', acknowledging the authorship of the Waverley Novels – scarcely a secret then, as the recent exposure of Constable's affairs had made the circumstance pretty well known, particularly in literary circles.

[...] In June 1841 a great public banquet was given to Charles Dickens in the Assembly Rooms, at which Professor Wilson presided, and which the novelist subsequently referred to as having been a source of sincere gratification to him.[11]

Slum Life in Edinburgh, or, Scenes in Its Darkest Places: Those paying tribute to Dickens in 1841 were not unaware that less than a mile from the Assembly Rooms were conditions of poverty as dreadful as any in London. By 1830 Edinburgh was entering a period of rapid industrialization. Rural poverty and the promise of work in the new industries caused a dramatic increase in population. An epidemic of cholera in the early 1830s spread rapidly and affected all ranks of the population. It was most virulent in densely populated areas, where Edinburgh was reported to have the most unsanitary living conditions of any city in Britain at the time. (Overcrowding in some areas was estimated to be four times greater than in the prison cells of the period.) There was also a recession in the 1840s, causing a slowdown in construction in the New Town, consequently no attempt was made to address the conditions in the slums until the 1850s.

11. Ibid., Grant *h*.

Slum Life in Edinburgh, or, Scenes in Its Darkest Places[12]
was based on firsthand experiences in Edinburgh in 1891.
They were published as a series in the *Weekly Scotsman*,
and the author only gave his initials – T. B. M

> A walk through the Grassmarket or Cowgate,or
> down the Lawnmarket and Cannongate, is at
> times a very depressing experience; but one has
> to explore the huge tenements that tower on
> either side of the street, to enter the houses and
> speak with the people, to arrive at an adequate
> idea of what life in some parts of the slums
> means. A night spent in such an exploration –
> climbing foul and rickety stairs, groping your
> way along a network of dark, narrow passages,
> and peering into the dismal dens which the
> wretched inhabitants (and their landlords) call
> 'houses' – a night passed in this manner will give
> an experience of horrors that will forever remain
> imprinted on the memory.
>
> Go into any one of the courts in the Lawn-
> market, for instance; glance up at the rows of
> windows, and then reflect for a minute or two.
> Windows everywhere – looking to front, to
> back into courts and closes; and each one of
> them probably represents a 'one-roomed house',
> inhabited by from two to eight or nine persons.
> The rooms, once the spacious chambers of the
> aristocracy of Edinburgh, have been partitioned

---

12. T. B. M. [*sic*] *Slum Life in Edinburgh, or, Scenes in Its Darkest Places:
with twelve illustrations form life* J. Thin Edinburgh, 1891 (They
were published as a series in the *Weekly Scotsman* and the author
remained anonymous.)

off into small box-like apartments, like the cell
of a honeycomb. Everybody is familiar with the
filth of the closes and courts: these, then, need
not be further described. The stairs are in a
corresponding state of foulness. The seemingly
interminable passages which penetrate in all
directions into these human warrens are narrow,
and in general very badly lighted; in many the
darkness seems almost to be palpable, so dense is
it. Along these corridors the doors of the rooms
are ranged within a few feet of each other. A
close, sickening odour pervades the passages.
It is an indescribable smell – a compound of
all the foul vapours escaping from numberless
reeking hovels. Sometimes when you enter a
room, fumes like the quintessence of all villain-
ous smells combined, make you gasp, and then,
rushing down to the very foundations of your
vitals, cause a sensation as if the stomach were
trying to turn a somersault. But conquering
an instinctive desire to shut the door and beat
a retreat, you enter the room and look around
you. The room, for which a weekly rent of from
one and three pence to half-a-crown is paid,
is small, dirty, and dingy. The walls are black
with the smoke and dirt of years; here and there
the plaster has fallen off in patches, and reveals
the laths beneath. The floor looks as if soap
and water were still unknown in these regions;
like-wise the crazy deal table – if there happens
to be one. There may be a chair with a decayed
back, but frequently a roughly-made stool or an
upturned box does duty instead. And the bed!
These lairs – for the word 'bed' may suggest
erroneous ideas of luxury – have long been a

marvel to us; in as much as it is difficult to imagine how blankets, which presumably were once white, have assumed a hue so dark. They appear to have been steeped in a solution of soot and water-blankets, pillows, and mattress, or what stand for such. Generally, the bed is a wooden one, a venerable relic of bygone fashions, bought for a trifle from the furniture broker on the other side of the street. But very often a bedstead is not included in the furnishings of the chamber, in which case the family couch consists of a mattress or a bundle of rags, or some straw laid in the least draughty corner of the room, and covered over with any kind of rags that can be gathered together.

There a whole family will lie down at night, and when the cold is intense, and the piercing wind whistles through the chinks in the window frames, right glad they are to huddle together for the sake of warmth. It is no uncommon thing to see five or six, or even seven, persons in one bed – father, mother, and four or five children, one foetid intertwined mass of humanity. The unspeakably horrible results of this over-crowding need not be described; they can be readily imagined. For it is not only children who are packed together within the four walls of one chamber. It is quite a usual thing to find grown-up people herding together in one small room, without any pretence of privacy or decency.

In a room in the Lawnmarket we found a man and his wife in bed, both unwell. The husband had been out of health and unable to work for

*Illustration from 'Slum Life
in Edinburgh, or, Scenes in Its
Darkest Places': a whole family
in one room.*

twelve months, and he and his wife were supported by a daughter of twenty years of age,
who earned seven shillings and sixpence a week,
and shared their room, and their bed, with
them. And they would think you had queer
notions if you expressed surprise at this natural
arrangement.

Another room – this one in the Castle Wynd –
presented a scene that is only too easily paral-
leled in any part of our slums. It was typical
of the poor man's home. The room was filthy
beyond description. From the blackened walls
the paper hung in shreds, and in one corner the
damp had discoloured the plaster beyond the
power of whitewash to restore. A feeble light
from a paraffin lamp shed its melancholy rays
over a group of two men, two girls, and a boy
cowering round a cinder fire which they were in
vain endeavouring to coax into a flame. Beside
them, on a bundle of rags on the floor, lay a
woman and two grown-up daughters; and on a

decrepit bedstead, curled up among a few foul cloths that no one would think of calling bed-clothes, a man was sleeping off the effects of a two-days' carouse.

In this dark, damp den, the weekly rent of which was two shillings and fourpence, the man, his wife, and five children, the eldest of whom was a girl of eighteen, lived - under what conditions we shall leave the reader to depict for himself. Yet this is almost a desirable residence com-pared with some of the abodes that may be seen any day of the week. In Lower Greenside, where there are some execrable specimens of one-roomed houses, we stumbled across a den about twelve feet square. It was a debatable point which was the more hideous, the room or its occupants. Furniture there was none, unless a shakedown of rags, a stool, and an empty orange box may go by that name. In the grate an old boot was burning, for the supply of cinders had run out. On one side of the fire sat an unkempt virago, with a baby at her breast and a pipe in her mouth. Opposite to her crouched an aged woman, whose grey, dishevelled hair, hooked nose, and brown, minutely wrinkled face gave her a very witch-like appearance. Cross-legged between them sat a boy of about ten years of age. This beldam, having reached an advanced stage of intoxication, was venting her spleen in a shower of oaths and curses upon her companion with the baby and the pipe, but the latter treated her volleys of vituperation with the calmness bred of use and wont. only at intervals removing her pipe from her mouth and commanding the

old woman to 'shut up', an injunction always followed by a fierce, complicated oath.

A feature of this low life that impresses one with
painful vividness is the total absence of anything
approaching rational enjoyment or employment.
When a man in comfortable circumstances goes
home from his day's work, he generally finds a
cheery hearth and a warm meal awaiting him.
Then, if he does not go out for a walk, or to
visit friends, or to some place of entertainment,
he puts his slippered feet on the fender and has
his pipe and his newspaper; or, if he is a family
man, he enjoys the company of his wife and children. At all events he is fed and warm, and his
mind is more or less at ease. The forlorn being of
whom we write returns to the hovel he calls his
home, after, it may be, a day spent in a fruitless
search for work. He finds nothing there to cheer
or attract him. Dirt and desolation everywhere!
His better-half not remarkable for her tidiness.
A swarm of ragged, hungry bairns are sprawl-
ing about the Hour. It depends on chance and
the luck of the day whether there is any supper
or not. Possibly there is not a crust in the house.
Though the night is bitterly cold, there is only a
handful of smouldering cinders in the grate, and
a dullness that penetrates to the very marrow
pervades the room. Books or newspapers he
has none; probably he could not read them if he
had any. The night is too cold for loafing at the
'close-mouth' – a favourite summer pastime of
our slum denizens; so all he can do is to kill time
till he shuffles off to bed. It sickens the heart to
see the hopeless, aim-less demeanor of a family

'Royal High School, Edinburgh' by the architect Thomas Hamilton, (pencil and watercolour on paper, submitted by the architect to the Royal Scottish Academy in 1831). (Wikimedia Commons)

group such as this. There they sit, as close to the meagre fire as possible, gloomy emptiness on all sides. They do nothing; of conversation they have little, only an occasional remark is dropped in a listless way. When one surprises a household in this attitude, he is impressed with the idea that this cluster of silent figures are expecting something – waiting for something to turn up. But if they are expectant, it is of something that never comes. At length, hungry, shivering, utterly wretched, they throw themselves upon the pallet of straw and rags, and for a time forget their misery in sleep.[13]

The Royal High School: Life in the New Town went on oblivious to the suffering. At the weekend,

13. Ibid., *Slum Life in Edinburgh.*

'The New Observatory and Playfair's Monument, Calton Hill: drawn by H Shepherd, 1828.

I imagine James and Elspeth among the crowds enjoying the view of the city from Calton Hill, adjusting and learning to act on this new and evolving stage and plays. They would pause by the National Monument still encased in scaffolding, and despite the news of the project's financial difficulties, there would be excitement in what it promised. They would then wander by several charming classical temples, the Dugald Stewart Monument, the Robert Burns Monument, the Political Martyrs' Monument. They would admire the Observatory designed by the nephew of its president, the architect William Playfair. At the southern edge of the hill, they would look over at the grim prisons, the Bridewell, designed by Robert Adam and the Calton Jail, both depressing and misplaced structures on this veritable acropolis of symbols and heroes. And below, they would see the roofs of the city's new High School. The grandest evocation of the ancient world in the city. (A school I attended between 1951 and 1956, but more of that later.) The architect was Thomas Hamilton. His father was both a carpenter and an architect successful enough from city commissions to send his son to the Old High School off the High Street. With the death of his uncle also a builder, the 28-year-old Hamilton inherited several properties in the New Town. He was a founding member of the Royal Scottish Academy in 1826 and a wealthy and respected figure in the city when he prepared the designs for a new High School.

The High School is one of the oldest schools in the English-speaking world,[14] with a history of almost 900 years. Historians associate its birth with the flowering of a twelfth-century renaissance in Scotland. It first enters the historical record as the seminary of Holyrood Abbey founded by the Augustinian canons of King David I in 1128. In 1505, the school was described as a 'high school', the first recorded use of this term in either Scotland or England. In 1566, following the Reformation, Mary, Queen of Scots, transferred the school from the control of Holyrood Abbey to the Town Council of Edinburgh, and around 1590, James VI accorded it royal patronage as the *Schola Regia Edimburgensis,* or King's School of Edinburgh.

This was the seventh location for the school since the sixteenth century. It was in the Vennel of the Church of St. Mary in the Fields between 1503 and 1516; in Kirk o' Field Wynd, from 1516 to 1555. In that year, it is surprising to find the school relocated in the former home of the last Scottish cardinal before the Reformation, Cardinal Beaton, in Blackfriars Wynd less than a decade after his death. This move was made on orders of the young Mary, Queen of Scots when she gave the school

---

14. The Edinburgh High School is believed to have been a model for the first public high school in the United States, the English High School of Boston, in 1821, before the current structure was built.

to the city just before she married the Dauphin Frances. in 1 It was then for a brief time at the Collegiate Church of St. Giles 1569–1578; and for the longest in Blackfriar's monastery 1578–1777, when it was given a royal title. And lastly, at the High School Yards till 1829 when the new school opened. This sequence of settings marks the move from the religious to the secular and shifting centres of power and influence in the city.

The foundation for the new school was laid on 28 July 1825.[15] The speech by Mr Brougham stressed one deeply significant aspect of the school and its history:

> [...] Mr. Brougham spoke this affectionately
> of High School: 'Yet a school like the old High
> School of Edinburgh is invaluable, and for what
> is it so? It is because men of the highest and low-
> est rank of society send their children to be edu-
> cated together. The oldest friend I have in the
> world, your worthy vice-president (Lord Douglas
> Gordon Halyburton of Pitcur, MP.) and myself
> were at the High School of Edinburgh together,
> and in the same class along with others, who still
> possess our friendship, and some of them in a
> rank in life still higher than us. One of them was
> a nobleman who is now in the House of Peers;
> and some of them were the sons of shopkeepers
> in the lowest part of the Cowgate – shops of the
> most inferior description and one or two of them

---

15. The *Edinburgh Journal* reported: 'Tho' the foundation of the intended High School was laid this day with great formality it seems extremely doubtful when the building will commence'. The author was doubtful if it could be paid for 'contributions for public institutions are not getting on at present with much spirit [...]'

'View of the Royal High School and Burns' Monument, Edinburgh' c.1830 Painting presumed to be by friend and colleague of Thomas Hamilton, David Roberts, Thomas Allom, Thomas Hamilton and David Roberts 1800 (image © Royal Scottish Academy of Art & Architecture)

were the sons of menial servants in the town. They were sitting side by side giving and taking places from each other, without the slightest impression on the part of my noble friends of any superiority on their parts to the other boys, or any ideas of the inferiority on the part of the other boys to them; and this is my reason for preferring the old High School of Edinburgh to other and what may be termed more patrician schools, however well-regulated or conducted'.

The Finlays could also have been part of the crowds on 23 June 1829 at the celebration of the opening of what many considered to be the nation's high school. *The Scotsman* newspaper reported:

The new High School, one of the most classical and perfect edifices to be seen in Europe, was opened yesterday, under the most favourable auspices. The sky, which had lowered and almost threatened, during the earlier part of the day, drew up its curtain of clouds just before the procession moved from Infirmary Street; and as the sun burst forth in all its glory, the streets, and not only the streets but the houses and public buildings of Edinburgh, windows and balustrades, presented a most interesting spectacle [...] When the Lord Provost, magistrates and Council were introduced to their seats and received by Mr. Hamilton the architect [...][16][17]

---

16. SCOTSMAN Digital Archive June 1829.
17. https://sites.google.com/site/joerocksresearchpages/thomas -hamilton- architect/royal-high-school-chronology

Though more than 50 years after the opening, James Grant showed his fondness for the building and its setting:

> [...] but, by far the most important, interesting, and beautiful edifice on this remarkable hill is the new High School of Edinburgh, on its southern slope, adjoining the Regent Terrace. The new High School is unquestionably one of the most chaste and classical edifices in Edinburgh. It is a reproduction of the purest Greek, and in every way quite worthy of its magnificent site, which commands one of the richest of townland country landscapes in the city and its environs and is in itself one of the most striking features of the beautiful scenery with which it is grouped. [...] It is of pure white stone, designed-by Thomas Hamilton, and has a front of 400 feet, including the temples, or wings, which contain the writing and mathematical classrooms. The central portico is a hexastyle, and, having a double range of twelve columns, projects considerably in front of the general facade. The whole edifice is of the purest Grecian Doric, and, even to its most minute details, is a copy of the celebrated Athenian Temple of Theseus.

> A spacious flight of steps leading up to it from the closing wall in front, and a fine playground behind, is overlooked by the entrances to the various classrooms. The interior is distributed into a large hall, seventy-three feet by forty-three feet; a rector's classroom, thirty-eight feet by thirty-four feet; four class-rooms for masters, each thirty-eight feet by twenty-eight feet; a library and two small rooms attached to each

of the classrooms. On the margin of the roadway, on a lower site than the main building,
are two handsome lodges, each two storeys in
height, one occupied by the janitor, and the other
containing classrooms. The area of the school
and playground is two acres and is formed by
cutting deep into the face of the hill. The building cost when finished, according to the City
Chamberlain's books, L34,199s and 6d. There
are a rector, and ten teachers of classics and
languages, in addition to several lecturers on
science.

The school, the most important in Scotland,
and intimately connected with the literature and
instruction in all departments of a commercial
as well as liberal education. Every branch of literature, including reading, orthography, recita-
tion, grammar, and composition, together with
British history, forms the prominent parts of the
system; while the entire curriculum of study –
which occupies six years – embraces the Latin,
Greek, French, and German languages, history, geography, physiology, chemistry natural
philosophy, zoology, botany, algebra, geometry,
drawing, fencing, gymnastics, and military drill.
In the library are seven thousand volumes.

The building was completed in 1829, and the
pupils proceeded thither [...] from the time-
honoured old school, in a procession arranged
by Sir Patrick Walker of Coates, preceded by
the band of the 17th Lancers, each class marching with a master at its head, followed by the
High Constables, the magistrates, professors
of the university, and all 'those noblemen and

gentlemen who had attended the High School, in fours'. A long and elaborate Latin inscription on the front of the buildings commemorates the founding of the edifice, with reference to the Old School, founded 300 years before; but two statues, which formed a part of Hamilton's design, and were to have been in front of the portico, have never been placed there and in all likely hood never will be.

Entrance to the school was based on examination, and open to all, it was a meritocracy. [I was one such beneficiary.] And the opening address again stressed the peculiarity of its constitution, as its classes embrace all sects and grades of society - the peer and peasant sit together in the same form, each possessing no advantage over his schoolfellow.[18]

The school has gone from the buildings now, moved out when they were briefly considered being converted into the new Scottish Parliament building. Sir Walter Scott would have been delighted to see a new parliament returning not only to Scotland but to his chosen site for a centre of Scottish power, Calton Hill, but it was not to be. A progressive Scotland could never countenance conducting business in recreated Greek Temple. Hamilton's majestic structure was vacated in 1968, and in 2021, having been empty for more than 50 years, the Edinburgh City Council agreed to convert the building into a National Centre for Music.

---

18. Ibid., Grant.

I was a student at the school from 1951 to 1956, and little had changed in my years there from the descriptions of 100 years ago. In truth, apart from the new occupants in the homes and businesses, the old civic order of the New Town was still intact. Despite having commanded the southern aspect of Calton Hill for 180 years, the Royal High School still seems detached from the reality of Edinburgh. Surprisingly, I don't recall any attempt by my teachers in Latin, history or art, explaining why we were part of such an extravagant classical theatre. I do recall that all the rooms in the Hamilton buildings were heated by coal fires in ornate fireplaces, and bullying sometimes involved holding a boy perilously close to the flames. Among the rituals and routines of High School life was the obligatory Latin, and the smoking clubs in the tunnels beneath the assembly hall, and in their final year the procession of graduates through the great doors of the hall, which were opened but once a year, just for them.

Once a week, every student had to run around Calton Hill, rain, slush and snow. I remember freezing as I stumbled up the steps by the house of the photographers Hill and Adamson, past the tomb of Dugald Stewart and the little temple housing the Royal Scottish Observatory; on past the enormous and gracious columns of Edinburgh's Parthenon (always seemed to me to be larger than the real thing). I do remember the feeling of superiority in being part of this ancient school culture, where Sir Walter Scott and the brothers Adam were taught.

Did the Finlays feel strange to be in the presence of such theatrical creations of the classical world? Did they take it for granted and were amused by being surrounded by such elaborate structures, or did they consider if more would be expected from them in this new reality? They were unwitting actors who had been given no

preparation for their performance; however, they would
now be wearing the new costumes, new fashions, many
inspired by the tartan fantasies created by Sir Walter
Scott for the visit of George IV in 1833. As they walked
and talked, did they try to make their *lallans* accent, the
broad Scots of the lowlands, sound more English? I presume they would have known and be pleased to be part of
what Scott named 'The Athens of The North'. (Latin and
Greek were obligatory subjects at the Royal High even in
my day). Nowhere in Scotland's past had public reality
ever been so symbolic or so formal.

*'The Royal High School',
photographed by Hill and
Adamson, 1843.*

V

Building Status

In 1832, the Finlays moved to Stockbridge. In the records of St Cuthbert's parish, James and Elspeth Finlay had a son born on 20 June 1832, who they named James. It states that they were living at No 8 Kerr Street, Stockbridge.

> *James Finlay, Writer, N 8 Kerr Street, Stockbridge and Elspeth Wallace his spouse had a son born 20th day of June last named James St Cuthbert's Parish*

What had happened to force the move from Hanover Street? The answer, their benefactor Andrew Bell died in January 1832, and his will decreed that all his assets be sold off to create foundations and gifts for the various causes he championed. Imagine the anxiety in the family with Elspeth pregnant and having to search for a new home. Having enjoyed the prestige of living in the centre of the New Town, they would have felt it necessary to remain close to the new city centre, yet with little money, there were limited choices.

Kerr Street and surrounding streets had been recently developed for people with more modest incomes. They were a recognition that this New Town would have to accommodate a wider spectrum of society. And Kerr Street would have been a reasoned choice. It was in the

*Edinburgh 1833, Kerr Street
is in the diagonal upper left,
Hanover Street is at the lower
left: W. & A. K. Johnston for
Gray's annual directory.*

valley of the Water of Leith, north of the area laid out
by Craig and part of a sequence of streets linking the
village of Stockbridge with the New Town. This ran
through Royal Circus and east of the spectacular facades
of Murray Place, both part of the glorious second phase
developed in the previous 25 years with great financial
success.

The buildings had just been completed in
1831 and the Finlays would have been impressed with the
newness of it all; by the sandstone walls freshly cut from
the Craigleith Quarry. Number 8 was and is still a four-
storey building with flats on each floor around a common
stair. It was small; one bedroom, and one family room,
where all the work of the house was done. The coal fireplace as well as heating the house was surrounded by the
pots and pans for cooking. (Ovens beside the fire were
not common till a few decades later, and Elspeth would

take her pies to the baker.) There may have been running water, but in these years, it was most common for water to be carried to each house by men called 'water cadies'. From the available evidence, there was no indoor toilet; the residents shared the facilities of the privy or the outhouse in the courtyard; otherwise, they would have used chamber pots. Before sewers were constructed later in the century, human waste was collected at night by scavengers or night soilmen employed by the town council.

Stockbridge around 1890. No 8 Kerr Street is in the block of flats left of center. (The trams were driven by cables in the groove between the rails.).

All washing was done from the common sink in the main room. When families did bathe they used a wooden or metal bath placed in front of the fire and filled with jugs of hot water. The Finlays may have been among the many that believed that having a bath was bad for them and that washing hair was dangerous. Hair would be cleaned by brushing it with oats or powder.

India Place opening off Kerr St to the South, just before demolition in the 1960s.

India Place looking south from Dean Terrace, rising above is the massive rear wall of Murray Place.

194

India Place, just south and west of Kerr Street, may have been designed for more modest incomes. I remember walking along it in my teens and being puzzled why such simple and strong buildings in a delightful setting – close to the river and to the wealthiest in the city could descend into such ruin and squalor. The reason must lie somewhere in the New Town's inability to accommodate the poor. I remember the fights outside the corner bar on Saturday evening, men drinking through their week's pay. I wonder if that was where James began to find solace in drink.

The gate to the Old Stockbridge market immediately behind Kerr Street

Immediately behind their flat was the Stockbridge Market, the gate still advertising 'Butcher Meat, Fruit Fish and Poultry'. And though modest, the family could look out of their windows across to the Water of Leith and to the west, Dean Terrace just built and glowing at the edge of a splendid further New Town extension planned and designed by the greatest of Scottish artists, Sir Henry Raeburn.

Dean Terrace Facing Kerr Street across the Water of Leith. (Photo author)

James Grant in *Old and New Edinburgh*[1] gives extensive coverage to Stockbridge:

> On both sides of the Water of Leith lies Stockbridge, some 280 yards east of the Dean Bridge. Once a spacious suburb, it is now included in the growing northern New Town, and displays a curious mixture of grandeur and romance, with something of classic beauty, and, in more than one quarter, houses of rather a mean and humble character.

1. Ibid., Grant.

St Bernard's Crescent 1900

Could he mean Kerr Street? He continues:

> One of its finest features is the double crescent
> called St. Bernard's, suggested by, Sir David
> Wilkie, [another gifted Scottish painter] con-
> structed by Sir Henry Raeburn, and adorned
> with the grandest Grecian Doric pillars that

*David Robert's Birthplace on
Duncan's Land Opposite Kerr
Street. (Photo author)*

View of the Edinburgh from Calton Hill: David Roberts, 1863. (With permission Guildhall Art Gallery)

are to be found in any other edifice not a public one.[2]

David Roberts: Not fifty yards from the Finlay home across Kerr Street, was the birthplace of the Scottish painter David Roberts, RA (1796–1864). The house was then called Duncan's land (now Gloucester Lane) and is the only building in Stockbridge that predates the New Town. It is a merchant's house built about 1790 from the stones of demolished buildings in the Old Town, again from James Grant:

> In Duncan's Land, in the old Kirk Loan – a pile built of rubble, removed during the construction of Bank Street, and having an old lintel brought from that quarter, with the legend, 'I fear god oxlye,1605' – was born, on the 24th October, 1796, David Roberts, son of a shoemaker. In the jamb of the kitchen fireplace there remains to this day an indentation made by the old man when sharpening his awl. In his boyhood David Roberts gave indications of his taste for drawing, and made free use of his mother's whitewashed walls, his materials, we are told, 'being the ends of burnt spunks(matches) and pieces of red keel'. He was apprenticed to Gavin Beugo, a housepainter in West Register Street, whose residence

---

2. Leading on to St. Bernard's Crescent is Danube Street (which leads off to right of the photo) was the address of one of Scotland's best known brothels, particularly popular among ministers of the church. Dora Noyce (1900–1977), the proprietor for about 30 years after World War II, was fined 47 times for living off immoral earnings. She is remembered as a local legend, and was also a good friend of Madame Doubtfire, whom I remember in the door of her used clothes shop at the foot of Howe Street not far away. She inspired the movie of the same name.

was a house within a garden, where the northwest corner of Clarence Street stands. [...] On
the expiry of his apprenticeship, Roberts took to
scene-painting, his first essay being for a circus
in North College Street; and after travelling
about in Scotland and England, working alter-
nately as a house and scene painter, he returned
to his parents' house in Edinburgh in1818, and
was employed by Jeffrey to decorate with his
brush the library at Craigcrook. He now took to
landscape painting, and his first works – Scottish
subjects – appeared in the Edinburgh Exhibition
in 1822, when, to his delight and astonishment
he found that they had been well hung, and
bought at the private view.[3]

In the 1830s, J. M. W. Turner and others encouraged
Roberts to give up working for the stage and become a
full-time artist, and in 1838 he began a journey across the
Middle East, producing numerous drawings and water-
colours to produce a series of not just beautiful, but highly
accurate illustrated plates published as *Sketches in the Holy
Land and Syria, 1842–1849*. He funded the work through
advance subscriptions, Queen Victoria being subscriber
No. 1.

   In 1832, Roberts was elected as president of the
British Society of Artists, and his celebrity in Edinburgh
would have been well known. The Finlays would not have
been unaware of the distinguished son of their near neighbours, given that this was a gossipy society, they would
have also known that Robert's wife was an alcoholic and

---

3. Ibid., Grant.

he had been forced to divorce her in 1831 – sending her back to Edinburgh from London. Again, from Grant:

> [...] His attachment to Edinburgh was strong and deep, and when he re-turned there he was never weary of wandering among the scenes of his boyhood. Thus Stockbridge and St. Bernard's Well received many a visit.

St Bernard's Well: Grant recalls that in 1832, the year the Finalys moved, 'the stream flooded all the low-lying land about Stockbridge and did very considerable damage'; and their home was and remains on the south bank of the river. And not 500 yards to the east is the most delightful folly – a modest reflection of the Temple of Vesta in Tivoli – St Bernard's Well. It is an early manifestation of the romantic dreams of Edinburgh's powerful. *The Scots Magazine* in 1760[45] speaks of the mineral well:

> lately discovered between the Water of Leith and Stockbridge, which is said to be equal in quality to any of the most famous in Britain. The Edinburgh Advertiser for April 27th, 1764, states 'As many people have got benefit from using of the water of St. Bernard's Well in the neighbourhood of this city, there has been such demand for lodgings this season that there is not so much as one room to be had either at the Water of Leith or its neighbourhood.

> The Doric temple was erected above the well in 1789. designed by the Scottish architect

4. *The Scots Magazine* 1760–02: Volume 22.
5. newspaperarchive.com/edinburgh-advertiser-dec-23-1823-p-14

Alexander Nasmyth, inspired by the Sybils'
Temple at Tivoli. 'The foundation stone was
laid', says the Advertiser for that year, 'inpres-
ence of several gentlemen of the neighbourhood'.
A metal plate was sunk into it with the following
inscription: 'Erected for the benefit of the Public,
at the sole expense of Francis Garden, Esq.,
of Troupe, one of the senators of the College
of Justice, a.d. 1759. Alexander Nasmyth.
Architect; John Wilson, Builder'.

'At Stockbridge', says the *Edinburgh Advertiser* for 1823:

> we cannot but regret that the rage for building
> is fast destroying the delightful scenery between
> it and the neighbouring village of the Water
> of Leith, which had so long been a prominent
> ornament in the environs of our ancient city [...]
> One of the leading features in this locality is St.
> Bernard's Well [...]
>   A fine statue of Hygeia, by Coade of London,
> was placed within the pillars of the temple. For
> thirty years after its erection it was untouched by
> the hand of mischief, but now it is so battered by
> stones as to be a perfect wreck.

The benefits of the water were examined in 1790 by John
Taylor[6] in 1790 for Lord Gardenstone. Taylor explained:

---

6. John Taylor, and John Fleming *A Medical Treatise on the Virtues of St
   Bernard's Well, Illustrated with Select Cases: Addressed to Francis Garden,
   Esq. of Gardenstone [...]. Proprietor of St Bernard's*; Edinburgh: Sold by
   William Creech and J. Ainslie.

*St Bernard's Well 1860,
the 'The Water of Leith' on
the right and Telford's Dean
Bridge in the distance. William
Leighton Leitch 1860.
(Wikimedia Commons)*

Building Status

The chief motive which induced me to publish
this treatise, was in compliance with the proprietor's desire to introduce St Bernard's Well
to public notice, being of singular efficacy in
removing the most obstinate diseases, after they
have foiled very eminent practitioners in the
medical art. Its situation being only a pleasant
walk from the City of Edinburgh, was likewise
an inducement to make the inhabitants of that
populous city acquainted with it. As this publication is meant chiefly for the benefit of the lower
class, who oft and most in need of it, its best rec-
ommendation will be plainness and perspicuity,
without the parade of much theory and science.
It will not, however, be amiss to take a transient
survey of the situation, course, and other circumstances of St Bernard's Well, for the information of men of superior rank, and to gratify
the curiosity of all who wish to be informed of
these particulars.

He discusses the use of the water in relation to a number
of ailments presumably common in these years – several
quite intimate. He gives good advice on 'Impotency'; for
example, he writes:

From the warm, kindly, and balsamic virtues of
these waters, good effects may be expended in
cases of impotency and barrenness, which do not
always proceed from debility, but are often the
effects of indulgence and high living, by which
Nature is oppressed, and drove out of her course,
that the faculties necessary to procreation cannot be exerted. If high seasoned food, strong

wines, and spirituous liquors, were exchanged
for plain, Simple, nourishing food, and the use
of these waters, with regular hours and exercise,
most excellent effects might be promised from
such a regimen.

And he describes the setting with great charm:

ST BERNARD'S Well is situated in a pleasant
vale, formerly called Stockdale, a short distance
from Stockbridge, a, small, neat village, which
terminates the valley, about a mile distant from
the City of Edinburgh, from the New Town not
above half that distance. The valley is formed
by steep hills on each side of a small river, called
the Water of Leith. The adjacent eminence are
covered with forest trees, underwood, shrub-
beries, garden grounds, and gentlemen's seats.
All the vicinity has a wild, romantic, and very
pleasant appearance. In this valley, from under
a green bank, and through a flinty rock, a small
fountain of clear water takes its rise. It runs in
six small veins, which are collected into two,
and run into a tub perforated a little above the
chyme in two places [...] There are many airy
pleasant walks, and fine landscapes beautifully
diversified, both from sea and land. The Firth
of Forth is only a mile distant; and the prospect is much enlivened by the ships palling and
repalling to and from Leith and the neighbouring seaport towns. In short, a more picturesque
and pleasing piece of scenery is scarce to be seen
anywhere.

View of the well in the Valley of Dean in 1790.

And just north of the well across the river are two beautifully classical terraces also designed by the painter developer Sir Henry Raeburn, give form to Anne Street, the culminating point of the suburb of Stockbridge. Though not far from the centre of the New Town, it was in the early nineteenth century a secluded place. Though removed from the ambitious society around Hanover Street, Stockbridge had its own surprisingly creative and rather libertine society. James Grant writes[7]:

> In withdrawing from the more fashionable part of Edinburgh, they did not, however,

---

7. Ibid., Grant.

exclude themselves from the pleasures of social intercourse with the world. In Anne Street they found a pleasant little community, that made residence there far from distasteful. The seclusion of the locality made it then – as it still seems to be – rather a favourite quarter with literary men and artists.

A member of this libertine society was Thomas Penson De Quincey124, the English essayist, best known for his *Confessions of an English Opium-Eater* published in 1821, who in the late 1820s moved to Edinburgh and lodged at first in the homes of the painter John Watson Gordon (future president of the Royal Scottish Academy) who resided successively in Nos. 17 and 27, Anne Street. James Grant continues:

> [...] In 1829 De Quincey made a very protracted stay at Anne Street, and Mrs. Gordon [the painter's daughter] thus describes the daily routine of the famous opium-eater there: 'An ounce of laudanum per diem prostrated animal life in the early part of the day. It was not infrequent sight to find him in his room lying upon the rug in front of the fire, his head resting upon a book, with his arms crossed over his breast, in profound slumber. For several hours he would lie in this state, till the torpor passed away. The time when he was most brilliant was generally towards the early morning hours; and then, more than once, in order to show him off, my father arranged his supper parties, so that, sitting till three or four in the morning, he brought Mr. De Quincey to that point at which,

The path from the Dean Village to Stockbridge passing by the Well in the 1870s, Kerr Street lies at the end.

in charm and power of conversation, he was so truly wonderful'.[8]

It is thrilling to contemplate that while my staid ancestors were cautiously trying to learn the habits and style of respectable society, they were just a short distance from such extravagant productions. Close enough, had they but known, to experience De Quincey's opium-inspired dreams. But the Finlays could not have imagined

8. Ibid., Grant.

such indulgent going on, and had they but known, it would have increased their anxiety and sense of inferiority.[9]

Kerr Street was much further from Register House than the old address on Hanover Street and there was a steep hill to climb. Finlay could have taken the coach, shown here struggling up Howe Street, but that may have been too expensive, so I presume he walked the 30 minutes there and back every day, as most people did. Then the Finlays began producing children and by 1836 had moved a few doors down Kerr Street to No 2.

'St Stephens Church from Howe Street' drawn by Thos. H Shepherd, 1833.

---

9. De Quincey formed a strong bond with Wordsworth, which led to his settling in 1809 at Grasmere, in the Lake District. I imagine he must have been acquainted with Andrew Bell. He died at Edinburgh in December1859.

No 2 Kerr Street was on the corner with Hamilton Place. It is probable that at one time all the windows facing the street had small decorative iron balconies. (Photo author)

They must have needed more room for the growing family, and they did not move far:

> *1836 James Finlay writer, residing at No. 2 Kerr Street, Stockbridge and Elspit Wallace his spouse had a daughter born on the 17th day of march last – named Margaret Norie.*

> *1842 James Finlay writer Residing in No 2 Kerr Street Stockbridge Elspit Wallace his spouse had a son born on the twenty fifth day of February last, named Kirk*

George Miekle Kemp and the Scott Monument:
As mentioned in the Introduction, during World War II, I was frequently looked after by my mother's aunt Susie. Elspeth and James Finlay were her grandparents, and Susie's maternal Grandmother's name was Susan Kemp Menzies. I can clearly recall her telling me that she was a

distant cousin of George Miekle Kemp, yet despite hours of searching, I have found no connection. She would have had no reason to make it up; it was her mother's mother after all. However, the more I learn of Kemp, the more I admire him and will keep alive the possibility that there is a family connection.

James Grant observed:

> Among the many interesting features in Princes Street are its monuments, and taken seriatim, according to their dates, the first – and first also inconsequence and magnificence – is that of Sir Walter Scott. This edifice, the design for which, by G.M. Kemp, was decided by the committee on the 30th of April, 1840, bears a general resemblance to the most splendid examples of monumental crosses, though it far excels all its predecessors in its beauty and vast proportions, being 180 feet in height, and occupying a square area of 55 feet at its base.[10]

And the monument continues to dominate the city and has lost none of its strange power and elegance.

The *Biographical Sketch of George Meikle Kemp*[11] by his nephew Thomas Bonnar published in 1892, does more than simply sketch the major events from the life. Keeping it in the family meant he was able to draw on Kemp's extensive notebooks and correspondence. Bonnar places Kemp's early years in Edinburgh, close to the Finlays on

10. Ibid., Grant.
11. Thomas Bonnar, *Biographical Sketch of the George Meikle Kemp Architect of the Scott Monument Edinburgh*. Edinburgh: William Blackwood and Sons, MDCCCXCII.

Kerr Street and to the streets of my childhood. He quotes from another remarkable local historian Cumberland Hill in his *Reminiscences of Stockbridge and Neighbourhood*[12] published in 1874:

> G. M. Kemp, the architect of the Scott
> Monument, lived for some time, during the
> earlier part of his comparatively short career,
> in the second flat of the stair entering from No.
> 18 Bedford Street, Stockbridge. Here he wrought
> upon and finished many of the fine drawings
> of interesting Scottish ruins and buildings he
> had visited in the course of his travels; and here
> he constructed the model of a new palace that
> at one time was proposed to be erected for the
> Duke of Buccleuch at Dalkeith.[13]

(I was born and grew up on Dean Park Street, which joins Bedford Street at its northern end. It was in my early years – the 1940s – the poorest street in the neighbourhood and dangerous. My mother gave me stern instructions to avoid it and be wary of the gangs of children my age. But I knew them, they were playing not 50 yards from my front door, playing *aleyavoi*, a sort of hide and

---

12. Cumberland Hill *Reminiscences of Stockbridge and Neighbourhood*, published in 1874 in 8 Volumes.
13. The Bonnar biography notes that 'The model was completed in about two years: two year working in the cramped quarters of Dean park Street, and was placed in the vestibule of Dalkeith Palace: to this day it remains at Dalkeith, in one of the Duke's workshops, and forms a most interesting object, unique in the high technical skill and delicate manipulation it displays in every part'.

seek. I have vivid memories of a 'stairheid rammy',[14] fights on the tenement stairs and blood in the hall, never free of the smells floating up from the communal toilets in the well. It was a miserable place, and in the 1970s, long after I had left Scotland, Bedford Street was demolished.)

Kemp was poor and the text brings an image to my mind of his future wife and he struggling to carry the model of Dalkeith Palace down the narrow stair in his tenement on Bedford Street and onto a carriage and off to please the aristocrats.

Reminiscences of Stockbridge continues:

After he married, he resided in the upper flat of No. 7 Saunders Street, Stockbridge.

---

14. The blog 'Blood and Porridge' translates: 'A stairheid rammy is a brawl that breaks out among the womenfolk in the staircases and on the landings of Scotland's urban tenement buildings'.

It was while living in the latter place that he executed the design for the Scott Monument, a structure not surpassed by anything of the kind in Europe; a monument alike uniting the genius of the great novelist, of the city of his birth, and also commemorative of the genius of Kemp.[15]

He married in 1832, arriving on Saunders Street the same months that the Finlays moved to the adjoining Kerr Street, close enough for Elspeth on a morning stroll to have seen the model of the proposed monument to Walter Scott being loaded onto a carriage after another struggle down a staircase. Kerr Street however was superior. Bedford and Saunders Streets were laid out around 1830, deliberately laid out for what was called the deserving poor. They were four-storey tenements, with four small flats per floor, all around a communal stair. Families that moved in could have been from the old town, but were most likely new arrivals to the city from the countryside, some even from Ireland. They were looking to better themselves, but most struggled for decades, and by the end of the nineteenth century, the poverty of the tenants and poor maintenance had decayed the buildings which were gradually abandoned. In the 1960s, Saunders Street was also demolished. Kemp would eventually move up in his world and into grander premises on the south side of the city.

---

15. Ibid., Hall.

Portrait of Kemp by his brother-in-law William Bonnar, circa 1840. (National Galleries of Scotland)

The article on Kemp in *A Biographical Dictionary of Eminent Scotsman*[16] states:

This architect, whose great work, the Scott Monument, one of the noblest ornaments of

---

16. *A Biographical Dictionary of Eminent Scotsmen,* Robert Chambers, Originally published: 1835.

Edinburgh, has secured the admiration of
Europe, and the approbation of the highest judges of architectural excellence in every
country, was the son of a lowly shepherd, who
pursued his occupation on the southern slope of
the Pentland Hills'. This is simply not true and is
evidence of the continual questioning of Kemp's
social standing. His grandfather was a successful farmer, his father's two brothers attended
Glasgow University studying for the professions.
Into his thirties despite being poor Kemp was
well connected. The project for Dalkeith Palace
came through his brother Thomas, Master of
Works to the Duke of Buccleuch. While working
as a cabinet maker, (a trade much respected in
19th century Edinburgh), Kemp was befriended
by William Bonner, several years his junior, a
scene-painter who was also gaining a reputation
as a portrait painter. In 1822 when George IV
visited Edinburgh, a very young Bonnar assisted
David Roberts in decorating the Assembly
Rooms for the grand state ball which was given
in honor of the occasion and Bonnar became
under David Roberts, one of the principal
assistants scene painters in Edinburgh's Theatre
Royal. And through Bonner, Kemp was introduced into the artistic intelligentsia of the city,
including David Roberts. And it was within this
circle that Kemp fell in love with and married
Bonnar's sister Elizabeth Wilson Bonnar. The
Sketch notes that 'It is almost needless to say that
these, as well as many subsequent designs by
Kemp, were indebted to the brush of his friend
Bonnar for their refined and artistic finish'. And
Bonnar was most pleased to add has painterly

hand not only to Kemp's drawings, but to his designs.

Kemp's letters are delightful, erudite and opiniated, particularly in defence of the Scots, (while writing from England). In a letter from London on learning of the laying of the foundation stone for a National Monument, he wrote 'They need not try to restore the Parthenon until they pay some attention to its cultivation, and a nation does not deserve a monument that cannot raise one to herself'. And later in an essay titled 'Hints Regarding the National Monument', he was highly critical of the city when the work was halted:[17]

> It is a pity that the great majority of people who have money to spare are so averse to lay it out on improvements of this sort. The more beautiful a city is, like some other things, it attracts the more lovers. As it is only the rich that can afford to be allured by beauty, so adding to a city like Edinburgh the beauties of Grecian art to the wonders that nature has so profusely lavished around her is the sure way to get her wed to a rich population.

The *Sketch* includes many poems, which I read out loud in my thin Edinburgh accent; they seem even now highly spirited and musical, very much in the voices of Ferguson and Burns:

> *My heart grows dull, and sickens at the thought Of life dragged out 'mong little tyrants, snools; Nor claim frae*

---

17. Ibid., Bonnar,

men o' wrath ae single thought, – I'd rather dwell wi'
worms beneath the mools.

At kintra fairs I've heard the hucksters cry That he
wha never ventured never won; Tho' poor and auld, I'll
venture yet and try – That wight daes weel wha daes the
best he can.

This plan of life, at nature's ca' designed –
Tho' rude the Scotch, you comprehend my aim –
Should your approval fix my wandering mind,
Be yours the praise; if not, Ise mine the blame.

The Scott Monument: Sir Walter Scott died in 1832, mourned by the nation not just as the writer of compelling medieval fantasies, but it was Scott who both in his words and deeds invented the myths and heroes of Scottish history and designed the costumes to go with them. (Myths that continue to colour the way Scottish character is viewed in the world and which too many Scotts accept without question.) The climax of his mythmaking was his creative direction of the events in Edinburgh celebrating the visit of King George IV in 1822. The first visit by a reigning monarch in almost 200 years. (Scott was rowed to meet the King's boat in Leith Harbor, and on seeing him arrive on deck, George IV cried, 'What, what, the one man in Scotland I most want to see'.)

In 1837, a competition was announced calling for designs for a monument appropriate to Scott's epic stature. The city fathers of Edinburgh had to find an imagination to conceive of a monument equal to the immensity of Scott's creativity and influence. In the three entries chosen in the first stage, was one with the pseudonym 'John Morvo', the name of the medieval architect of Melrose Abbey. Kemp was Morvo. It was probable that

Scott Monument Competition., The Playfair entry on the left, David Roberts Design (on the right) for the Competition for the Scott Monument, Edinburgh (National Galleries of Scotland, Creative Commons by NC)

Kemp had feared his lack of formal qualifications and reputation would disqualify him, so he used a false name, and as Morvo he was invited to develop designs for the second phase. The jury though not unanimous, chose the Kemp design and awarded him the contract in 1838, but not before a fierce attempt was made to deprive him of the work.

The attack was promoted by a minority of the building committee, led by the architect of the Royal High School, Thomas Hamilton, who had been sufficiently impressed by Kemp earlier to buy one of drawings, but not enough to allow a social inferior create a monument to a national hero. Along with a written complaint to the building committee, Hamilton called on two celebrated figures in Scottish art to produce rival designs, David Roberts and William Playfair. The invitation to David Roberts is surprising as he was not known as an architect.

King George IV Entering Princes Street, Edinburgh, August 1822; An event stage managed by Sir Walter Scott's direction. Register House is on the left. (William Turner 1789–1862)[18] (Art UK with permission)

---

18. William Turner (29 November 1789 – 7 August 1862) was an English painter who specialized in watercolour landscapes. He was a contemporary of the more famous artist J. M. W. Turner

and his style was not dissimilar. He is often known as William Turner of Oxford or just Turner of Oxford to distinguish him from his better-known namesake.

From the biography:[19]

> The complaint was based on two issues –
> 1. That the artist was an obscure man; and 2.
> That the design was a plagiarism. In a letter
> Kemp made a forceful defense: In regard to the
> charge of plagiarism which has been brought
> against me, and which Mr Hamilton, in his let-
> ter read at last meeting, rather insinuates than
> ventures to assert, I deem it unnecessary for me
> to enter upon at length. It is for the gentlemen
> of the committee to decide how far it is fair in
> Mr Hamilton to alter and rearrange his plans in
> order to bring them into some show of conform-
> ity with mine, and then on this forced resem-
> blance to ground a charge of plagiarism against
> me. John Knox's Church is professedly taken
> from Antwerp Tower, which was as open to me
> as to any other architect.

And he was successful, the commission proceeded as
planned, (I must add that the Antwerp Tower, or the
sixteenth-century clock tower of Cathedral of Our Lady
Antwerp Belgium, clearly influenced not just Kemp's, but
also the Roberts' proposal.) It is curious that Kemp, who
was admired by all who knew him both for his character,
his wit and intelligence, should have faced such prejudice.
Burns seemed never to suffer so, but such snobbery was
in the essence of the Edinburgh character and became
worse after the building of the new town. All who sought
to advance within the city had to contend with it.

---

19. Ibid., Bonnar.

The foundation stone was laid in 1840, and in it was deposited a plate, bearing the following inscription by Lord Jeffrey, remarkable for its tenor:

> *'This Graven Plate, deposited in the base of a votive building on the fifteenth day of August, in the year of Christ 1840, and never likely to see the light again until all the surrounding structures have crumbled to dust by the decay of time, or by human or elemental violence, may then testify to a distant posterity that his country-men began on that day to raise an effigy and architectural monument, to the memory OF SIR WALTER SCOTT, BART., whose admirable writings were then allowed to have given more delight and suggested better feeling to a larger class of readers in every rank of society, than those of any other author, with the exception of Shakespeare alone, and which were therefore thought likely to be remembered long after this act of gratitude on the part of the first generation of his admirers should be forgotten'.*

A contemporary description does note the influence of Melrose Abbey:

> [...] the lower arches in the diagonal abutments, with their exquisitely-cut details, resemble the narrow north gable of Melrose. The groined roof over the statue is of the same design as the roof of the choir of that noble abbey church so much frequented and so enthusiastically admired by Sir Walter. The pillars, canopies of niches, pinnacles, and other details, are chiefly copied from the same ruin, and magnificent views of the city in every direction are to be had from its lofty galleries.

The drawing states, 'Scott Monument from a drawing by the architect for His Royal Highness Prince Albert, a Subscriber to the Auxiliary Fund for elevating the Structure to its full Altitude'. (The Royal Collection Trust)

Just months before the building would be completed, Kemp died suddenly and mysteriously. From the biography:[20]

> Mr. Kemp had thus passed, by a single stride, from the condition of a humble mechanic to the highest rank in architectural talent and distinction; and having won such an elevation while life was still in its prime, a long perspective of professional achievements, and the rank and profit by which they would be accompanied, was naturally anticipated for him by his friends, and perhaps by himself also. The building, too, which he had planned, was rapidly rising from base to summit, while at each step the public eye detected some new beauty, and waited impatiently for the completion. But here the life

20. Ibid., Bonnar.

*The Monument in construction,
looking northeast with Calton
Hill and the unfinished national
monument in the distance: Hill
and Adamson, 1844.*

*Looking west to the finished
Monument: Hill and Adamson,
1845.*

Looking east on Princes Street: Gentlemen's Clubs on the left, the Royal Institution and the Scott Monument on the right: Photograph by William Donaldson Clark, about 1858 (Edinburgh City Libraries and Information Service, Creative Commons)

of the artist was brought to a sudden and most disastrous termination. He had been absent from home, employed in matters connected with the structure; and on the evening of the 6th of March 1844, was returning to his dwelling at Morningside, through Fountainbridge, when, in consequence of the darkness of the night, he had diverged from the direct road, and fallen into the canal-basin at the opening. His body was found in the water several days afterwards, and the whole city, that had now learned to appreciate his excellence, bewailed the mournful event as a public calamity. It was intended to deposit his remains in the vault under the Scott Monument, as their fitting resting place; but at the last hour this purpose was altered, and the interment took place in St. Cuthbert's church-yard; while every street through which the funeral passed was crowded with spectators. Such was the end of this promising architect, when his first great work, now nearly completed, surpassed the latest and best of those of his contemporaries, and gave promise that architecture would no longer be classed among the *artes perditae* in Scotland.

There was speculation as to the cause of the death; the public was encouraged to assume that he was drunk. A more probable explanation is that he was beaten, robbed and his body dumped in the canal.

1840, North Melville Place: Excessive drinking was commonplace in Edinburgh. I have no direct evidence except my mother warning me of the perils of alcohol and of someone in our families past who was ruined by drink, he was also, in her telling someone who had wanted to be an artist, and I remember paintings on the walls of my great aunt's flat. So, James Finlay, my great aunt's grandfather is the most likely candidate. Finlay's drinking habits probably began with months of his joining the club of the young law clerks Register House. Even in my student years, Edinburgh was a drunken town; the pubs closed at ten o' clock, and in the half hour before the closing bell, everyone in a frenzy consumed as much as possible; the preferred tipple was a pint with a chaser of whisky.

Things were not so different in the 1830s. Although he was writing mainly about the eighteenth century, in the last chapter of *Bacchanalia, Taverns, Clubs of his Traditions of Edinburgh*,[21] Robert Chamber writes:

> [...] All the shops in the town were then shut at eight o'clock, and from that hour till ten, when the drum of the Town-guard announced at once a sort of licence for the deluging of the streets with nuisances, and a warning of the inhabitants home to their beds – unrestrained scope was given to the delights of the table. No tradesman thought of going home to his family, till after he had spent an hour or two at his club. And he admits that looking back to first half of the 19th century – it was unsafe to walk the streets of Edinburgh at night, on account of the numerous drunken parties of young men, who then reeled about, bent on mischief, at all hours, and from whom the Town-guard were quite unable to protect the sober citizen.

---

21. Ibid., Robert Chamber.

(In some parts of Edinburgh, this was still true in the 1960s, and based on a walk down Rose Street on a Saturday evening in 2017, it is probably true to this day.) Chamber writes that Tavern Dissipation, [...] 'prevailed in Edinburgh to an incredible extent, and engrossed the leisure hours of all professional men, scarcely excepting even the most- stern and dignified. No rank, class, or profession, indeed, formed an exception to this rule'. And he singles out lawyers and their clerks:[22]

> The debaucheries of the great lawyers were imitated and followed out by all their satellite and dependents; and it was quite possible that a few Lords of Session and advocates of high practice might be bousing over stoups of French claret, or playing at High Jinks, in Mrs – 's best room, while the very next apartment contained a set of equally joyous spirits, namely the clerks and apprentices of the said great men, who transacted the same buffooneries, drank the same liquor, swore the same oaths, and retailed the yesterday's jokes of their masters.

With the birth of Elspeth in 1847, the Finlays had produced eight children. The 1851 census lists the others – Elizabeth 15, James 13, Catherine 9, Margaret 7, Keith 5, Elspit (and inventive derivation from Elspeth) 3, like clockwork one every two years. So, by 1840 with child number four on the way, the house on Kerr Street would have become too small; they had to move. (Some indication of the pressure on the family may be seen in the census of 1841, for the household of Elspeth's father Robert

---

22. Ibid., Robert Chamber.

Wallace. It lists two of the Finlay children, Elizabeth and James, living with their grandfather in St Andrews.)

> *1847 James Finlay, writes Residing at No 4 North Melville Place and Elspit Wallace his spouse had a Daughter Born on the Fourth of April current named Elspet Wallace*

An economic depression in the 1830s brought construction in the city almost to a standstill. I can imagine Elspeth, between pregnancies, frequently walking around the streets near Kerr Street, checking progress on the new buildings in the expanding New Town to the west. It would have been a familiar walk that took her by St Bernard's

North Melville Place. (Photo author)

Well, underneath the majestic arches of Thomas Telford's Dean Bridge, so recently opened in 1832, and into the Dean Village. Then up Bell's Brae to immediately face the partially completed terrace of Melville Place.

The terrace was a few yards from the path of the Dean Bridge, flying effortlessly across the Dean Valley, and the photograph shows it was and remains an arrangement of flats above shops on the street level around a common stair. (It remains a handsome building much more in the style of the better streets of the New Town.) The large windows in the first floor suggest an elegant living room facing the street, with probably two bedrooms behind the smaller windows above. They leased it new, just completed in 1840, and roomy enough for their four children. It was also a brisk twenty-minute walk to Register House for James – along George Street, passed their old flat on Hanover, and no hills to climb. The living room would face the charming park on Randolph Crescent. The Finlays were coming up in the world, and like so many ambitious families, they gauged every house move as a mark of their rising social status. They were back in the New Town, and back in the midst of affluence.

The new town was riding over the old. This both delighted and troubled Robert Louis Stevenson:[23]

> But at the Dean Bridge, you may behold a
> spectacle of a more novel order. The river runs
> at the bottom of a deep valley, among rocks
> and between gardens; the crest of either bank
> is occupied by some of the most commodious
> streets and crescents in the modern city; and a

---

23. Stevenson, Robert Louis, 1850–1894. *Edinburgh: Picturesque Notes.* London: Seely, Jackson & Halliday.

handsome bridge unites the two summits. Over this, every afternoon, private carriages go spinning by, and ladies with card-cases pass to and fro about the duties of society. And yet down below, you may still see, with its mills and foaming weir, the little rural village of Dean. Modern improvement has gone overhead on its high-level viaduct and the extended city has cleanly overleapt, and left unaltered, what was once the summer retreat of its comfortable citizens.

There are moments in my reimagining the city of my family's history in which the past and the present coincide in quite unexpected ways. *The book of the Old Edinburgh Club*[24] describes the harsh cries of the street traders in the old and new city. It regrets that 'the disappearance of the oyster beds from the Firth of Forth […] greatly affected the sale of this shell-fish, and although a number of years ago the oyster was bought freely by all classes, the cry of 'Caller has entirely ceased in old Edinburgh', however, he adds ': know, however, that this historic cry is not altogether extinct, and anyone wandering around say Moray Place or Randolph Crescent early on an evening in late autumn, might chance to hear this ancient cry'. For years I would walk by Melville Place on my way to the college, and immediately opposite the Finlay apartment, I would pass an old women – I remember her clearly selling from buckets on her cart, not oysters, but the surviving shellfish from the Forth, mussels, cockles and whelks.

Late 1840s the Finlays moved to Leith Walk. By 1847 they had eight children, which must have made life

---

24. *The Book of the Old Edinburgh Club*. Electric Scotland. https://electricscotland.com › bookofoldedinbur03olde PDF

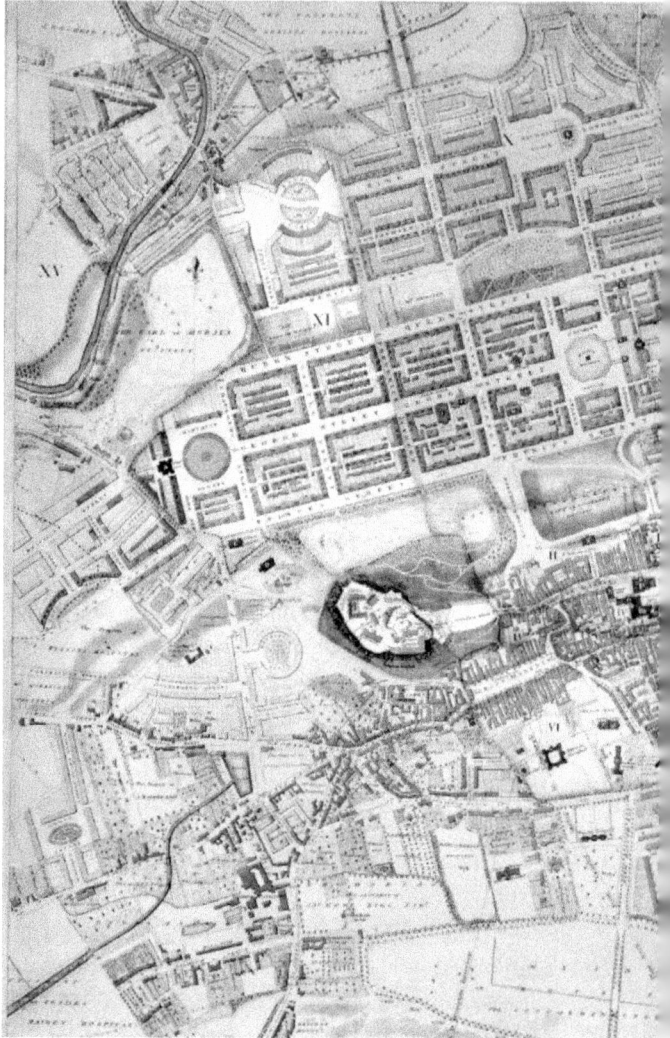

Kirkwood's Plan of Edinburgh in 1882. Upper right, Playfair's plan for extending the New Town north along Leith Walk and the activity at the Westend. (Reproduced with the permission of the National Library of Scotland)

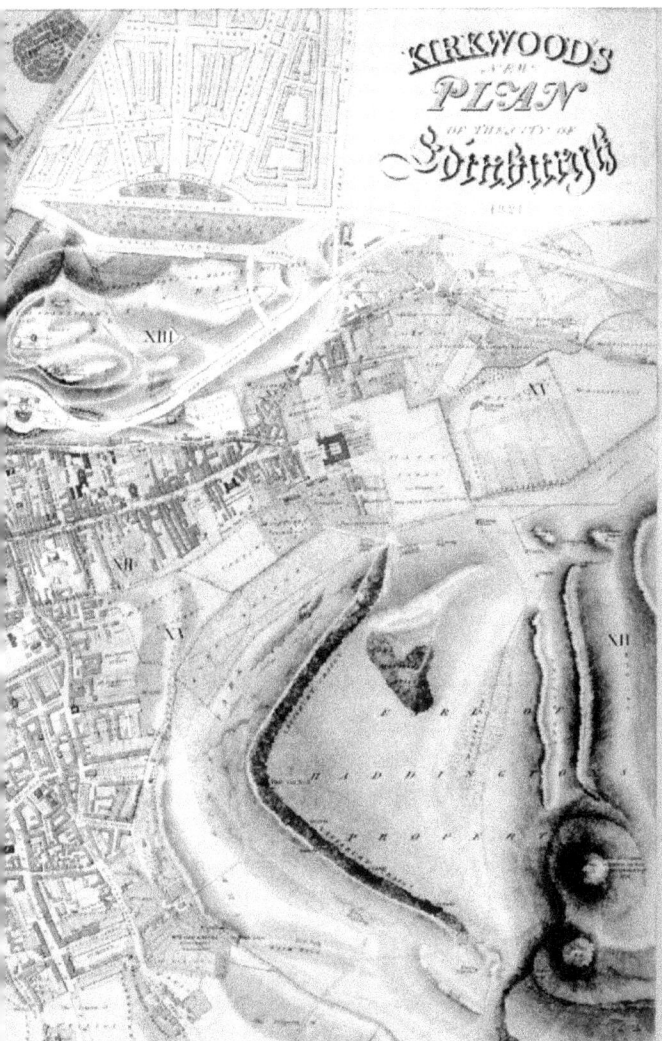

impossible on Melville Place. They would have to move again, but where? A place had to be found within easy reach of Register House, not only large enough to accommodate a family of ten but also able to maintain the status of being in the New Town. Again, they looked at new construction at the weakening edges of the New Town. It must have been Elspeth Finlay who took on the task of house hunting; her husband would simply not have had the time. And her decisions, looking back from almost two centuries, were good. She had to find an affordable home that would maintain the family status on what must have been the barely adequate income of a civil servant. Even a humble law clerk was a gentleman's profession and many of Finlays colleagues would come from modest wealth. They had private incomes and families to fall back on, the Finlays had no one.

All of Edinburgh would have known of the plan by Scotland's most favoured architect William Playfair to extend the New Town to Leith in a series of grand avenues, crescents and squares. However, Playfair was keenly aware of the competition with developments in the west of the city. He wrote in assessing his plan for the eastern extension, 'There is a formidable rival to contend with, in the buildings which are now going forward in the western end of the present new town. There, a circle of fashionable and wealthy people has been collected and they will tend to stay'.[25] Playfair's plan first appears on Kirkwoods map of the city for 1821 and again richly engraved on William Home Lizars maps from the mid-1820s. It finally vanished from the maps in 1832, several years after the project was abandoned.

---

25. Playfair, William Henry (1790–1857). .https://discovery.nationalarchives.gov.uk/details/c/F32249

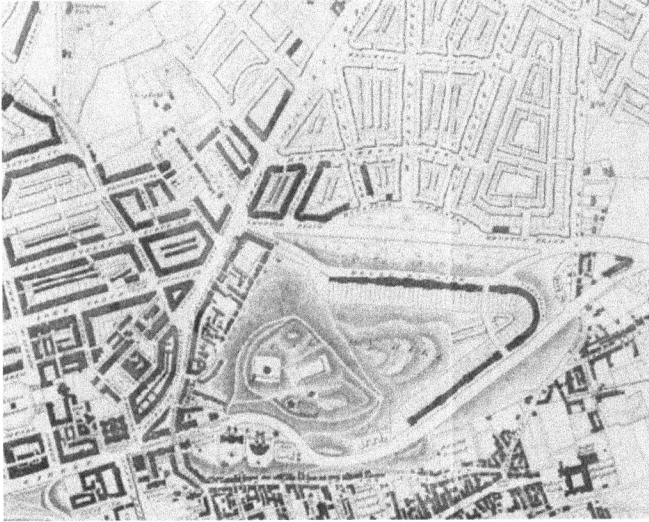

Detail from William Home Lizars plan of 1830–1831 showing the start of development on the Playfair plan with the cranked terrace of George Place top centre. (Reproduced with the permission of the National Library of Scotland)

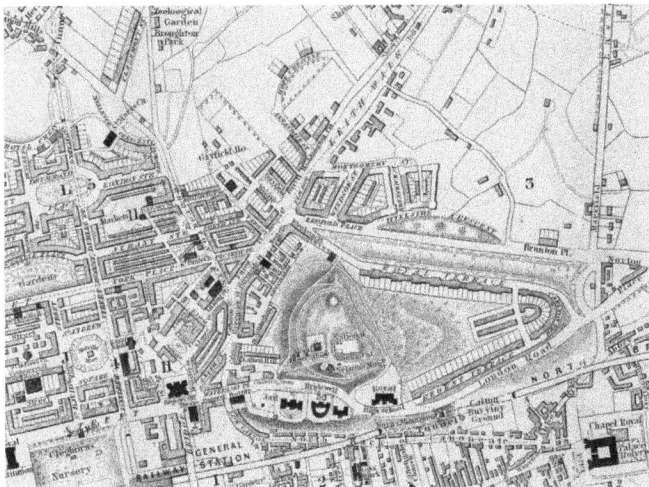

Lizars map of 1851, Playfair's plan abandoned, George Place looks over market gardens. (Reproduced with the permission of the National Library of Scotland)

Leaving behind an elegant wall of buildings on the east side of Leith Street, Leopold Place, and the south blocks of the street plan, the dream of the New Town was slowly dying, but slowly. I imagine Elspeth encouraging James to explore Leith Walk after his work on a Saturday afternoon. The area would have a sense of promise lingering from the Playfair plan. They would pass Blenheim Place and look east at fragments of the plan, blocks of terraces still incomplete after 25 years, though Gayfield Square on the west was complete and occupied by modest gentry (according to Grant). An even more pathetic site was visible just north at the centre of Major Hope's development began in 1825, Hope Crescent (now Hopetoun), looking like broken teeth with only four units completed by the late 1840s. Beyond that, they would pass the remnants of what had been lands of several small estates from the eighteenth century, Gayfield House, Broughton House, Broughton Park and close to the substantial structure of Shrub Hill.[26] Several isolated terraces had been constructed in the character of New Town, facing the open fields and market gardens on the east, which supplied the city with fruit and vegetables. (Isolated and perhaps waiting to become part of renewed vision create development stretching all the way to Leith.) And it was in one of these terraces, George Place, a short block on Leith Street, that the Finlays leased or bought. This was close enough to Registrar House, though for James it was a long, steep walk up the Leith Street. (Horse-drawn trams would not appear until the 1870s.) For Elspeth, it was the same walk every day to the meat, fish, fruit and markets under the North Bridge.

Perhaps they looked at these lonely structures in relation to Playfair's plan and imagined the prospect of George Place facing the garden of the proposed Heriot

---

26. Shrubhill is a distinct area of Leith Walk, just south of Pilrig. It was once the site of a gibbet known as the Gallow Lee, literally the 'field with the gallows', where several infamous executions took place. Bodies were buried at the base of the gallows, or their burnt ashes scattered.

The townhouses on George Place, the family home was number 2 is on the left. (Photo author)

Crescent and the street leading to Trinity Square with its circular park in the middle. It was all so convincing, having lived through the astonishing transformation of the city since the beginning of the century; they may have held on to the belief that Playfair's plan or something equivalent could be realized. But they were aware that they had been actors in a dream world that would in that very decade, die.

The census of 1851 lists the Finlays as having eight children along with two visitors or boarders (one a German chemist) living at 2 Georges Place. A house big enough to house 12 people – a townhouse with its own front door and in New Town style. They had been living there for four years. James' occupation is given as 'Managing Clerk, Abridgement of Leasing Office in the General Register House'.

As some point not long after the census, James Finlay left the house on George Place and in July 1854, died:

1854 July 28 Finlay James, Clerk [age] 48, 5 Moray Street [cause of death] Decline.

Was it just James or had the whole family moved
to Moray Street? According to the death certificate, James
was living at 5 Moray Street (no longer standing), just a
few yards from George Place. Was it just James or had
the whole family moved to Moray Street? He is referred
to somewhat abruptly as 'clerk'. The certificate does not
name his wife, the head of the family, no mention of the
eight children or if there were witnesses and declines to
give the cause of death. I have searched all the available
databases looking for an obituary and have found nothing. It may be that in their grief the family was unable to
fully respond. He seems to have been abandoned.

This is the James Finlay who through the beneficence of his great uncle, Andrew Bell, was able to rise
out of poverty, and when of an appropriate age, study for
a position in the law. After serving for at least 25 years
as a public servant, he had reached the rank of managing clerk in an office which dealt with property rights. He
would have been secure in this position for life. Yet aside
from prestige and security, the need to continually move
to house his ever-expanding family must have put great
strain on a modest income. Also, in a city where status
and success were measured by where you lived, he had to
find a place that maintained an association with the New
Town. The evidence shows however that with each move,
the family had been pushed further and further from the
heart of the new city.

Something devastating must have happened
to force James Finlay out of the home on George Place
and into a house on an adjoining street (which no longer
exists). We shall never know why a relatively successful
father of eight should die quite suddenly at the age of 48,
(though life expectancy for a man mid-nineteeeth century
was not much more than 50). The most reasonable explanation would be that his death was sudden, from many

possible causes – heart failure or even cholera. However, it is also possible that, burdened by debt, which forced the move and another child on the way, James Finlay took his own life.

A month after the death, August 1854, the new child, Hedderwick McCredie Young Finlay (my great grandfather) was born:

> *Finlay, James, (the late) Writer Residing at No*
> *5 Moray Street [the document spells it Murray] Leith*
> *Walk and Elspeth Wallace his spouse had a son born*
> *fourteenth August Eighteen hundred and fifty-four named*
> *Hedderwick McCredie Young Baptized by the Rev.*
> *James Grant DD of St Mary's Church Edinburgh on the*
> *16th November thereafter.*

(No explanation for the name; no record either of Hedderwick ever being used as the first name,[27] and I have yet to find any family connections to the names McCredie or Young. As Elspeth would have made the choice, a possible explanation is that they were names in the Wallace family.)

The baptism of grandfather Hedderwick, was in the St Mary's Church on Bellevue Crescent in the New Town, the major church closest to their home. It took place almost three months after the birth, perhaps the delay was a reflection of a family in grief. Elspeth was left with nine children, no husband and no income.

---

27. The only notable Hedderwick in the year of the Christening was the poet and successful newspaper editor James Hedderwick, whose poems were published in the 1840s, perhaps they were favourites of Elspeth.

A view east on Princes Street looking toward Waterloo Place with Register House on the left, taken around the time of James Finlay's death and the birth of Hedderwick. (The statue of Wellington in front of the building was unveiled in 1852.).

VI

The Other New Town

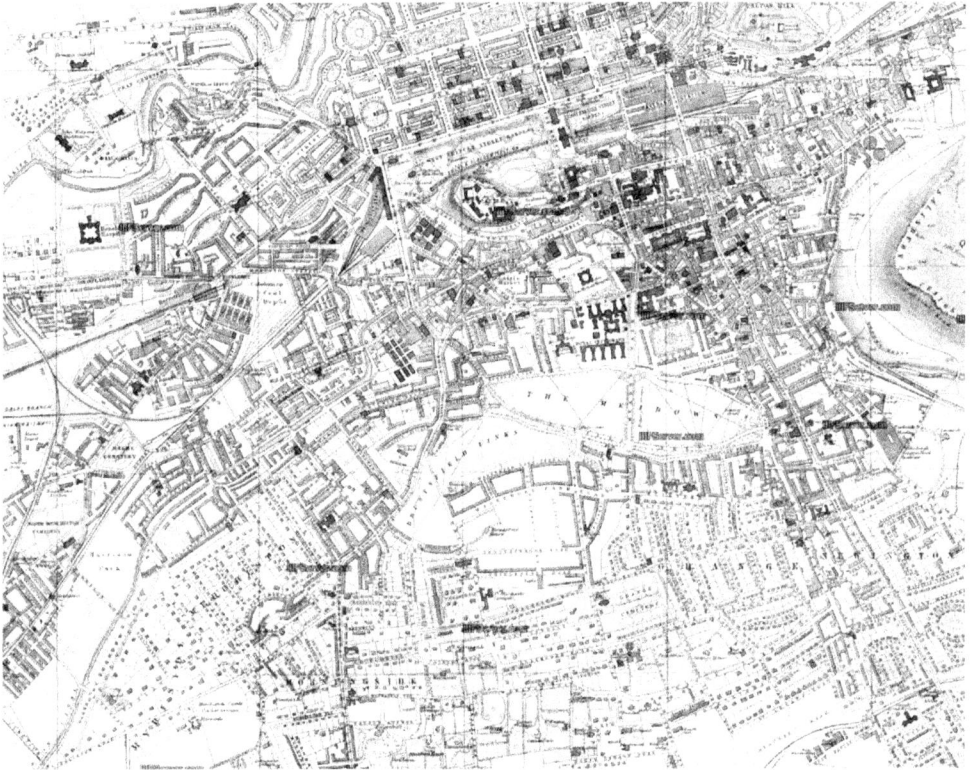

Think of this image not as a plan of a city, but as a diagram of a transforming organism. The seed at the core is the castle at the centre; it even appears embryonic. Its defensive shell is a great rock, the remains of an ancient volcano. It is only open on the east, where a passage follows the slope of the land through a dense mass of building that has been forming for a thousand years, to the royal palace. All was defined by the need for defence, wholly introverted, unable to escape its bounds, rising layer upon layer until and after many centuries it choked from decay and began to collapse. Although chaotic, the old city on the path from castle to palace created out of circumstance was a richly social place and deeply human.

On being released from the constraints of the ancient walls, the new city became selective, and in a Darwinian manner, the wealthy were first to move emulating theatricality of the English and European elite, building great urban rooms in which to parade and socialize. They were built for public pleasure. The poor at first were left behind, but they found employment and mobility in the newly created industries, moving from the tenement slums of the old city to their modern equivalent. They were built only to profit the landlords, often supporting their extravagancies in the New Town. And in the midst of all this change, almost unnoticed, a lower middle class emerged; many were new arrivals in the city, each watching each other's status. Edinburgh followed London in developing on the south side large areas of detached and semi-detached villas for this third new society, giving a home with a garden and a reality to be shaped to their private pleasure.

It is there in the image, the new reality evolving from the straight regimented structures immediately north of the castle, into increasingly fanciful circuses and crescents and curving terraces, ending, after almost a century on the left of the image with a flourish in several oval-shaped parks before being blocked by the coming of the railway, and the return of the poor.

The harsh intrusion of not one but two railways following the path of least resistance west out of the city. And with the railway came major industries and the end of a romantic vision for a city in nature. They bought land along the path of the rail west (lower left on the map), and the need to house an expanding industrial workforce began to create another very different new town. This was immediately across the rails from the final flourish of a dying vision of Classical Edinburgh and from the desire to live in harmony with nature. This other new town was built for workers who had no need for elaborate terraces and gardens. It was built to provide basic accommodation, minimal space required to house a standard family of three or four, no matter if in use there happened to be twice that many, in tenements that were only marginally better than the slums they were designed to replace. Accommodation for so-called 'rent slaves' never able to buy. Early examples of the model tenement and associated industry were built within curving ironbound in the centre left of the image. This is where both sides of my family found themselves at the end of the nineteenth century.

This was a time of dramatic change. By the mid-nineteenth century, Scotland's towns and cities were facing a housing crisis. Between 1845 and 1849, the Irish famine brought thousands into the cites of England and Scotland looking for work. Edinburgh, slow to industrialize, did not have the housing to absorb this rising labouring population, leading to overcrowded tenements with poor or no sanitation and the consequent spread of malnutrition and disease. A mid-nineteenth-century flat in a tenement on Edinburgh's southside was listed as having just one person living in it, but the valuation rolls listed the names of 27 inhabitants, mostly semi-skilled including painters, plasterers, masons, cooks and seamstresses. Whole families were paying relatively high rents to live in one or two rooms, with a single open coal fireplace, freezing in winter, without running water and all using common latrines outside. The worst were the households with only one room and a window, the so-called single end which served as kitchen, bedroom and living space for a family of four or more (valuation roles reported on both the number of rooms and windows). Most such buildings were owned by absentee landlords.

The city was being changed in other ways:

- The two major industries, where both my families were to find employment, began production in 1856 – the American-owned North British Rubber Company Rubber Mill and McEwan's Fountain Brewery.
- The last public hanging was carried out in 1864 in front of large crowds on the High Street opposite St Giles, a site that had been used for centuries.
- The railways had first entered the city in 1842, stopping west of the centre in Haymarket. Edinburgh's major station opened on the Princes Street in 1870.
- In the same year, the city's Royal Infirmary was completed, the biggest hospital in Europe under one roof. The scale of it can be seen on the map in the two blocks of fork-like structures centre right.
- The first street tramways began operating in 1871, horse drawn in the early years; by 1888 it was converted to the endless cable system.
- Also in 1888, an astounding fact from the last months of horse-drawn trams, the Flying Scotsman train reached Edinburgh from London in 6 hours 19 minutes.

- And by 1895, the main streets of the New Town saw electric street lights replacing gas lamps (however, gas lamps were still lighting the streets of my childhood in 1945).

And in 1879, 29-year-old Robert Louis Stevenson, published his *Edinburgh: Picturesque Notes*[1], years before the books that made him famous. He writes with painful immediacy on the collapse of a tenement (in Scots a 'land') on the High Street: 'The land had fallen; and with the land, how much! Far in the country, people saw a gap in the city ranks, and the sun looked through between the chimneys in an unwonted place':

> There was nothing fanciful, at least, but every circumstance of terror and reality, in the fall of the land in the High Street. The building had grown rotten to the core; the entry underneath had suddenly closed up so that the scavenger's barrow could not pass cracks and reverberations sounded through the house at night; the inhabitants of the huge old human bee-hive discussed their peril when they encountered on the stair; some had even left their dwellings in a panic of fear, and returned to them again in a fit of economy or self-respect; when, in the black hours of a Sunday morning, the whole structure ran together with a hideous uproar and tumbled story upon story to the ground. The physical shock was felt far and near; and the moral shock travelled with the morning milkmaid into all the suburbs. The church-bells never sounded

---

1. R. L. Stevenson, *Edinburgh: Picturesque Notes 1878.*

more dismally over Edinburgh than that grey forenoon. Death had made a brave harvest; and, like Samson, by pulling down one roof destroyed many a home. None who saw it can have forgotten the aspect of the gable: here it was plastered, there papered, according to the rooms; here the kettle still stood on the hob, high overhead: and there a cheap picture of the Queen was pasted over the chimney. So, by this disaster, you had a glimpse into the life of thirty families, all suddenly cut off from the revolving years.

And one feels his pain and his anxiety as he observes the fractured city:

There, when the great exodus was made across the valley, and the new town began to spread abroad its draughty parallelograms and rear its long frontage on the opposing hill, there was such a flitting, such a change of domicile and dweller, as was never excelled in the history of cities: the cobbler succeeded the earl; the beggar ensconced himself by the judge's chimney; what had been a palace was used as a pauper refuge; and great mansions were so parceled out among the least and lowest in society, that the hearthstone of the old proprietor was thought large enough to be partitioned off into a bedroom by the new. These sentences have, I hear, given. It is true that the over-population was at least as dense in the epoch of lords and ladies, and that now-a-days some customs which made Edinburgh notorious of yore have been fortunately pretermitted. But an aggregation of

comfort is not distasteful like an aggregation of
the reverse. Nobody cares how many lords and
ladies, and divines and lawyers, may have been
crowded into these houses in the past – perhaps
the more the merrier. The glasses clink around
the china punch-bowl, someone touches the
virginals, there are peacocks' feathers on the
chimney, and the tapers burn clear and pale in
the red fire-light. That is not an ugly picture in
itself, nor will it become ugly upon repetition.
All the better if the like were going on in every
second room; the land would only look the more
inviting.

Times are changed. In one house, perhaps, two
score families herd together and, perhaps, not
one of them is wholly out of the reach of want.
The great hotel is given over to discomfort from
the foundation to the chimney-tops; everywhere
a pinching, narrow habit, scanty meals, and
an air of sluttishness and dirt. In the first room
there is a birth, in another a death, in a third a
sordid drinking-bout, and the detective and the
Bible-reader cross upon the stairs. High words
are audible from dwelling to dwelling, and children have a strange experience from the first:
only a robust soul, you would think, could grow
up in such conditions without hurt. And even if
God tempers his dispensations to the young, and
all the ill does not arise that our apprehensions
may forecast, the sight of such a way of living is
disquieting to people who are more happily cir-
cumstanced. Social inequality is nowhere more
ostentatious than at Edinburgh. I have mentioned already how, to the stroller along Princes

Street, the High Street callously exhibits its back garrets. It is true, there is a garden between. And although nothing could be more glaring by way of contrast, sometimes the opposition is more immediate sometimes the thing lies in a nutshell, and there is not so much as a blade of grass between the rich and poor. To look over the South Bridge and see the Cowgate below full of crying hawkers, is to view one rank of society from another in the twinkling of an eye.

By mid-century, the sanitary and health problems in the city were so bad that there had to be an enquiry. How bad were they? An account from the *Builders Journal* of 1861[2] reported: 'We devoutly believe that no smell in Europe or Asia can equal in depth and intensity, in concentration and power, the diabolical combination of sulphurated hydrogen we came upon one evening about ten o'clock in a place called Todrick's Wynd' (a close off the High Street).

Report on the sanitary condition of the City of Edinburgh: Henry Littlejohn was described in the *British Medical Journal* as 'one of Edinburgh's and of Scotland's great men'. He was a police surgeon for 54 years, and as medical advisor to the Crown in Scotland, an expert witness in cases of murder and suspicious death. (He is believed to have been the inspiration for Conan Doyle's *Sherlock Holmes*.) His *Report on the sanitary condition of the City of Edinburgh*,[3] is viewed as one of the

2. *The Builders Journal 1861*: The Internet Archive has volume 19.
3. Littlejohn, Henry D. (Henry Duncan), Sir, 1826–1914; *Report on the sanitary condition of the City of Edinburgh, with relative appendices*, Colston & Son Edinburgh, 1865.

most significant reports on the health of any city from
the nineteenth century. Described as 'acute in analysis,
precise and pin-sharp in its prose, unusually non-judge-
mental towards the poor, and firm [...] in its advice to
the authorities'. Its findings relate directly to the life of
both my families, but in particular, the Jamiesons and the
Balfours who, after arriving in the city years, lived in the
decaying streets of the old town. They then moved to the
workers' tenements surrounding the new industries producing beer and rubber, where sanitary conditions were
not much better.

Littlejohn's primary concern was the city's sanitary arrangements. 'Even in the New Town' he writes,
'though the buildings are handsome they are devoid of
ways of keeping clean or disposing of human waste':

> [...] At the time of the building of the New
> Town, both at its commencement and at its
> subsequent rapid enlargement in 1825, imperfect
> notions prevailed as to the internal and exter-
> nal drainage of houses. The domestic use of
> baths was apparently unknown, and the con-
> veniences were few in number and awkwardly
> placed, either as to deprive a principal room of
> its amenity, or in such a confined space as to
> be entirely without ventilation. Princes Street,
> George Street, Queen Street, York Place, and
> Heriot Row can still furnish specimens of such
> faulty arrangement. When unhealthy competi-
> tion prevails in the building trade, and houses
> are erected with undue haste, many points of
> essential importance to their sanitary condi-
> tion are very apt to be overlooked, while oth-
> ers which bulk largely on the eye of intending
> purchasers, such as external decoration, receive

an undue amount of attention. This, I have no
doubt, was the case during the building mania
in 1825. Stately houses were erected of the finest
freestone, with rooms of excellent ventilating
proportions, but the sanitary arrangements were
invariably defective. Besides this, no definite
drainage plan for such a large town had been
prepared, and where street drains were constructed they were imperfectly built, and their
communicating branches with the houses, being
hastily put together with the chips coming from
the stones in the process of being shaped, were of
the most faulty description.

He worried about the impression the filth in the old city
makes on visitors:

Our closes are narrow, and their poor inhabitants naturally ventilate themselves in the High
Street, which, for its proportions and width,
contrasts remarkably with the contracted streets
of the same period in other capitals. Those
places of refreshment, which are too frequently
the resort of the poor, are all situated in the chief
street. Hence it is not to be wondered at that
the visitor, after inspecting Holyrood, when he
walks to the Castle, sees Edinburgh poverty and
Edinburgh vice in its most repulsive form. Our
principal educational institution, the University,
and our busy Law Courts, in which the judicial
business of the kingdom is transacted, cannot be
reached but by crossing this great thoroughfare.
Besides this, the traditional and historical associations of our city are to be found in the meanest

localities. At every step, therefore, poverty is
met, and is justly made the subject of remark.

But it was the poor and their sanitary arrangements that
troubled him most:

> Our poor are so lodged, that to inhale the
> atmosphere in their houses is enough to produce
> a lethargic depression, to escape from which is
> but to be exposed to the temptations of the High
> Street and Cowgate. With no comfort at home,
> the poor labourer is forced to go elsewhere for
> enjoyment. To his sleeping-place he returns,
> to find himself in a crowded apartment, where
> there is no attempt to maintain the ordinary
> decencies of life. With so many and varied
> proclivities to vice in all its forms, it is a heart-
> less task to talk to such and one of righteousness,
> temperance, and judgment to come.[4]

This was the plight of the Balfours and the Jamiesons –
they could pay rent, but there was no acceptable housing available. Littlejohn wrote: '[…] the question is forced
upon us – is a class, which can afford to pay such rents,
not capable of being provided with suitable accommodation, on the ordinary principle of supply and demand?'
He writes specifically of the areas where the Balfours and
the Jamiesons lived:

> It will be observed how readily pauperism
> gravitates to the poorest districts, and where, as
> in Canongate, Tron, St Giles, and Grassmarket,

---

4. Ibid., Littlejohn.

A view looking west to the High Street around 1890. Canongate is in the center of the view immediately to the left of the Canongate Tolbooth, with the dock and tower.

we have the greatest overcrowding and the most
deficient house accommodation, we have also
superadded pauperism and its attendant evils,
mental depression, imperfect nourishment,
scanty clothing, and in too many instances,
intemperance. The large mortality of these dis-
tricts is amply accounted for, and it is not to be
wondered at if in epidemics of cholera and fever,
as shown by\the same table, the percentages
of cases should be universally high. Were the
poorest and most degraded of the class removed
to better quarters, I am convinced that a great
improvement would be effected in our Old
Town. So long as there is a population with such
a percentage of pauperism scattered through it,
the best sanitary regulations are disregarded,
and it is useless to enforce them by the stron-
garm of the law.

His language is poetic and powerful:

The pittances that are given to paupers through
the proverbial economy of boards, representing
the ratepayers of our city, are only intended to
allow of life being maintained at a legal flicker,
and by no means at a steady flame.
    He considered the result of using containers
for human waste supplied to houses,
    [...] a piece of mechanism which must be
handled with some degree of care, otherwise it is
apt to get out of order – it becomes no longer air
tight, and a leakage of foul gas takes place. This
occurs to a notorious extent in the best parts of
the New Town [...] But in the houses of the poor

this leakage would be constantly occurring in an already vitiated atmosphere, where the inhabitants are overcrowded, and prone to disease. He describes a failed attempt to install new system of toilets: No sooner were the rooms tenanted, than a large pool of sewage, both solid and liquid, collected at the foot of the main passage, in consequence of the choking of the pipes [...]

At length, after the authorities had repeatedly interfered, several of the conveniences were closed, and the number of parties frequenting the remainder curtailed: but, in spite of these precautions, a state of matters is produced, by overflow and leakage, of the most nauseous description.

He concludes in despair:

My experience of the poor of this city, and of their house accommodation, has led me to the conclusion that they are not as yet prepared to make a proper use of conveniences. The poor require preliminary education in keeping their houses and stairs clean, before they can be trusted in the manner proposed.[5]

It was the fault of the poor.

Tracing my father's family movements in the last decades of the nineteenth century shows that they were slowly able to escape the worst of the Edinburgh slums.

---

5. Ibid., Littlejohn.

From the 1871 census, William Balfour was living with his wife Isabella at St Anthony's Place, a street on the border with Leith, which no longer exists. William was still a plasterer, the trade he brought from Torryburn. John, my illegitimate grandfather, was 12 years old and listed not as a scholar but as a messenger boy. He had left school as soon as he was able. His grandmother, 78-year-old Margaret Jamieson, was also living with them. Five people in a house with two windows. William never had children of his own.

By the 1881 census, they were living in Morningside at an undecipherable address, but a step out of poverty. And Grandfather John had left home and was living as a boarder in White Park, working as a boot machine operator. My father told me his father was a shoemaker, which triggers a long-forgotten memory – for years lying in the corner of the coal cupboard was a rusty, cast-iron three-footed cobbler's last. (White Park is no more; the houses, presumably slums, demolished to make way for the North British Distillery was near my mother's birthplace in Downfield Place.)

In 1881, John Jamieson Balfour married Marion Brown, daughter of Joseph Brown, a forester:

> *John Jamieson Balfour, shoemaker (Journeyman)*
> *(Bachelor), 22, of 6 Oliver Terrace Edinburgh, [par-*
> *ents] William Balfour Plasterer, and Isabella Balfour*
> *M.S.[Maiden Surname] Jamieson, after Banns*
> *according to the Forms of the Church of, Marion Brown*
> *Domestic Servant (Spinster) 20, of 48 Brunswick*
> *Street, Stockbridge, Edinburgh, [parents] Joseph Brown,*
> *Forester and Helen Brown, M. S. Brewer*

From the '91 census, John and Marion were living in a typical tenement on Yeaman Place, south of

the Dalry Road, close to both the North British Works
and the distilleries. He is then described as a 'Packer to
Ironmonger'. They had three children, son William J,
and two daughters, Catherine and Marion. The number
1 marked on the right side of the census form indicates that
the flat had only one room with a window. By 1895 they
had moved to Dundee Street, immediately adjoining the
North British Rubber Mill, when Marian suddenly died
from a ruptured stomach ulcer.

In 1896, John remarried Catherine Scott,
who was born in Biggar but grew up in the village of
Innerleithen:

> *On the 12th June 1896 at 35 Bristo Street Edinburgh*
> *After publication of the according to the terms of the*
> *Episcopal Church of Scotland, John Jamieson Balfour,*
> *Shop Porter widower, 37, and Catherine Scott Domestic*
> *Servant Spinster [Both living at] 105 Washington*
> *Cottages [his parents] William Balfour, Plasterer, and*
> *Isabell Balfour, [her parents] John Scott, Shepherd, and*
> *Catherine Scott M.S. Johnstone. N J Gourley, Priest*
> *in charge of St Martins Episcopal Church. Witnesses*
> *Andrew Balfour[6] and Maggie Scott.1*

Washington Cottages no longer exists.

It would seem that John had maintained his
connections in the Borders, marrying first the daughter
of a forester and then the daughter of a shepherd. His
new wife Catherine (my maternal grandmother) was,

---

6. Andrew, the witness, would have been William's elder brother who
was working as a damask weaver in Torryburn in 1841. Maggie
Scott was Catherine's sister.

no matter how lowly, a member of Clan Scott,[7] which includes Sir Walter Scott and the hereditary clan chief, the Duke of Buccleuch. John Scott would have considered him a kinsman. The surname Scott first appears in the twelfth century in the Scottish Borders around Peebles, and they became one of the most powerful of the Riding Clans raiding, battling and defeating neighbouring clans.

Their marriage in the Episcopal Church of Scotland means that Catherine was Episcopalian and explains why my father was in the choir of the St Mary's Episcopal Cathedral of the Scottish Episcopal Church in Edinburgh, Scotland, part of the worldwide Anglican Communion. (The foundation stone of the Cathedral was laid in 1874 by the Duke of Buccleuch and designed by the English architect Giles Gilbert Scott.) The church was once pejoratively referred to in Edinburgh as the 'English Kirk', and was also sometimes known as the 'Laird's Kirk' because of its historical associations with the landed aristocracy of Scotland, whose membership of the church exceeded that of other denominations. (In the mid-1800s, it was recorded that three-quarters of the 'landed proprietors of Scotland' were Episcopalians.)

John Scott and his fathers before him would have been one of the lowly members of the Scott's Clan, labouring on the estates of their feudal superiors and would have followed their religion. And he raised his children in Innerleithen, the village that serves the Traqair House, the oldest continually occupied house in Scotland, as one of the many shepherds on the estate he would have worked his whole life like his father before him, in a state of semi bondage.

---

7. Derived from the Latin, *Scotti*, as word the Romans used to describe the Gaelic speaking Irish.

Driving the sheep in the path out of Innerleithen to Edinburgh. A remote road though only 20 miles from Edinburgh. (Photo author)

Traquair House: is southeast of Peebles, and though no part of the present building can be dated with certainty before the fifteenth century, it was built on the site of a hunting lodge used by the Scottish kings from the twelfth century in the style of a fortified mansion. Alexander I (1078–1124) was the first Scottish king to stay and hunt at Traquair. The house later became a key link in the chain of defence that guarded the Tweed Valley against English invasion.

In 1469, James III of Scotland granted the estate to William Rogers, who lived there a few years before selling it to James Stewart, 1st Earl of Buchan. The Earl gave the manor to his son, also James, who later died at the Battle of Flodden in 1513. The estate was elevated in 1633 when John was given the title of 1st Earl of Traquair. (The last of the family, Lady Louisa Stewart, died aged

99 in 1875 and the lands passed to her kinsman, Henry Maxwell. Henry adopted the name Stuart, and the Maxwell Stuarts still live in the house today.)

The concealed nature of the power and beliefs of this aristocracy is revealed in such places, 'The King's Room', where Mary, Queen of Scots stayed in 1566; it contains her rosary, crucifix, purse, a silk quilt and letters bearing her signature. Such was the Stewart family's affection for their kinsman, the Catholic Charles Edward Stuart (Bonnie Prince Charlie), that new entrance gates were installed to prepare for his visit in 1738. They were closed after the Bonnie Prince passed through in 1745, and the Earl vowed they would never be opened until Scotland had a Catholic Stuart king. Their choice of religion was hardly secret; immediately following the Catholic emancipation, the family added a Roman Catholic chapel in 1829.[8]

Despite it being the dominant clan in the area, there are no Scotts associated with Traquair in recent times. One must move east to find the lair of the Scotts on the Bowhill estate near Selkirk. Bowhill House is the home of the Duke of Buccleuch.[9] It has been owned by the Scott family since the twelfth century (apart from a brief respite in the eighteenth century when it was owned

---

8. In the present, the Traquair estate has 4,500 acres surrounding the house including four sheep farms, possible among them the farm where my grandfather was a shepherd, 20 cottages for estate workers and sole rights to fishing on a stretch of the river Tweed.
9. The Dukedom was created for the Duke of Monmouth, who was the eldest illegitimate son of Charles II of Scotland, England, and Ireland, and who had married Anne Scott, 4th Countess of Buccleuch. The Duke also holds the Dukedom of Queensbury created in 1684. one of only five people in the UK to hold two or more different dukedoms.

Traquair House (Photo author)

by the Murrays). In 1322, King Robert the Bruce granted
estates in Ettrick Forest to the Buccleuch family. The forest reverted to the Crown in 1450, and for hundred years,
it was a favourite hunting ground of the Kings of Scotland.
In about 1550, it was returned to members of the Scott
family. Sir Walter Scott, a frequent visitor, admired the
house so much that he christened it 'Sweet Bowhill' in his
famous poem, 'The Lay of the Last Minstrel'. The house
has one of the world's most distinguished private art collections, including works by Gainsborough, Reynolds,
Raeburn, van Dyke, Canaletto and Lely. Traquair and
Bowhill are two of the several feudal estates that are the
majority landowners in the borderlands between Scotland
and England. The Bowhill estate totals 58,000 acres,
almost 90 square miles.[10]

In its present form, Bowhill House dates mainly
from 1812 and was greatly expanded during the nineteenth century by architects that included William Burn

---

10. This includes non-adjoining areas extending from Melrose's
Eildon Hills to Branxholm Castle, near Hawick.

and David Bryce. Burn was much involved in the later years of the New Town; he was architect of the Church of Saint John the Evangelist in 1818, which marks the west end of Princes Street, and the great shaft of the Melville Monument dominating St Andrews Square. Despite the power of the family and the scale of Bowhill House, the thin Georgian architecture has little distinction, certainly no ostentation, yet it appears to have more than a hundred rooms – for what purpose?

The Feudal Estates: Growing up in Edinburgh, I had no idea that some thirty or so miles south of the city were several vast palaces held by feudal lords, occupying thousands of acres of land that the families had held for centuries. These are the estates of a shadowy Scottish aristocracy whose independence and arrogance lie at the foundations of the vision to create a classical city. These great houses remain to this day firmly in possession of a few feudal families. Consider how strange it is to find such vast estates with great houses, their numerous rooms are filled with elaborate furniture and major works of art, the rival of anything in England, hidden away in the Scottish countryside. Hidden because the Scottish aristocracy was able to remain mostly independent from the king and church. Even into the nineteenth century, these feudal princes did all they could to remain laws unto themselves. Consider these feudal lords, in their palaces, many created by the architects of the New Town, as a major inspiration for the creation of the classical city.

To fully appreciate the social and economic foundations that made classical Edinburgh, it is necessary to acknowledge the essentially feudal nature of Scottish society. Historically, Feudalism was the dominant social system in which the nobility held lands from the Crown in exchange for military service, and vassals were in turn tenants of the nobles, while the peasants (villeins or serfs) could not own the land they worked and were obliged to pay homage, labour and a share of the produce to the lord. In Scotland, many feudal lords held land not gifted by the Crown; they were powers unto themselves. It was not until November 2004, the *Abolition of Feudal Tenure etc. (Scotland) Act 2000* came into full force and effectively ended Scotland's feudal system. After that date, the former vassal of an estate became the sole owner of the land, and the former lord's rights were extinguished.[11]

There may have been a time when the clan was a family and when the privileged were obliged to help the poor. Around the time of building these great houses, farming methods were being dramatically improved, and without hesitation, the feudal landlords drove their unwanted labourers, clan or no clan, off the land and these displaced agricultural workers were among the many that migrated to Edinburgh and into the decaying streets of the old city at the end of the eighteenth century. But even in Edinburgh, the migrants could not escape feudalism, and much of the land on which the city was expanding was owned and leased by the same landlords. (I recall

---

11. Historically in the system of feudalism, the lords who received land directly from the Crown were called tenants-in-chief. They doled out portions of their land to lesser tenants in exchange for services, who in turn divided it among even lesser tenants. This process – that of granting subordinate tenancies – is known as subinfeudation. In this way, all individuals except the monarch were said to hold the land 'of' someone else. It was usual for there to be reciprocal duties between lord and tenant. There were different kinds of tenure to fit various kinds of duties that a tenant might owe to a lord. For instance, a military tenure might be by knight-service, requiring the tenant to supply the lord with a number of armed horsemen. The concept of tenure has since evolved into other forms, such as leases and estates.

how anxious my mother was every month when time came to pay the few duty, her payment to the landlord.[12])

Families Converge: It is not clear how Elspeth Finlay, without a husband or an income, survived the years immediately after James' death. Her parents must have helped, but she was resilient; from the 1861 census, she was back living in Stockbridge, at 20/5 Hamilton Place, not 20 yards from her home on Kerr Street, and she had a profession; from the census, she is 'Elspeth Finlay, Head, Widow, 50, Legal Assistant' helped presumably by James' colleagues in Registrar House. Her daughter Catherine Finlay, a teacher 25 years old, was living with her, but the census makes no mention of Hedderwick, who was seven years old and would have needed looking after. In the 1871 census, Elspeth is described as an 'annuitant' – someone who receives an annuity – which must have been generous for the family to move to 120 Mayfield Road, Liberton, far to the south of the city in a new and afflu-ent district. With her were her daughters Elizabeth and Margaret and son Hedderwick, who at 16, was already an apprentice law clerk, seems young, yet again his father's colleagues at Register House must have made this possible.

The census records from 1871 to 1911 detail changing addresses, household size, and jobs, and show a slow convergence in the lives and the fortunes, or lack thereof, of both the Finlay and Jamieson Balfour families,

---

12. Few Duty in Scots law was a fixed annual payment granting the right to the use of land.

Feu was long the most common form of land tenure in Scotland, as conveyancing in Scots law was dominated by feudal-ism until the Scottish Parliament passed, as mentioned above, the Abolition of Feudal Tenure etc. (Scotland) Act 2000.

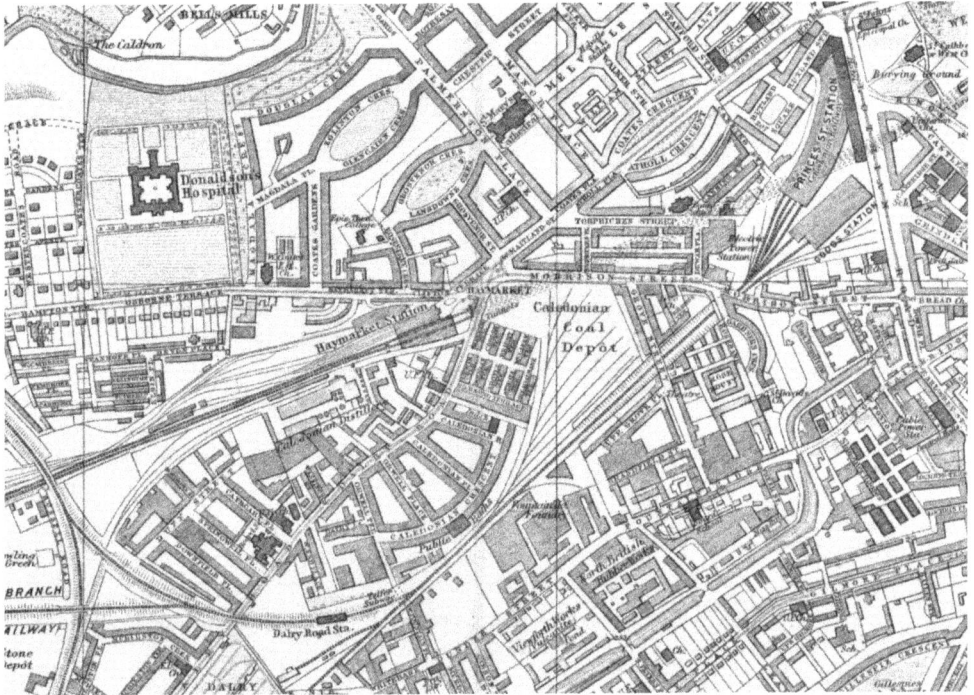

as they move into a new area of the city being to be close to the factories where they will find work.

The Bartholomew Plan shows the last fanciful terraces of the New Town across the top. Haymarket Station is centre left and beyond the extensive marshalling yards of the then named Princes Street Station. The Finlays raised their families within this enclave surrounded by the railways in the lower left; it was called Dalry. They lived in the tenements on Caledonian Crescent at the eastern edge of the enclave and in Downfield and Springwell Place (surrounding the massive Caledonian Distillery). The Jamieson Balfours, raise their families in the meaner tenements One Dundee Place and then Upper Grave Place, the lower right close to the North British Rubber Mill.

Bartholomew – Post Office Plan of Edinburgh, 1910– 1911. (Reproduced with the permission of the National Library of Scotland)

Hedderwick's view from Register House in 1880. (From Eon. Photo, reproduced by courtesy of the Yerbury family.)

Declining Fortunes

In 1876 Hedderwick Finlay married Margaret Thomson Menzies:[13]

> *1876 Fourth January N, Cumin Place, Grange*
> *Edinburgh, After Banns according to the Terms*
> *of the Church of Scotland, Hedderw. Finlay Law*
> *Clerk, Bachelor, 21, Caledonian Road Edinburgh,*
> *(father) James Finlay, Clerk general, Register House,*
> *Deceased, and Elspeth Finlay, MS. Wallace; Margaret*
> *Tomson Menzies, Domestic Servant, Spinster, 24, No*
> *12 Lonsdale Terrace Edinburgh, Hugh Menzies , mason*
> *and Susan Menzies MS. Kemp. [witness sigs]*

Hedderwick is listed as a 'Law Clerk General, Register House', a position similar to that once held by his father; his wife Margaret Tomson Kemp Menzies was a domestic servant. And in March 1876, only three months after the wedding, their daughter, Susan Elspeth Finlay was born (my great Aunt Susie). With this marriage, the Finlays united with the Kemp family, and as mentioned earlier, my aunt was confident in telling me that her mother, Susan Kemp (after whom she was named) was related to George Meikle Kemp.

In April 1881, my grandfather James Hugh Finlay was born at 20 Caledonian Crescent:

> *James Hugh Finlay April 25th 10hr 15 min an [at]*
> *20 Caledonian Crescent , [father] Hedderwick Finlay,*
> *Law clerk, Margaret Thomson Finlay M.S. Menzies,*
> *1876 January 4th Edinburgh. Hedd.k Finlay present*

---

13. The Menzies family (pronounced Mingis, the *z* replacing a lost letter from the Gaelic alphabet) my Aunt claimed were relayed with the most successful newsagents in Scotland.

In the census of that year, Elspeth Finlay was 70; her household was living at 44 Broughton Road, a dramatic come-down from Mayfield Road. She had lost her dream of returning to the New Town. This is a year in which the Finlay family fortunes were clearly in decline. What could have caused such a change in fortune? The two children living with her were contributing very little to the household income. Her daughter Margaret, 40, was unmarried, working as a lady's maid (in 1871 over 55 per cent of female workers in Edinburgh, were employed as domestic servants). Her older son Kirk, 39, was listed as an unemployed brass fitter, and Hedderwick could not offer much help. Growth of jobs in industry was creating opportunity for a much larger segment of the population and the once privileged position of law clerk paid little more than a skilled worker in industry.

Beginning with the move to the flat on Broughton Road, both the Elspeth and Hedderwick's families lived in a succession of properties in the other new town, in streets of joyless repetitive tenements, block after block, following the growth of industry on the east side of the New Town. In the years 1885–1886, Hedderwick and family were tenants in an apartment at 13 Caledonian Crescent. This forms the eastern edge of the enclave surrounded by rail in the lower centre of the *Post Office Plan*.[14] These were all rental properties in which the tenants, according to Scottish law, paid 'feu' duty to the landowner as well as rent. (An obligation which only ended in 2005).

This detail of the map from 1910 shows very clearly the contrast between the last sylvan fantasies of the New Town immediately to the north, and the harsh reality of the workers' world across the tracks. Caledonian

---

14. An area recently developed by Edinburgh's then Lord Provost, James Steel.

Crescent, Downfield and Springwell Place, Yeoman Place
and Dundee Place, and on and on. These were the streets
where both sides of my family lived, worked and raised
children at the turn of the new century.

The 1891 census records Hedderwick living
at 18 Downfield Place, Dalry, with his wife Margaret,
daughter Catherine and my grandfather James who was
9.[15] Downfield Place was an even more modest address
than Caledonian Crescent. Fortunes continue to decline.
Their daughter, my aunt Susan Finlay aged 15, was living with her 80-year-old grandmother on an adjoining
street, Elspeth Wallace Finlay, born in St Andrews and
along with her husband, had benefited from the largess of
Andrew Bell, died in 1893.

In 1901[16] the nine members of the Jamieson
Balfour family, were all living together in two rooms at
27 Springwell Place, essentially next door to James Finlay
at number 20. This included the four children of the first
marriage and two from the second, my Auntie Nellie, my
Uncle Jock and grandmother Catherine Scott's brother.
(Could the two families have met at this time? It would be

15. In 1909, my mother's sister, Euphemia Stewart Finlay was born
(Auntie Effie) also at 18 Downfield Place.
16. 1891 census: John and Marian Balfour were living south of the
Dalry Road in the tenements on Yeaman Place. They had three
children: William, 8; Catherine, 7; and Marian, 2. All half brothers and sisters of my father of whom I did not know existed. The
number '1' on the census form records rather painfully that this
family of five lived in a flat with only one window. By 1895 they
had just moved to Dundee Street immediately adjoining the North
British Rubber Mill when Marion died suddenly from a ruptured
stomach ulcer. A year later, John married Catherine Scott.

Caledonian Crescent. Mother birthplace 1907. (Photo author)

twenty and more years before my Jamieson Balfour father and Finlay mother would meet.)

In 1903, my grandparents James Hugh Finlay and Ellen Stewart were married:

> *29 October at the Caledonian Halls Dalry Road*
> *Edinburgh after Banns according to the Forms of the*
> *United Free Church of Scotland [Grandfather] James*
> *Hugh Finlay, a cabinetmaker bachelor age, 22 of*
> *20 Springwell Place Edinburgh marries Ellen Stewart,*
> *rubber worker spinster age 18 years of 11 Stewart Terrace*
> *Edinburgh Hedder'k Macreadie Young Finlay, Law Clerk*
> *Margaret Thomas Finlay m s Menzies. James Stewart,*
> *Mason deceased, Euphemia Stewart ms Grainger,*
> *Edward Rankin Minister Emeritus of the United Free*
> *Presbyterian Church of Scotland, Sheils, Belhelvie.??*

Ellen was 18, listed as a rubber worker. Did it concern senior law clerk Hedderwick Finlay, that his son had fallen into the working classes? James, an apprentice cabinet maker, marrying a woman working in the rubber mill. Of course, it did. The 1901 census records that

Downfield Place. (Photo author)

North British Rubber Works, on the shop floor making golf balls 1930 (Edin Photo). My grandmother and my father's half-sister could be among them. (Reproduced by courtesy of Scotsman Publications Ltd.)

my father's half-sister Marian, also worked at the North British Rubber Works.

The origins of the company date from January 1856 when two American shoe and bootmakers acquired a large plot of land on the Union Canal in Fountainbridge, Edinburgh. At its peak, it employed up to 8,000, the largest employer in the city. A mill worker in the North British Rubber Co was a low-grade job. It paid a reasonable wage for its skilled employees, but the work was unhealthy and dangerous, and it stank. An average worker would go about their daily lives smothered in a mix of rubber, sulphur and soapstone – a pungent talcum powder-like substance which hung heavy in the air and coated everything. The workers produced goods ranging from golf balls, hot water bottles and combs to hoses, rubber sheeting, tyres for automobiles. If grandmother Ellen and my father's half-sister had to work, they must have needed money, but it may have been more than that.

The mill offered one of the few jobs available to women that paid more than domestic service, and it gave the possibility of real independence. That opportunity would have been significant for women in both my mother and father's family.

On 4 January 1906, the younger Finlay's first child James Hedderwick Finlay, was born:

> *James Hedderwick Finlay January 4, 18 Downfield Place, Edinburgh, James Hugh Finlay, Cabinetmaker, Ellen Finlay M.S. Stewart [signed] James Hugh Finlay Father*

The address is the home of his father Hedderwick, at 18 Downfield Place. After three years of marriage, James and Ellen were still living with his parents. And they were still at that address when in October of 1907, my mother Margaret May Finlay was born:

> *Margaret May Finlay 1907, October thirteenth, 18 Downfield Place, Edinburgh, James Hugh Finlay, Cabinetmaker. Ellen Finlay M.S. Stewart [mar.] 1903 October 29 Edinburgh, James Hugh Finlay, Father, Present*

I noted that no other family members were present. By 1911 the James family had found a home of their own on Robertson Avenue, a street close to Ellen's mother. I surmise that this would have allowed her to look after the children while both parents were at work. In 1911 John Balfour and most of his family moved back to Dundee Place to be next to the mill. The family now included my one-year-old father, Henry. John was listed as an ironmonger; his daughter Marion, a rubber worker;

North British Rubber Works from the air 1925. The plant covered all the land running diagonally across the view. The Finlays lived just across the track on the top left of the view. Grandfather John Balfour and family lived on Dundee Place, now demolished, at the edge of the Mill entrance at the left edge of the view. (Reproduced by permission of Royal Commission on the Ancient and Historical Monuments of Scotland, 0006-017-000 405C Aerofilms 27139).

Robertson Avenue. The same grim tenement they had left behind. (Photo author)

Robertson Avenue. The same grim tenement they had left behind. (Photo author)

her sister toiling in an industrial laundry. Marion, my father's half-sister was 22, and my grandmother Ellen was 26, close enough in age to have known each other and certainly they could have been working together.

Distressed families Eight Balfour's living in a flat in which only two of the rooms had a window. Of my father's half-siblings: Catherine Balfour, born on McNeil Street in 1883, became a domestic servant and married James Watson, a housepainter. Marion Balfour, born on Yeaman Place in 1887, married a night watchman named Purvis, and died in Queensbury House Hospital, aged 53, in 1940. From the death report, it appears as if she either had a fall or was beaten to death: 'cause of death, Concussion and Severe Cerebral Contusion'. I found no further information on either George, born 1891 or Elizabeth born 1893. Some of my father's half-brothers and sisters would have been alive and well when I was growing up, but these are names that I have never known. It is as if my father severed all connections with his step-family. I have no memory of my father ever mentioning his father (except saying he was a cobbler), and before I began this search, I could not have named him. The list also names Emily Jamieson Balfour, also unknown to me, and learned that my father had a second sister, and the more I have learned of Emily, she appears in my imagination so different and delightful.

In 1911, Hedderwick's daughter Susan (auntie Suzy) was living with her father until she married a 55-year-old railway clerk James Bell, taking her out of her parents' home and into a flat on Hillside Street – a development which retains the street plan laid out in Playfair's northern extension 30 years earlier.

War: Sometime in 1915, my grandfather James Finlay was called to service in the 17th (1st Rosebery) Battalion, Royal Scots (Lothian Division). He had not been drafted earlier because he was too short, but the desperate situation on the battlefronts between France and Germany demanded that all those who were able to serve should serve. The 17th (1st Rosebery) Battalion, Royal Scots, was raised in Edinburgh in February 1915 by Lord Roseberry, as a Bantam Battalion from men who were under the normal regulation minimum height of 5 feet and 3 inches. After initial training close to home, they moved to Glencorse in April 1915. In June, they joined the 106th Brigade, 35th division at Masham and went on to Chisledon, for further training in August. Ordered to Egypt in late 1915, but the order was cancelled and they proceeded to France landing in Le Havre on 1 February 1916, the division was concentrated to the east of St Omer.

Throughout 1916, Private James Finlay, 'Wee Jimmy' as they called him, suffered through a succession of the worst battles of the war; on the Somme at Bazentin Ridge, in Arrowhead Copse, and Maltz Horn Farm and Faflemont Farm. Late in the year, the division received new drafts of men to replace the losses suffered on the Somme, but the officers soon discovered that the new recruits were not nearly as fit as the original Bantams, most of whom had come from the mines and the farms. A medical inspection was carried out, and 1439 men were deemed unfit and transferred to the Labour Corps. Wee Jimmy must have been a survivor – if only he had failed the test.

And the war came to Edinburgh in other ways: On the night of 2–3 April 1916, two German airships, the L14 and the L22, dropped 23 bombs on Leith and the City of Edinburgh. Reinhard Scheer had been appointed commander in chief of the German fleet at the end of February 1916 and, anxious to provoke the Royal Navy, he attacked the British mainland, using surface ships, submarines and airships in a combined operation.

Warning of the impending air raid was received at 7 pm on Sunday 2 April 1916, and the police in Leith and the City of Edinburgh instituted air-raid precautions: the Electric Light Department lowered all lights, traffic was stopped and lights on vehicles were extinguished. The Central Fire Station and the Red Cross were notified and all policemen, regular and specials, were called up. The first reports of bombs exploding were received by the police just before midnight. The L14, having crossed over the coast at St Abbs Head in Berwickshire on route for Rosyth and the Forth Railway Bridge, was unable to see its targets and dropped its bombs over Leith and the centre of Edinburgh. The L22 crossed over the mainland at Newcastle and dropped its bombs over the south of the city.

Seven incendiary and seventeen high explosive bombs were dropped on the city, many of them on the south side. This included a bomb which landed on the roadway approximately 400 yards from Edinburgh Castle and an explosive bomb which fell in the grounds of George Watson's College, breaking a number of windows and damaging stonework on the steps. The White Hart Hotel in the Grassmarket and the County Hotel in Lothian Road suffered substantial damage, as well as a number of tenement buildings in Newington. During the raid, seven residents of Edinburgh were killed, including five men at 16 Marshall Street in Newington, from a fragment of a shell and died eight days later from peritonitis and heart failure.[17]

In 1917, Private Finlay was in action during the pursuit of the Hindenburg Line, at Houthulst Forest, the second Battle of Passchendaele. On the 24 and 25 March 1918, the town of Bapaume was evacuated and occupied by German forces; on the following day, German troops advanced against the Fifth Army. On the 28 March, Private James Finlay was in the thick of a desperate effort to hold the line in what would be called the Battle of Arras. The Fifth Army had been spread thin on a 42-mile front lately taken over from the exhausted and demoralized French. They were forced to fight a rearguard action, contesting every village, field and, on occasion, yard [...] With no reserves, and with eighty German divisions against fifteen British. They fought the Somme offensive to a standstill on the Ancre, not retreating beyond Villers-Bretonneux, stopping the Germans from breaking the line. And in that extreme effort, Private James Finlay died, just to the east of the Arras.[18]

17. *The Scotsman* newspaper April 2 1916. https://www.scotsman.com › archive
18. Roberts, A. *A History of the English-Speaking Peoples Since 1900.* London: Weidenfeld & Nicolson, 2006.

Recorded on the Pozieres Memoria: In Memory of Private JAMES HUGH FINLAY 40994 17th Bn., Royal Scots who died on 28th March 1918 (Photo: T Brueleman, with permission)

The Pozières Memorial in the Somme depart-
ment of France lists the names of 14,657 British and South
African soldiers of the Fifth and Fourth Armies with no
known grave who were killed between 21 March 1918 and
7 August 1918 during the German advance known as the
Spring Offensive. It includes the name of: *Private JAMES
HUGH FINLAY 40994 17th Bn., Royal Scots who died on 28th
March 1918.*

Before he was called to war, James knew that
Ellen suffered from epileptic fits. Sometime after learning
of the death of his son, Hedderwick Finlay determined
that Ellen's illness made her unfit to look after the family
by herself and arrangement were made to place all the
children, James, May and Effie in Edinburgh's monumental Donaldson's School, an asylum for the deaf and
dumb.

My mother was 11.

VII

Into The Twentieth Century

Donaldson's Hospital: In 1918, my mother and her brother and sister destitute and alone were taken into care. Grandmother Ellen's epileptic fits though infrequent at first, must have become so uncontrollable that she would have had to leave the job at the rubber mill. With her husband at war, she was left alone at home with the children, continually in fear of an attack with only the pittance paid by the army to live on. With the news from the War Office that James had died in battle, a decision was made to treat the children as orphans and place them in care.

I can imagine the grandfather Hedderwick Finlay, the law clerk, never happy with the marriage, reviewing options with his two daughters, Susan and Catherine, both now married. Catherine had a family of her own and simply could not have accommodated three more children, and Susan's husband, very conservative and too old to accept the presence of children. There was no other way, they had to be taken into care. So, the decision was made to apply to Donaldson's Hospital, a celebrated charitable institution matching deaf and dumb children in equal numbers with normal children. With the help I presume of Hedderwickhe Finlay children were accepted and committed just a few months after learning about their father's death, sentenced to a childhood within the walls of the last and the strangest monument created within the vision of the New Town.

Donaldson's Hospital was founded in 1851 and paid for by the publisher of the *Edinburgh Advertiser* Sir James Donaldson. The design, an absurd baronial confection, built at enormous cost, was the last work of William Playfair, the greatest of Edinburgh's nineteenth-century architects.

The rules were set down in great detail in *DOCUMENTS Relating To DONALDSON'S HOSPITAL.*[1]

In 1833 the Hospital Trust obtained from the Governors of Heriot's Hospital, a. feu of about 17 Acres of the Lands of Coates, as a site for the Hospital. The Trustees agreed that it would be proper to erect a building of a size sufficient to accommodate 400 Children, 200 Boys and 200 Girls, although, until the expiry of the Annuities bequeathed by Mr Donaldson, the Hospital Funds would not be more than sufficient for the maintenance of 300 Children.

Three architects applied to by the Trustees furnished designs and models for the Hospital, viz., Mr. Playfair, Mr. Gillespie Graham, and Mr. Hamilton,[2] of Glasgow; and the Trustees having [...] considered the whole designs submitted to them, on 31st July 1838 unanimously adopted that of Mr. Playfair as best suited for the

---

1. *DOCUMENTS Relating To DONALDSON'S HOSPITAL.* Edinburgh: Neil and Company, 1851.
2. Three equally distinguished architects.

purposes intended.[3] By it, accommodation was
provided for 150 Boys and 150 Girls, and the
building admits of an addition being made to it,
sufficient to accommodate 100 more Children,
50 Boys and 50 Girls; and there was included in
the plan at Chapel in direct connection with the
Hospital. The Hospital, including the Chapel,
has now been erected upon the piece of ground
above mentioned, in conformity with the Plan
by Mr. Playfair.

There was a further proposal:

A proposal having been made to the Governors
of the Hospital that a proportion of Destitute
Deaf and Dumb Children should be received
into the Institution for maintenance and education, they, after full and careful consideration and discussion of the subject, resolved, on
the 4th July 1848, 'that, as suggested by the
Committee, one side of the Hospital, which will
contain 96 beds, shall be fitted up for the reception of Deaf and Dumb Children'; – and directions were in consequence given to Mr Playfair
to make arrangements for the accommodation of
that number of Children of that Class, one half
Boys and one half Girls, which has been done.

Work began on site in 1842, and the building was opened
(when not quite complete) by Queen Victoria in 1850.

---

3. This initial invitation was sent on 19 November 1833, but it was
   not until 31 July 1838 that Playfair was declared the winner; he
   had submitted a total of seven different designs to the Trustees.

Edinburgh essayist Henry Thomas Cockburn described her visit, recording: 'The Queen went over his [Playfair's] hospital [...] admiring everything. [...] It has even been rumoured that so impressed were Victoria and Albert that they suggested exchanging Holyrood Palace for Donaldson's Hospital'. Indeed, R. L. Stevenson noted that 'it has more the appearance of a Royal palace than a building for the reception of children [...] whose parents are in the humbler walks of life'.[4] The school was finally able to admit its first pupils in 1851, 20 years after the architectural competition.

The rules were strict and the critical qualification entry was, 'destitution':

> The Governors are not confined, by any statute or regulation, to the selection of the Children of parents of any particular classes of the community. Destitution is the only essential requisite for the admission of Children into Donaldson's Hospital, and that without regard to the situations in life which their parents may at any time have occupied, or to the particular localities in which they may have been at any time placed; provided that, at the time of application for admission, and as to the age, and state of mind and body of the Children, to qualify them for participating in the benefit of the Charity.

Although their mother Ellen was still alive, she herself must have been in care for the children to be treated as orphans. They were destitute because other members in their family refused to be responsible for

---

4. Ibid., R. L. Stevenson.

them. It was a decision based on the rules that '*the parents and children are in the circumstances required by the Deed of Constitution of the Hospital, as to destitution*'. The rules were clear: 'No Children shall be admitted into the Hospital whose Parents are able to maintain them, and none shall be admitted till they have attained the age of six years complete'. It then adds 'nor after they have attained the age of nine years complete'.[5] Two of the Finlay children were older, so someone had been persuaded to bend the rules.

The many rules that governed the running of the school had not changed since 1851 when my mother passed through the gates in the winter of 1918:

> On the day of admission, the old Clothes of the Children shall be taken from them and returned to their friends. The Children shall then be carefully washed in the Baths, shall have their hair cut and combed, and shall put on the Clothes of the Hospital, which shall be previously made to fit each Child.
>
> [...] such children to be clothed and maintained in the said Hospital, and taught and instructed in such useful branches of education as may be considered by the said Governors to be suitable to their station, sex, and age [...] *nor shall any of the children remain therein after they have attained the age of fourteen.*[6]

For those not deaf and dumb, it was a practical education:

---

5. Ibid., *DONALDSON'S HOSPITAL.*
6. Ibid., *DONALDSON'S HOSPITAL.*

William Playfair's Donaldson's Hospital 1870.

DONALDS

QSPITAL.
Street Edinburgh.

Entrance hall of Donaldson's Hospital.

Education of the Girls not Deaf and Dumb. The Committee recommend that these Girls should be taught by the Female Teachers English, the Elements of Geography, Sewing and Knitting; and that the Male Teachers should instruct these Girls in Writing and Arithmetic, and should also instruct the more advanced Classes of them in English and Geography; and that the *Girls should also be taught Washing, Ironing, the management of the Kitchen Department and the duties of House Maids.*[7]

The girls were being prepared for domestic service, still the major employment for working women in the post-war years: 'the elder Girls be instructed in all kinds of Female House-work, such as washing, ironing, the management of the kitchen department, and the duties generally of House-maids; and that they perform them with cleanliness, neatness, and dexterity'. The speaking children also had to learn sign language, and I remember when I was very young, mother showing me how she spoke to her deaf and dumb friends.

---

7. Ibid., *DONALDSON'S HOSPITAL.*

It was a disciplined regimen, with some rules difficult to comprehend, especially those discouraging frequent visits by the family:

> The relations and friends of Children in the Hospital shall be admitted to visit them in the Hospital once a month, on a day to be fixed by the House Governor. The Children shall *not* be permitted to reside, during the vacation, with their relations [I wonder why?] or friends who live in Edinburgh, but may be permitted by the House Governor, if he thinks fit, to visit such relations or friends, in the day time, more frequently during the vacation than at other times and further, for the purposes of healthful recreation and exercise to the Children, the House Governor shall have at all times a discretionary power to relieve them occasionally from their Classes in the afternoon, that they may enjoy the benefit of a walk to the country.

And there is a severe edict:

> The relations or friends of the Children, on all occasions of their visiting the Hospital, shall be *strictly prohibited from giving to any of the Children money* or any article of food, drink, or medicine, and from interfering in any way with their management, under pain of all future intercourse with them being prevented.[8]

---

8. Ibid., *DONALDSON'S HOSPITAL.*

And on religion:

> [The Chaplain] shall every day perform, or in
> his necessary absence cause one of the Teachers
> to perform, Morning and Evening Devotions in
> the Chapel, at the hours to be ordered by the
> Governors;
> And shall:
> [...] give, daily, the requisite instruction in the
> Bible and Shorter Catechism; and, in addition
> to this, he shall, as often as he deems it expedi-
> ent – but regularly on the Sabbath Evenings –
> convene them all in the Chapel, and give them
> such religious instruction, in the way of address,
> exposition, exercises, or otherwise, as may tend
> to encourage them in the cultivation of piety – to
> imbue their minds with correct views of Divine
> truth, and to form them to those dispositions
> and habits upon which their wellbeing and hap-
> piness throughout life so essentially depend.[9]

When the building was complete, Playfair felt that the
interiors were too dark and they would remain so during my mother's time. The only colour in the chapel had
come from stained glass filling the great oriel window in
the photograph above. However, a few years before my
mother arrived, these were destroyed in the Zeppelin
bomb raid in April 1916.

By the end of the first year, my mother would have
become institutionalized. There may have been occasional visits by great aunt Suzy. (My mother to my recollection never mentioned the name Hedderwick, I believe
he played no part in her childhood.) Her sister Euphemia,

---

9. Ibid., *DONALDSON'S HOSPITAL.*

The Chapel.

The Oriel window in the Chapel.

refused to adjust and continually soiled the bed. The family guardians were summoned, and the trustees of the hospital asked for her to be removed. She was removed and, under orders from Hedderwick, was adopted by a family in Edinburgh about whom I know nothing except that they were affluent enough to send her to a respected private school. Euphemia (she was called Effie) grew up estranged from her family, demeaning my mother.[10] For

---

10. I saw this at first hand when we visited her Devon, I was 11.

most of her remaining years in the hospital, mother's only source of comfort was her brother, Jim.

I will never know how this 11-year-old responded to being placed in such a highly regulated Victorian fantasy. She did talk about it from time to time and was never critical, for all its rules, it appears to have been a supportive place. She could not have begun to comprehend the architect's intention in creating such a spectacle nor have been aware how daily life on this elaborate stage was affecting her.

In *Cassell's Old and New Edinburgh*,[11] James Grant has a different and unconvincing version of those eligible for admission: '1. Poor children of the name of Donaldson or Marshall, if appearing to the governors to be deserving'. He then adds, 'Such poor children as shall appear to be the most destitute'. He describes the place:

> On the gentle swell of the ground, about 600 yards westward of the Haymarket, amid a brilliant urban landscape, stands Donaldson's Hospital, in magnitude and design one of the grandest edifices of Edinburgh, and visible from a thousand points all round the environs to the westward, north, and south. It [...] forms a hollow quadrangle of 258 feet by 207 exteriorly, and 176 by 164 interiorly. It is a modified variety of a somewhat ornate Tudor style, and built of beautiful freestone. It has four octagonal five-storeyed towers, each 120 feet in height, in the centre of the main front, and four square towers of four storeys each at the corners; and most profuse,

---

11. Ibid., Grant.

graceful, and varied ornamentations on all the four facades, and much in the interior.

Grant's description is sensible, but does not attempt to explore what was in the architect's mind. Consider Donaldson's Hospital as the last invention arising from the eighteenth-century dream to create a New Town. An ideal place that would take Edinburgh not just out of medieval decay, but into a distinctly Scottish reality that would inspire the future of the nation. The eighteenth-century ideal was Greek democracy, and the architecture of the New Town (an illusion as feudal Scotland was far from democratic). The Royal High School, set within a robust version of the Temple of Neptune, in Paestum. That was 1824; however, by the 1840s with the rise of a more militant Scottish church, the classical ideal faded and Playfair, a master classicist, had to search for a more appropriate national style. He did not have to look far. His perfect model for an authentic Scottish style, had been standing in the middle of Edinburgh since at least 1630. Established in 1628 as George Heriot's Hospital[12] (now George Heriot's School) in the reign of the Stewart king Charles I. Its form derived from the Flemish Renaissance. Historian Joe Rock has written, 'What the Trustees [for Donaldson's Hospital] sought was an association with the Renaissance as seen through the eyes of the Stuart dynasty. [...] The irony is that the term "Elizabethan"

---

12. Originally called the Heriot *Orphanotrophium*. It was the work of a succession of Scotland's earliest and most celebrated architects, William Wallace, until his death in 1631, succeeded as master mason by William Aytoun, who was succeeded in turn by John Mylne. And in 1676, Sir William Bruce produced a final plan.

is used to describe this development in picturesque taste when Jacobethan is probably more accurate'.[13] [14]

Playfair first experimented with the style when he designed a north gate to Heriot's in 1829. Then in 1838, he produced the vast and extravagant display of it in the design for Floors Castle in Kelso (as seen in the previous chapter). Playfair may have convinced himself that he was creating a future style for the nation, but in fact in Donaldson's Hospital, he had built a monument to the tastes and values of the Scottish aristocracy, some still wishing for the return of a Stewart monarchy. (And it is notable that after the 1840s, classicism fell out of favour, and major buildings, particularly churches, preferred not the Stewart Renaissance but Gothic dress, which must have made the gods feel much more at home).

Donaldson's Hospital remains a curious monument from the final years of the New Town. What was in the beginning a progressive vison, albeit for a privileged few, ended with a spectacular work of romantic nationalism to provide a home for destitute children. Its symbolism would have lost all meaning in the second decade of the twentieth century as my mother was marched back and forward down these ominous hallways, day after day, month after month, for four years.

I have tried to picture the scene of a 14-year-old girl being turned out into the world after an extremely sheltered education. However, the Donaldson's Hospital was remarkably altruistic for the wards under its care. The rules state:

---

13. Joe Rock's Research pages: observations-on-the-donaldson-s-hos pital-ti meline&usg=AOvVaw3FgdtE8KJ1THDZn2vsTKth
14. Its evolution can be seen in houses built at Caerlaverlock (1620), Moray House, Edinburgh (1628) and Drumlanrig Castle (1675–1689).

Donaldson's Hospital on the right bank of the Water of Leith with Edinburgh Castle in the distance: David Roberts 1853. (National Galleries of Scotland.)

And we hereby declare, that the said Governors and Managers shall have full power, if they at any time deem it to be advisable, to give to the children when they leave the Hospital, or to any person or persons for their behoof, such sum of money or assistance as they see proper, to enable them to get situations or employments, by payment of apprentice fees, or otherwise ; and that either in one sum, or by payments made to them, or to any person or persons for their behoof, annually, for four or five years ; and also to give to the children any rewards or premiums for good conduct, while in the Hospital, or after-wards, which they may think proper.

[...] otherwise, they would have been destitute.[15]

_____

15. The building was closed and put up for sale in 2003, and by 2018 had been converted into luxury apartments.

Donaldson's Hospital 1910.

Alone in the City: Thus, in the spring of 1922, according to the rules, at the age of 14, my mother left Donaldson's Hospital. Someone in the family must have agreed to take her in. I believe it must have been her aunt Suzy; no other member of the family was as close to my mother. Childless herself, she could have felt that mother was the daughter she never had. If so, mother would have lived for a brief time within Playfair's plan for the eastern extension of the New Town on Hillside Street, a home I visited nearly every weekend in my childhood. She may have gone back to school, but I doubt it. I have a fragment of memory in which she regretted leaving school at fourteen. Whoever was willing to look after her would have quickly helped her find a job and, when able, moved her into her own accommodation. On her wedding certificate, seven years after leaving Donaldson's, she is described as a dyers and cleaners shop assistant.

Her major preoccupation must have been her mother's condition. She had experienced Ellen's epileptic fits before she was taken into care. From her earliest childhood, she must have been terrified by a mother lying on the floor having a fit; it would happen when the children were alone with her. She watched helplessly as her mother's body moved in ways she couldn't control, sometimes violently. She would lose consciousness and muscles would stiffen and jerk, memories printed indelibly in the child's mind. She was convinced the condition was hereditary, coming from the male side of the Stewart family, and she was terrified that her children – my sister and I, would be so afflicted. In our early years, she watched us for anything that reminded her of her mother's behaviour and seizures.

Could she have returned to her mother? Alas, there is scant evidence of Grandmother Ellen's health or whereabouts from the time the children were taken from her until her death at the age of 47 in 1931. Her death certificate lists her 'usual residence' as on Wardlaw Place, so she may have been living independently. What is known is that sometime in the 20s Ellen Finlay was committed to a mental asylum, the Bangour Village Hospital and there my mother would experience another kind of institutional reality where, unlike Donaldson's Hospital, family visits were not just encouraged, but seen as supporting treatment.

In the years of Ellen's commitment, my mother was quite alone, sister Effie had disowned the Finlay family, and her beloved brother James, the one constant in her life, joined Shell Oil in the mid-1920s and sailed off to Venezuela.

Bangour Village Hospital,
the administration block with
turrets slightly reminiscent
of the towers on Donaldson's
Hospital.

Bangour Village Hospital: On her visits, my mother would have been unaware that she was again entering another interpretation of the Stewart Renaissance. It is described as being 'designed in a restrained Scots Renaissance style and as an outstanding example of a psychiatric hospital built as a village and espousing a complete philosophy of care'. It was based on the Alt-Scherbitz Hospital near Leipzig in Germany, established in 1870s, which encouraged psychiatric patients to be cared for within their own community setting, with few physical restrictions and where village self-sufficiency was encouraged, and there were no external walls or gates.[16]

The hospital was the major mental asylum in the city. During World War I, it had served as a military

---

16. Co-opted by the Nazis in 1936 and over 1,800 of its patients were sent from there to be gassed.

hospital, reopening in 1922 and sometime thereafter, Grandmother Ellen was committed.

The Edinburgh Lunacy Board had concluded that a new psychiatric hospital was required to cater for the increasing number of patients from Edinburgh and the hospital was opened in 1906. There must have been a reason for an increase of madness in the city, was it a product of poverty or drink? I was surprised to find my father's half-brother William Jamieson Balfour, was sent there in 1906. He would have been one of the earliest patients; he died there in August 1908.

The hospital was planned and designed as a village, by Edinburgh architect Hippolyte J Blanc, won in competition in 1898. Blanc was a respected architect best known for his Gothic revival churches. He was described as an antiquarian and many of his designs attempt to evoke an earlier Scottish style, much less elaborate but not dissimilar to Playfair's Donaldson's Hospital. This was only mildly evident at Bangour. Competent though they are, the buildings lack the character of a village.

The administration buildings were at the centre, and the medical buildings for patients requiring supervision and treatment were to the east. The villas to the west were each home for around 30 patients who required less supervision and who were able to work in some sort of industry. The complex included a farm, bakery, workshops, recreation hall, school, shop, library and its own water and electricity systems. For the first 15 years of its existence, it had its own railway; it was some distance from Edinburgh, and for a time, the railway was the only way to get there on public transport.

(The hospital continued as a psychiatric hospital until 2004, when it was closed and abandoned. The site was used as a filming location for the 2005 film *The Jacket*, starring Keira Knightley and Adrien Brody. And

Bangour Village Hospital, the gift shop on the entry path in 1944.

Bangour Village Hospital, the gift shop on the entry path in 2018.

in 2009, the grounds were used as the site for 'Exercise Green Gate', a counter-terrorist exercise organized by the Scottish Government to test decontamination procedures in the event of a nuclear, chemical or biological incident.)

I visited the now desolate collection of buildings on a bleak rainy October in 2017, and imagined my mother making frequent trips into this dispiriting world throughout the 1920s. It was a long way into the country from Edinburgh and she would have taken trams and buses to get there. She would have met her mother in the

*Bangour Village Hospital,
the path of the administration
block.*

library or in the shop which still stands all boarded up,
and they may have gone back to the villas they would talk
sitting on the bed. She knew nothing more could be done.
Perhaps her last trip was in 1930 with my father, her new
husband.

On 25 December 1931, Hellen (Ellen) Finlay died
in Bangour Village Hospital:

> *Helen Finlay widow of James Finlay, Cabinet maker*
> *dies December 28th at Bangor Village, West Lothian.*
> *Usual residence 28 Wardlaw Place Edinburgh.*
> *47 years, both parents James Stewart, Mason (deceased),*
> *Euphemia Stewart, previously Ramsay, MS Grainge*

*r(deceased), Epilepsy, Transverse Myelitis, Pyelitis.
Death certificate signed by J Gerrard Secretary to the
Hospital1*[17]

There is no evidence of any family member being present.
Ellen's mother had recently died, and her father died long
ago. Of her children, her son Jim was in Venezuela, no
idea where daughter Euphemia was; however, daughter
May, my mother, was in Edinburgh and, I presume, chose
not to be present. No family member signed the death
certificate.

Where was she buried, was it a pauper's grave?[18]

Into the 1920s at the Palais de Danse:
Although it was 1918 when my mother entered
Donaldson's Hospital, she lived for these four years a distinctly nineteenth-century life, and when she came out at
fourteen, the world and Edinburgh were being changed
by the eager promise of the twentieth century. It was an
egalitarian promise which unsettled the class division that
the New Town had created. It was in this changing society that she began to build a life of her own. Nowhere in
the history of the Finlays is there any evidence of deep
religious faith, so it is unlikely she would have found community in the church. Her fellow shopworkers would have
been her companions and in the new Edinburgh they
would find entertainment in pubs, the cinemas and in one
dance hall in particular *The Palais de Danse*. And it was
there that I believe my mother met my father.

---

17. Apart from epilepsy, her death was also caused by transverse
myelitis; an inflammation of the spinal, a neurological disorder
that damages the covering of the nerve cell fibres.
18. Not only do I not have an answer, but I also cannot recall visiting
the grave of any family member.

Looking back over the previous hundred years, there are only three major places created for the city to gather, listen to music and sometimes to dance. In 1787 the Assembly Rooms opened in the heart of the New Town, on George Street. For the first 20 years, it was the only place in the city, outside of the church, and the taverns for social gatherings. A grand portico was added in 1818, and a music hall was constructed at the back in 1843. The Assembly Rooms and Music Hall were the centre of all social and musical events for the privileged classes throughout the nineteenth century. Designed by John Henderson, the Assembly Rooms opened in 1787 in the centre of the New Town (which was still in construction). Shepherd's engraving carefully illustrates the dress and posture of the people in the street in front of the elegant facade in 1825, all willing subjects of George IV.

In 1914, just as war was threatening, the city began the construction of the first monumental building of the twentieth century, the Usher Hall.

The Usher Hall competition entry drawing of the entrance from the architects Stockdale Harrison & Howard H Thomson of Leicester, 1911.

Not the product of aristocratic patronage but from the profits of whisky. The hall was funded in a bequest from Andrew Usher, whose 'desire and intention [was] that this Hall should become and remain a centre and attraction to musical artistes and performers and to the citizens of Edinburgh and others who may desire to hear good music [...]' Usher died in 1898, and it was not until 1910 that an architectural competition[19] was announced with the requirement that the hall be simple but dignified.

The design is in distinctly un-Scottish Beaux Arts style, a fashion caught between the nineteenth and twentieth centuries. On 19 July 1911, George V and Queen Mary laid two memorial stones, an event attended by over a thousand people. Beneath the stone, it is a concrete structure on an awkward site where the dome helps to give it position. It is a restless object, never at ease with the city around it.

---

19. The winning bid came from Stockdale Harrison & Howard H Thomson of Leicester.

I knew it well the Royal High School would hold an annual concert on its stage and, in my years there with a gifted and ambitious music teacher, Bill Bowie, we would rehearse and give the first performance of a major choral work in Scotland. It extended and in some superseded the role of the Assembly Rooms, not quite as privileged; it has housed a greater range of activities from Oswald Mosely rallying the Fascists to heavyweight boxing matches. And there in the foreground of the competition drawing are the satisfied *soignee* Edwardians of the city in the 1920s. They are so smart and casual.

Palais De Danse at the centre, across the bridge over the Union Canal on Fountainbridge in 1930: a bridge both my parents would cross often. The entertainment heart of the workers' city was located on the southeast corner of the North British Rubber Works.

The *Palais de Danse* opened just after World War I ended. Located close to the eastern end of the North British Rubber Mill, it was built to entertain the majority poor in the city. It began as a cinema ballroom with seating for 1,800. History records that 'dancing came to the venue in style on Hogmanay 1920 as the inaugural Grand New

Year's Ball of the new Palais de Danse, "Scotland's most exclusive ballroom and social rendezvous".[20] It gained prestige during the Twenties and Thirties, attracting, at some point (for no good reason I can think of) the Duke of Windsor and the Duke of Kent. Maybe it was royal politics, or maybe they were there to pick up women. On the streets are the workers trusting supporters of the Labour Party and the Scottish prime minister Ramsay MacDonald.

The 'Palais' (it was always referred to as the Palais) has a graphic one-dimensional classical façade, an amusing demonstration of the cooption and corruption of a style that once defined classical Edinburgh. It is appropriate that a city which for a century had reproduced robust, classical structures to elevate and enrich the public life of the elite, would give this popular people's palace such a cheap reproduction.

I remember a conversation with my father when I tried to learn the trumpet. He talked fondly of one Nat Gonella,[21] the English Louis Armstrong, who he had heard playing at the Palais, and how for a few years he and mother would go dancing there. And as this was the only dance hall in the city and near both their homes before they married, it would seem highly likely that this was where and how they met. (Looking at the map, I see the dance hall is just a few minutes from father's home.)

A recollection of an evening at the Palais in the 1930s:

> The dance floor was so big, perhaps 80ft by 200ft, that it took some nerve to walk across the empty floor to ask a girl on the other side to

---

20. In 1933, Gonella published a book called *Modern Style Trumpet Playing – A Comprehensive Course*.
21. *The Scotsman* Feb., 2015.

PALAIS DE DANSE. FOUNTAINBRIDGE. EDINBURGH
"UNDER ROYAL PATRONAGE"

dance and you had to have a plan B so that if someone beat you to it, or the girl looked unwelcoming, you had to be pretending to be looking for someone else, in order to save face.

On a good night the Palais would attract over 900 people cavorting away on its enormous sprung dancefloor, listening and dancing to the music on the hand-cranked revolving stage. This allowed the bands to seamlessly swap over, without interruption to the dancing. There was a bar, non-alcoholic called Cupid's Corner, serving only fruit juice. (from my own experience at that age, the men would have smuggled in whisky.) It was a setting where many relationships began.[22]

The dance floor at the Palais De Danse in 1930, 'Under Royal Patronage'. (Post Card)

22. *Edinburgh Recollections* – Palais De Dance – EdinPhoto.

And on 6 December 1929, Margaret May Finlay married Henry Irvine Jamieson Balfour,

> *6th December at 31 Leamington Terrace Edinburgh,*
> *After Banns according to the Forms of the Church of*
> *Scotland, Henry Irvine Jamieson Balfour, Motor Car*
> *Driver, Bachelor, 23, 15 Upper Grove Place Edinburgh,*
> *[father] John Jamieson Balfour, Ironmonger's Packer,*
> *(deceased) [mother] Catherine Balfour M.S Scott*
> *(deceased) Scott. [marries] Margaret May Finlay, Dyers*
> *and Cleaners Shop Assistant, 22, 39 Temple Park*
> *Crescent, Edinburgh, [father] James Hugh Finlay,*
> *Cabinet Maker (deceased), [mother] Ellen Finlay, M.S.*
> *Stewart. (signed) Henry Heath, Minister of Chalmers*
> *Church of Scotland, West Port, Edinburgh. (Signed)*
> *Thomas Howie, 6 Comiston Gardens Edinburgh,*
> *Witness, and Margaret E B Fleming, 39 Bryston Road*
> *Edinburgh, Witness.*

Ellen Finlay was still alive, but too ill to attend, even if she had been invited. She died a few months later, and no other family member is recorded as being present. I knew the witnesses throughout my childhood, Thomas Howie, and Margaret Fleming (Aunty Meg and Uncle Tommy.) Meg was mother's best friend at Donaldson's Hospital and for life.

Mother was 22, and my father 23. His occupation was listed as a motor car driver. He drove for the Distillers Company Limited, which in the 20s and 30s claimed to be the 'largest whisky distiller in the world'. It dominated the whisky industry, owning among others Haig, John Walker, Buchanan–Dewar and White Horse Distilleries for many decades. At the time of the marriage, he was living at his father's home on Upper Grove Place (My

On the day of the wedding Father was living in the family home at 15 Upper Grove Place, on the right side of the photo. (Photo author)

And Mother was a boarder at 39 Temple Park Crescent on the left in the distance. (Photo author)

only recollection was his description of crashing a van in Scottish Borders, so I assume he was in distribution. He must have resisted the temptation that many succumbed to – of sampling the wares.)

Mother's occupation is given as a dyers and cleaners shop assistant (I remember how my mother would dye clothes in the bath to try and make them seem new.) She was living as a boarder not far away from my father on Temple Park Crescent. As the photograph shows, this was a superior address; how she came to be there and who she was living with, I will never know. They were both poor and got engaged despite the objections from mother's aunts, especially Suzy. 'Marrying beneath herself' was a phrase I often heard as a child. Yet they found comfort and security in each other at a time when this was more important than anything else.

The months before and after the wedding had been difficult for both father and mother. On 13 June 1929, father's mother Catherine Balfour died from cancer of the intestine. On 22 October, little more than a month before the wedding, his father John Balfour died of a cerebral haemorrhage. Upper Grove would have been a house filled with sadness. And on 7 January 1930, a month after the wedding, mother's grandfather Hedderwick died of heart disease. He was 75.[23] He was living at 156 Dalkeith Road, a small step up socially from the homes he had always lived in. And as noted earlier, on 25 December 1931, Ellen Finlay died in Bangour Village Hospital.

On the 14 February 1933, my sister Margaret Balfour was born and given the middle name of Valentine. Our parents had moved into a house on Dean Park Street, where I would be born five years later. It was a rental flat in a typical 1860s tenement, significant in being constructed immediately adjoining the abandoned walls of the south block of St Bernard's Crescent from the last phase of the New Town.

---

23. The 'signature of informant' present at the death was his brother James Finlay, of whom I know nothing.

In 1938, my father's sister Emily died.[24] Emily, who I had never knew existed until I began this task. Beautiful and mysterious Emily – in her portrait a flapper, if ever there was one. My sister Margaret must have known her. Emily died in childbirth along with the baby, she was 33. She married, Alexander Stevenson, a brewery foreman and they were living at 21 Gardner's Crescent at the time of her death. This is a most surprising and rather forlorn terrace of housing from the very last years of the New Town. This, as the fates would have it was a Jamieson Balfour, not a Finlay who finally found a place back in the New Town.

21 Gardner's Crescent in right in the centre. (It is just visible top centre in the aerial view of the North British Rubber Works.)

---

24. Cause of death from the death certificate: *Pulmonary Embolism, Pelvic Thrombo, Phlebitis Puerperal Septic Endometritis,* all connected to childbirth.

Plan of the City of Edinburgh, including all the latest and intended improvements. Edinburgh: T. Brown, 1823. (Reproduced with the permission of the National Library of Scotland)

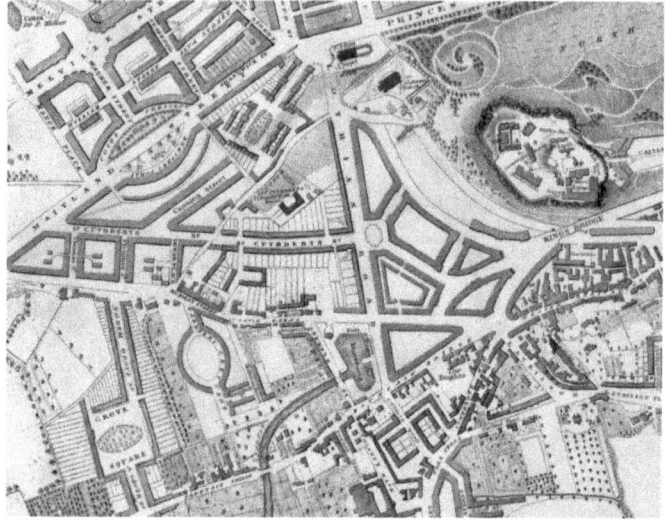

Plan of the same place transformed by industry in 1866, only forty years later. Gardener's Crescent just left of centre, facing the six terraces of Rosebank Cottages above the quadrangle of the Rosemount Buildings. John Bartholomew FRGS 1866. (Reproduced with the permission of the National Library of Scotland)

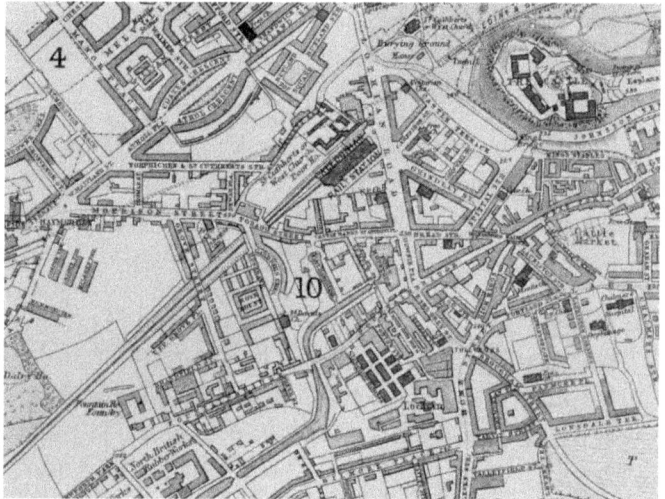

Built in the 1820s, Gardner's Crescent was an outlier from the New Town developments on the west. Originally intended to have a matching crescent on the east side, visible on the lower left of the city map of 1823. It was part of the rather disordered New Town development to the west of the Castle conceived a few years before the railways ploughed through and transformed the area abruptly, ending the development. The map shows the aggressive penetration into the city by the railway cutting across the end of what would have been the other half of Gardner's Crescent. Two experiments in providing house for the poor were built in its place, the six terraces of Rosebank Cottages and immediately to the south, the quadrangle of the Rosemount Building.

Now largely forgotten, Gardner's Crescent is a monument not only to the end of the vision of the New Town, but to the continual struggle to deal with housing the poor. Standing in the garden in front of the Crescent, one can see three distinct realities. On the east is the crescent, a fragment of an ideal city for the privileged. On the southwest, two rows of cottages, conceived on the romantic notion of offering the urban poor a simpler life, the illusion of a return to the country. And on the northwest, an English import, a worker's collective arranged anonymously around the galleries of a courtyard.

Even by 1850, the tenement buildings which were forming the other new town (where my families found housing for almost a century) were seen by Scottish housing reformers as unsatisfactory. They reminded many of the squalid tenements in the old town, and were too small for the large families who had no choice but to move in. Out of this came a movement to create model working-class housing which would end the density of the tenement streets and give every family a front door and a garden. They would be called 'Colony Houses'.[25]

---

25. There are several suggestions for the use of the term 'Colony'. It may have derived from the fact that they were Colonies in the sense of a community of similar people (artisans). I think it

In 1857, on the land that had been planned for the other half of Gardner's Crescent, architects Sir James Gowans and Alexander MacGregor designed Rosebank Cottages. This was the second such development in an initiative which had the stated aim of providing 'flatted cottages for the better class of mechanics'. Each flat had a living room, two bedrooms, a scullery and a water closet. They were built as double flats, one above the other, with front doors and gardens on opposite sides. Rosebank Cottages were deliberately formed in a Scottish vernacular tradition, stone-built, windows framed in whitewash and the chimneys on the gable ends. Gowans wrote, 'The idea that I had was to get working men into small self-contained houses, where they would have their own door to go in by, every room being independent of the others, having a door from the lobby for privacy, and having a little green attached'.[26]

Rosemount Buildings located immediately south of Rosebank Cottages, on the other hand, appears to have been directly influenced by London's 'Metropolitan Association for Improving the Dwellings of the Industrious Classes' (founded in 1841), and was constructed in very un-Scottish polychrome brick. In total contrast to the Cottages, the plan of the Rosemount Buildings showed no concern for either the individual or nature. This is an early socialist vision, a quadrangle of small flats arranged anonymously around a shared drying green whose

---

has a more specific class meaning, from the dictionary: Colony: 'a group of people of one nationality or ethnic group living in a foreign city or country' applied to Edinburgh, these were houses for artisans living in what had been planned middle-class neighbourhoods.

26. https://www.wikiwand.com/en/Colony_houses

Rosebank Cottages, facing Gardner's Crescent on the west. There are six terraces each with four separate dwellings.

Rosemount Buildings also facing Gardner's Crescent on the west.

creators, I presume, believed would produce communal solidarity.

A wall was built in between these two experiments in workers' housing and the New Town crescent to prevent any mixing of the classes. People still remember the divisions which lasted well into the twentieth century; the poorer children from the Rosebank Cottages and Rosemount Buildings were never allowed to set foot in the gated gardens of the Gardner's Crescent.[27]

St Andrew's House, 1939: I have applied a simple but strict rule guiding all the tales that form this biography; all places and events must in some way touch or relate to a member of my two families. I began without knowing whether this limitation would provide enough substance to justify the effort; however, as it has turned out to my advantage, we have played out our lives on many of the city's major stages. This has had much to do with a struggle for status in Edinburgh's class-conscious society. Elspeth Finlay moving houses in a determined effort to keep her family within the fabric of the New Town, though never getting beyond the edge. Her granddaughter, sixty years later, encouraging her docile older husband to buy a flat within the Playfair plan of the failed New Town to the east. And my father's sister Emily finding a place in the

---

27. There were other Colonies, one of which I knew very well. Mary Scott (the wife of father's cousin Tommy Scott, part of maternal grandmother's Catherine Scott Balfour's family) lived in the earliest, Glenogle Colony. I visited her often when I was young. She appeared to others to suffering emotionally and prone to bursting into tears yet, in my recollection she seems quite normal. Every so often she would decide to share with me her one great treasure. From the cupboard in her tiny kitchen she would bring out an old tin box, worn and scratched. Opening the lid, she would lift out a small bundle of cloth which she carefully unwrapped, layer after layer, and then held in her hand a tiny glass, probably for whisky rather than wine. Bringing it close to my face, I could see scratched below the rim a signature, spidery, though quite clear – Robert Burns. She then told the story – someone in our family had been a servant in a tavern in Edinburgh's High Street and had purloined the glass which had been left on a table after an evening of indulgence. The year would have been 1793.

last fragment of the New Town before the railways forced all into a new order.

And it was not just the desire to be within the New Town but with the Finlay's need to return the family to a position in the law profession that it had held for over a century. It must have been in the mind of Catherine Finlay Haston, Grandfather James' second sister, when her daughter, Margaret Haston married the lawyer James Shaw in 1947. He was working in the very new headquarters of the Scottish Government, St Andrews House.

St Andrews House was built both to house the Scottish Office, including the offices of the Secretary of State and to symbolize the government in Scotland. The need to build such a symbol was the result of a post–World War I policy of devolved administrative, but not legislative power to Scotland from London.[28]

This is the last great monumental building in Edinburgh city before World War II, built on the foundations of the city's two main jails, the Bridewell, a debtor's prison designed by Robert Adam, and the Calton Jail. The Bridewell as described in James Grant's *Old and New Edinburgh*:[29]

> The great prison buildings of the city occupy the
> summit of the Dow Craig, [below Calton Hill]
> The first of these, the 'Bridewell', was founded
> 30th November, 1791, by the Earl of Morton,
> Grand Master of Scotland, heading a proces-
> sion which must have ascended the hill by the
> tortuous old street at the back of the present

---

28. https://www.gov.scot/publications/70-years-of-st-andrews
    -house/
29. Ibid., Grant.

St Andrews House, the grand entrance, the Royal crest dominates the front door, the figures crowing the pilasters, have always been unrecognizable under layers of soot: Daboss.

Convening Rooms. […] The architect was Robert Adam. It was finished in 1796, at the expense of the city and county, aided by a petty grant from Government.

It was a panopticon:

Semicircular in form, the main edifice has five floors, the highest being for stores and the hospital. All round on each floor, at the middle of the breadth, is a corridor, with cells on each side, lighted respectively from the interior and exterior of the curvature. Those on the inner are chiefly used as workshops, and can all be

328

surveyed from a dark apartment in the house of the governor without the observer being visible.

Robert Adam, section through the Bridwell.

On the low floor is a treadmill, originally constructed for the manufacture of corks, but now mounted and moved only in cure of idleness or the punishment of delinquency. The area within the circle is a small court, glazed overhead. The house is under good regulations, and is made as much as possible the scene rather of the reclamation and the comfortable industry of its unhappy inmates than of the punishment of their offences.186 What Grant does not mention it that the unstable politics of the time led it to being conceived as a defensive structure as well a prison.

The Calton Jail, adjoining the Bridewell at the east end of Waterloo Place, was called 'the town and county gaol'. It opened in 1817. Grant describes it 'as an extensive building, and somewhat castellated – in short, the whole masses of these buildings, with their towers and turrets overhanging the steep rocks, resemble a

Calton Jail from the entrance Calton Hill in 1880 Adam's Bridewell is on the right, behind it the towers that housed the prison governors.

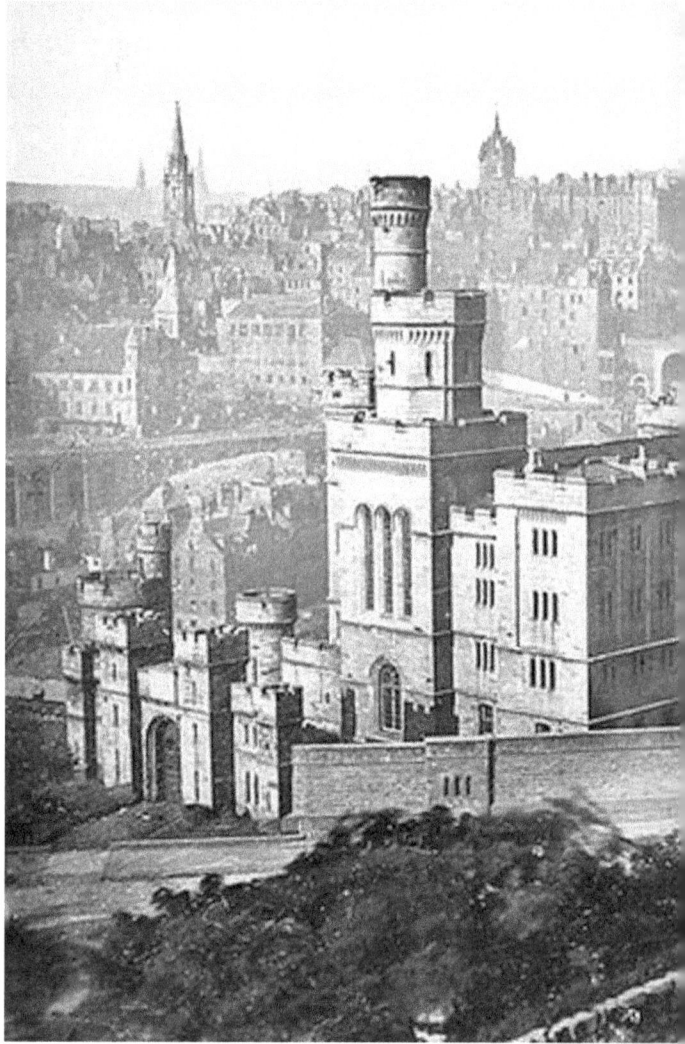

feudal fortress of romance, and present a striking and interesting aspect'. The decision to build the then largest jail in Scotland on such a prominent site was encouraged by Lord Henry Cockburn, solicitor general for Scotland, who later complained, 'It had been a piece of undoubted bad taste to give so glorious an eminence to a prison'. However, there were others who thought a little differently. On a visit to the city in 1859, French novelist Jules Verne was impressed, describing it as resembling a small-scale version of a medieval town.[30] It was such an impressive fortress-like pile that visitors to the city would sometimes mistake it for Edinburgh Castle. Despite its brutal function, the architecture seems to have been formed to provide a romantic contrast to the facades of Waterloo Place and the Regent Bridge, all created by the architect, Archibald Elliot. It was one of the most brutal jails in Victorian Scotland. Throughout much of the nineteenth century, most of the prisoners were women, almost all imprisoned for minor offences; with being 'drunk and incapable', with running unlicensed premises known as 'shebeens', illicit pubs where alcohol was sold without a licence, and more unusual crimes including 'concealing a pregnancy' and 'impersonating a man'. Prostitution and petty crime were rife in the city and the reason so many were forced into petty crime was that there were few jobs for women, and those that there were, paid a pittance. [31]

Calton was the prison for desperate women and for hanging. Public executions had ceased in the city in 1864, but hangings continued within the walls of the

30. https://www.scotsman.com/lifestyle/lost-edinburgh-calton-jail-1-3071270
31. https://www.scotsman.com/lifestyle/book-tells-forgotten-hell-of-edinburgh-s-calton-jail-1-4016450

Calton prison to the end of the nineteenth century and were visible from the slopes of Calton Hill above the Royal High School. In the twentieth century, executions were taken indoors, the last in 1923.[32] The prison closed in 1926 and was demolished in the 1930s. Portraying a hellish prison as a romantic folly recalls Baudelaire's observation 'Art dulls the terror of the void better than anything else'.

The architect of St Andrews House was Thomas S. Tait,[33] of Burnet Tait and Lorne, architects. This was one of the most influential modern practices both in Britain and internationally. Their work on the Royal Masonic Hospital at Ravenscourt won the RIBA Gold Medal for the best building of 1933, and in 1934 they won the design competition for St Andrews House. The building sits physically on the lower walls of the Calton Jail that arose, retaining for no good reason the picturesque towers of the house of the prison governor. Work began in November 1935, and the building was completed in 1939. It was by far the most significant public building and the most modern design constructed in Edinburgh between the Wars. There is much originality in Tait's majestic design. It is not without influences, a hint of Frank Lloyd Wright, but the greatest debt would seem to

---

32. The last to be hanged on 30 October 1923 was Philip Murray, sentenced to death for murder by throwing a man out of a window on Jamaica Street, who he had discovered in bed with his wife.

33. Born in 1882 in Paisley, the son of a master stonemason, he studied architecture at the Glasgow School of Art after serving an apprenticeship. In 1918, he joined the London practice of Sir John James Burnet. Tait became a partner, and in 1930 Scottish-born Francis Lorne returned from America to become a third and the practice was renamed Burnet, Tait and Lorne.

St Andrews House, view from the South with Calton Hell in the background, traces of the prison governors house on the left. (The Scotsman Publications Lid)

be to Willem Marinus Dudok and the Hilversum Town Hall in Holland, completed in 1931, which had won the RIBA Gold Medal in 1935. The public façade, facing Regents Road, is unambiguously disciplined, even fascist. Imagine swastikas hanging from the battery of flagpoles across the front. To the rear, looking over the Waverly Valley, two massive, flanking blocks enclose what could be a splendid public stage, alas it is always empty.

It is a morose though dramatic place, perhaps unable to transcend the merciless history of the place. It seems to have been admired, but its significance as a national symbol was lost with the declaration of war. An official opening ceremony timed to take place on 12 October 1939 was 'cancelled due to War' (Britain's first air raid of the war took place only four days later over the Forth Bridge). Instead, it was officially opened by King George VI and Queen Elizabeth on 26 February 1940.

It may be the dirt of Edinburgh that makes it seem so cold. For five years, I would walk by it every day, passing the circular towers of the former house of the Calton prison governor, giving a picturesque flourish to the view. St Andrews House has always seemed to me aloof, a brooding and cold place, unable to escape the tragic history of the place. I cannot recall seeing a single person entering or leaving. The vast facade is silent, nothing to say about itself or the nation it represents. The phalanx of vertical columns that guard the entry is crowned by a series of blackened heads now unrecognizable staring ominously up at the unfinished National Monument at the crest of Calton Hill – in mourning or as a warning. This then was the symbol for Scotland's future before the world was again transformed by war.

On 18 March1939, I was born at 16 Dean Park Street. And by the years end, my father was called to war and gone from my life for much of the next six years. Mother left alone to cope with two children and live on a soldier's pay of eleven shillings a week.

VIII

Reflections

These stories are not unusual; they record the struggles experienced by most families over the last few centuries. What makes them of interest is that these lives were shaped by the building of the New Town and suffered its consequences. Given that I began knowing nothing more than the name of one of my grandparents, this has been a more revealing journey than I could have imagined. I did not anticipate producing a book of any length, just a series of short essays written for the family, putting whatever I learned into a historical context. I could not have predicted the discovery of Andrew Bell, and his three-volume biography which gave both detailed written evidence on my mother's family history and a sense of adventure to the project. There was satisfaction in discovering an illustrious ancestor, an educationalist and learning that he benefited my family. I must be one of the very few who have struggled through the three volumes of the biography. His correspondence reads like a continual complaint, and I can't imagine what would have been the basis of his friendship with the romantic poet William Wordsworth; I recall he was close enough to ask the poet to edit his papers. He seems to have been at ease in America though the biography has only a passing reference to the Revolutionary War and says very little about his employer Carter Braxton, a signer of the Declaration of Independence and one of the largest slave owners in Virginia.

He died believing his lasting achievement would be the founding of Madras College in St Andrews. I visited Madras College in the fall of 2018. I had written to the headmaster to say that I was a descendant of Dr Bell and was greeted with enthusiasm. The school historian said that as far as he knew, my family were the last surviving relatives of Bell. He believed that the Madras System of teaching had faded from the college in the nineteenth century. The college became a state public school in the years after World War II. (At the time of my visit, 2018, the cost of maintaining the old building had become a burden, and all the facilities had recently been sold to St Andrew's University.)

I was born and for 16 years lived at 16 Dean Park Street, on the north side of the city, just behind St Bernard's Crescent at the northern edge of the New Town. The photograph shows Dean Park Street looking south in 1900: This is exactly as it was in my youth. On the second shop on the right, you can barely make out the sign for the St Cuthbert's Co-op where we bought groceries, the bakery on the opposite side of the road. There is a small shopfront on its left where large churns of milk were delivered every morning. The window of the stationers on the right is exactly as I remember it: postcards, note paper, pencils, some children's books and the smell of newsprint; newspapers would arrive several times a day. I see in my mind's eye a foggy evening and clusters of men snapping the evening pink sports paper, checking the scores against their football coupons. The opening of the right led to a mews lane where the horses for the milk carts were stabled. And on the left, the opening to Bedford Street, where George Miekle Kemp once lived.

Dean Park Street looking south 1910. The incomplete south end of St Bernard's Crescent was just to the left in the distance.

My formative years were spent on the rough and unsettled edge between the New Town and the working-class town built around it. I could see at the end of the street the unfinished gable wall with empty windows at the south end of St Bernard's Crescent, marking one abrupt ending of the New Town, long since demolished. And just as the children in the 'colonies' were not allowed into the gardens or walk on the pavement in the adjoining Gardner's Crescent, I don't believe I ever thought of entering the gardens in St Bernard's Crescent just a few yards from my home, the vast colonnade of Doric columns seemed a menacing. Even in memory, it remains an alien place. Though gangs of children from the streets surrounding Dean Park Street, played together, I don't remember seeing the children playing on the Crescent, perhaps there were no children.

Though I have returned to Edinburgh occasionally, I have given little thought to the city until I began this work. I was 12 years old when I first put on the black blazer with the arms of the city on its pocket and set out on my journey from home to the Royal High School, a journey repeated every week of every term for the next five years. The number 24 tram would stop at the foot of Frederick Street, and I would walk briskly along Princes Street past Registrar House, up Waterloo Place to the school. Five years in all weathers, gives plenty of time to know and explore a place, to form lasting memories. Over these years, I would often pause by the arch of the Regent Bridge; the bridge is the most dramatic demonstration of the New Town being built alongside and over the slum structures of the older city. The drawing by Thomas Shepherd is a view looking north, up Leith Wynd (now Calton Road). It shows the bridge and the back of the New Town terrace of Waterloo Place rising above an ancient lane, and the female figures in the foreground appear to have bare feet. Again, in the words of Robert Louis Stephenson: 'This is only the New Town passing overhead above its own cellars; walking, so to speak, over its own children, as is the way of cities and the human race'.

Further up I would pass the gates to the Old Calton Cemetery, cut in half by the construction of Waterloo Place. A statue of a standing Abraham Lincoln, glimpsed from the gate, freed slaves at his feet, tempted me to linger there awhile after school. And I was surrounded by massive tombs of the wealthy and powerful from Edinburgh's past. Built to give them immortality that only the stones themselves remember. In all my visits, I seemed to be alone. The walk took me by the railings at the Burns Memorial, then down the hill into the New Calton Cemetery; this is still a lost place with such an air of sadness. (At lunchtime, we senior schoolboys would take a variety of paths down to the Cannongate and buy

Regent Bridge, from the Leith Wynd' in 1829, Thos. H Shepherd

little packs of the cheapest cigarettes and smoke them in the hidden corners of the sixteenth-century White Horse Close.)

In the fall of 2018, I revisited the old High School. The gates were closed, so I climbed the steps onto Calton Hill and looked down at the empty buildings, showing signs of neglect. My romantic imagination saw Rome in the Sixth Century when all the gods had gone, and the temples had ceased to have meaning and were abandoned. Later that same week, I visited the new so-called

'Royal High School', an extremely ugly building lost on the west of the city. (I cannot understand why they kept the name.) However, I had an enjoyable discussion with the headmistress, who was sad to admit that the principles on which the old school had been founded and which so widely influenced the idea of a public 'High School' have gone.

Even though the Art College I attended was on the edge of the old town, I rarely walked down the High Street or into the Grassmarket. I am surprised now to recognize that these ancient places embodying complex histories were of no interest to me then because I was encouraged by New Town culture to see them as remnant of a past that offered nothing to the future. In my final year at Art College, I was awarded the Edinburgh Corporation Silver Medal for Civic Architecture, and one might assume that the history of the city and its buildings would have been a central part of my studies, but not so, no attempt was made to teach the history of the city at either the High School or at the college. I took for granted the heroic structure of the High School and all the monuments on Calton Hill above it, never questioning why they were there. I knew nothing of the transformations that produced Edinburgh, nothing of the forces that shaped the vision, ignorant of the succession of brilliant architects who created the theatrical reality of the New Town from that vision for more than a century. My education gave me no scholarly guidance in making critical judgements on architecture or architectural history. (I was a finalist in a national competition to design a theatre in the manner of Palladio, and I just made it up.) This was the damning effect of modernism on design teaching in these years, an active rejection of the immediate past. Researching the history of the city and the Scottish nation has given me some pleasure and not a little discomfort. (It has, to my surprise, left me a strong wish to visit that strange world of castles, palaces and art collections scattered along the border between Scotland and England.)

It is satisfying though rather sad, to learn the histories and circumstances out of which I have emerged. My families lived and were shaped by a city and a nation in almost two centuries of continual transformation. A transformation in which many suffered. Only now, in this work, have I realized Edinburgh's appalling poverty in the eighteenth and nineteenth centuries was the product of deliberate plans and those making the plans were aware of the possible consequences. It is an extraordinary ability within the human imagination to conceive in the abstract visions of man's place in the world and move them into physical realities, mostly pragmatic but at their most ambitious, they can be realities that embody dreams, the aspiration, intended to shape the future. Edinburgh is a potent demonstration of this. From my knowledge of European cities, Edinburgh is unique in building such an extensive idealized reality for such an extended time, almost ninety years. A reality which succeeded in not only dividing the city but in dividing people.

The city in the present is formed from four realities: the medieval remnants of a feudal nation, an enlightened eighteenth-century New Town built for the privileged subjects of the Georgian kings, and in the middle of nineteenth century, the emergence of two very different new towns to contain the workers in the new industries and a rising middle class. Again, unique to Edinburgh, each part was and remains as separate physically as for the most part socially.

The medieval city was mostly the product of circumstance. Only three objects were conceived of as projecting a symbolic presence. The castle displaying strength, the palace displaying the elegance and worldliness of the king court, and at the centre the great church, the home of God. They have remained in place into the present. The rest was a resilient mass of stone and wood endlessly changeable, rising and alas eventually falling victim to the ambitions of an elite culture that sought to escape from the squalor and the ambiguity of medieval reality. In the old town, God is dominant in the crusty old cathedral.

The New Town on the other hand was conceived deliberately to be elegantly ordered, serene and unchanging, and has remained so, both physically and socially for the last 200 years, and will continue in this self-satisfied state as far into the future as we can see. It was created to be the antithesis of the old town. Though not central in the New Town, in the ideal plan, God's place became a useful accessory to the streetscape of the intended main passage of the new city – George Street. The differences between these two realities the Old Town and the New were profound, resulting in different cultures, different poetry, music and different forms of love and violence.

Compare the development of New York City with the planning and building of the New Town in Edinburgh. The Commissioner's Plan for New York was produced a little more than thirty years after the Craig's plan for Edinburgh. Constructing these two new cities ran concurrently for 20 or 30 years. While Edinburgh sought to create a permanent unchanging stage for the elite of the culture, New York saw the establishment of the order of the city as a levelling device, as a frame for speculation, a temporal thing rising and falling with the demands of the culture and the economy.

The other new towns housing the workers and the rising middle class were shaped in the beginning by the railways, industry and by the poverty of the tenants. They have remained as unchanging and unchangeable as the town of privilege, keeping the class division in place as long as the buildings stand. And those toiling in industry were comforted by many grubby little churches seemingly squeezed into every tenement block and now largely abandoned. Both the vision and the perpetual presence of the New Town have proved so powerful and all-consuming that, based on confused projects from the last forty years, Edinburgh appears to have lost the ability to produce confident plans for its future – ideal or otherwise.

In reviewing the events of the last two hundred years, I realized that the building of the New Town coincided with migrations into the city of the tens of thousands from the villages across central Scotland who had suffered under the bondage of the *Collier and Salter* Laws (including my grandfather). They made their way to Edinburgh and other cities to find work that would pay a living wage and work was scarce Their presence added to the seams of deep poverty in the city that have never been erased. In the years after World War II, public housing estates were built on the west edge of the city in areas such as Muirhouse, rehousing people from the slums of the inner city, and within a few decades, they too degenerated into drug-infested slums. This is the setting for the Irvine Welsh novel, *Trainspotting*, described in an endless stream of filthy language, much of it in broad Scots. A brief extract describes the need to lie about the school you attended to get job; one of the schools mentioned, Heriot's like the High School, is hundreds of years old. Changes in Edinburgh is either extremely slow or not at all.

> – *Actually man, ah've goat tae come clean here. Ah went tae Augie's, St. Augustine's likesay, then Craigy, eh*

Craigroyston, ken. Ah jist pit doon Heriots because ah thoat it wid likes, help us git the joab. Too much discrimination in this town, man, ken, likesay? As soon as suit n tie dudes see Heriots or Daniel Stewarts or Edinburgh Academy, they kinday get the hots, ken. Ah mean [...].[1]

---

1. Irvine Welsh, *Trainspotting*. Secker & Warburg, 1993.

Methods and Sources

Some years before her death, my sister had a genealogist friend construct a family tree. It was a confusing document but did provide centuries' worth of names and dates for me to begin to explore, which I did with the support of the website *Scotland's People* (https://www.scotlandspeople .gov.uk) created by the Scottish Government. This is an astonishing resource with church and legal records going back to the sixteenth century. Here I not only followed my family tree back to the late seventeenth century but was also able to recover obscure documents from church records, recording successions of births, deaths and marriages and peculiar laws of past ages, all recorded in spidery handwriting with all manner of flourishes. From these two sources, I had names, addresses, occupations, causes of death for all the major figures in the families of my mother and father back to the eighteenth century. As I wrote earlier, it was a recollection of a conversation when I was no more than eight that led me to *THE LIFE of THE REV. ANDREW BELL, D. D. L.L.D. F. As. S. F.R.S.E D* in three volumes which contained intimate details of my mother's family back to the eighteenth century.

To put all these people and places in context, I had the help of the website *Town Plans and Views, 1580– 1940* from the National Library of Scotland, a marvellous

collection recording decade by decade the transformation
of Edinburgh first from building the New Town and then
with the arrival of the railways and the growth of industry (https://maps.nls.uk/towns/info.html). Giving life
and colour to the narrative are the many delightful drawing and paintings as the city attracted artists in the eighteenth century, and nineteenth centuries followed in the
1840s by the extraordinary images of Hill and Adamson,
among the world's earliest photographic documentation
of a city.

My objective in this work is to give future generations not only the names and years of their ancestors
but also a feeling for their hardships, and life was mostly
hard. To make palpable the character of their homes,
streets and workplaces and the villages and towns they
came from before being drawn to the city and embed
their lives into the dramatic creation of a new Edinburgh.
As mentioned in Chapter 2, I discovered that my third
grandfather, another James Finlay, had lived in a flat on
Hanover Street in the heart of the New Town in 1829,
so in November 2017 I rented a flat on George Street,
just a few yards from Hanover Street, whose interior had
remained essentially unchanged since 1795. Then I set
out to visit and experience the many pasts and places
where my families had lived.

Bibliography

One of the great pleasures of this work was to discover the brilliant writing in so many histories and commentaries on both Scotland and Edinburgh. Over several months, I read a broad range of sources and am astonished by the passion with which historians have examined the nation and its capital city over these last three centuries. The writing is blunt, often ironic and as pungent as smells of the demanded. The authors never hide the poverty or the severe injustice that was Scotland's fate from the seventeenth even into the twentieth century, no one more so than Henry Grey Graham in his *The Social Life of Scotland in the Eighteenth Century.*

Principle sources:

The Journal of John Wesle, Wesley, John 1703–1791; Parker, Percy Livingstone, 1867–1925, editor. Chicago: Moody Press

Henry Grey Graham, *The Social Life of Scotland in the Eighteenth Century.* London: Adam and Charles Black, 1901.

A History of Peeblesshire by William Chambers of Glenormiston. Edinburgh and London: William and Robert Chambers Publishers, 1843.

Sibbald *Memoria Balfouriana,* the Royal geographer 1590.

Culross and Tulliallan Volume 1, by David Beveridge, is a replication of a work published before 188, Books on Demand.

THEATRUM SCOTIA containing the PROSPECTS..... by John Slezer, Captain of the Artillery Company. London: Published John Leake, MDCXCIII.

1843 Poor Law Commission Extracts from *Poor Law inquiry (Scotland.)* Appendix, part III.

The New Statistical Account of Scotland for Fife, FHL book 941 B4sa, 2nd series, vol. 9. 1843

*THE LIFE of THE REV. ANDREW BELL, D. D. L.L.D. F. As. S.
F.R.S.E.D. Prebendary of Westminster, and Master Sherburn Hospital
Durham. COMPRISING THE HISTORY OF THE RISE AND
PROGRESS OF THE SYSTEM OF MUTUAL TUITION.* The
First Volume by Robert Southey, Esq., P.L., LL.D. The Two Last
By His Son, The Rev. Charles Cuthbert Southey, B.A. Oxford.
London: John Murray; Edinburgh: William Blackwood & Sons,
MDCCCXLIV.

*Ordnance Gazetteer of Scotland: A Survey of Scottish Topography, Statistical,
Biographical and Historical,* edited by Francis H. Groome and
originally published in parts by Thomas C. Jack, Edinburgh:
Grange Publishing Works, between 1882 and 1885.

James Grant, Cassell's *Old and New Edinburg: Its History, Its People, and
Its Places, 1822–1887,* published 1881–87. London: Cassell, Petter,
Galpin.

Proposals for Carrying on Certain Public Works in the City of Edinburgh.
Edinburgh: Lord Gilbert Elliot Minto, 1752.

Hugo Arnot. *The History of Edinburgh, from the Earliest Accounts to the Year
1780.* Printed by Thomas Turnbull.

J. Youngston, *The Making of Classical Edinburgh, 1750–1840.* Edinburgh
University Press, 1966.

https://blog.nls.uk/robert-adam-rome-and-piranesi/

The Book of the Old Edinburgh Club. Electric Scotland. https://
electricscotland.com › bookofoldedinbur03olde PDF

T. B.M. *Slum Life in Edinburgh, or Scenes in Its Darkest Places: With Twelve
Illustrations form Life.* Edinburgh: J. Thin, 1891.

The Scots Magazine 1760-02: Volume 22, newspaperarchive.com/edin
burgh-advertiser-dec-23-1823-p-14

John Taylor, and John Fleming *A Medical Treatise on the Virtues of St
Bernard's Well, Illustrated with Select Cases: Addressed to Francis Garden,
Esq. of Gardenstone ... Proprietor of St Bernard's.* Edinburgh: Sold by
William Creech and J. Ainslie.

Thomas Bonnar, *Biographical Sketch of the George Meikle Kemp Architect of
the Scott Monument Edinburgh.* Edinburgh: William Blackwood and
Sons, MDCCCXCII.

Cumberland Hill *Reminiscences of Stockbridge and Neighbourhood,*
published in 1874 in 8 Volumes. [8 volumes on my neighbourhood
of more that 20 streets!]

A Biographical Dictionary of Eminent Scotsmen. Robert Chambers,
Originally published: 1835.

Stevenson, Robert Louis. Edinburgh: Picturesque Notes. London:
Seely, Jackson & Halliday, 1850–1894.